YO-BZM-336

THE ROUGH GUIDE TO

NEW ORLEANS

Forthcoming titles include

The Algarve • The Bahamas • Cambodia
Caribbean Islands • Costa Brava
New York Restaurants • South America • Zanzibar

Forthcoming reference guides include

Children's Books • Online Travel • Videogaming
Weather

Rough Guides online

www.roughguides.com

Rough Guide Credits

Text editor: Yuki Takagaki
Series editor: Mark Ellingham
Production: Rachel Holmes
Cartography: Melissa Baker
Proofreading: Derek Wilde

Publishing Information

This second edition published September 2001
by Rough Guides Ltd,
62–70 Shorts Gardens, London WC2H 9AH

Distributed by the Penguin Group:

Penguin Books Ltd, 27 Wrights Lane, London W8 5TZ
Penguin Putnam, Inc., 375 Hudson Street, New York 10014, USA
Penguin Books Australia Ltd, 487 Maroondah Highway,
PO Box 257, Ringwood, Victoria 3134, Australia
Penguin Books Canada Ltd, 10 Alcorn Avenue,
Toronto, Ontario, Canada M4V 1E4
Penguin Books (NZ) Ltd,
182–190 Wairau Road, Auckland 10, New Zealand

Typeset in Bembo and Helvetica to an original design by Henry Iles
Printed in Spain by Graphy Cems

© Samantha Cook 368pp, includes index
A catalogue record for this book is available from the British Library.

ISBN 1-85828-744-8

THE ROUGH GUIDE TO

NEW ORLEANS

by Samantha Cook

ROUGH
GUIDES

We set out to do something different when the first Rough Guide was published in 1982. Mark Ellingham, just out of university, was travelling in Greece. He brought along the popular guides of the day, but found they were all lacking in some way. They were either strong on ruins and museums but went on for pages without mentioning a beach or taverna. Or they were so conscious of the need to save money that they lost sight of Greece's cultural and historical significance. Also, none of the books told him anything about Greece's contemporary life – its politics, its culture, its people, and how they lived.

So with no job in prospect, Mark decided to write his own guidebook, one which aimed to provide practical information that was second to none, detailing the best beaches and the hottest clubs and restaurants, while also giving hard-hitting accounts of every sight, both famous and obscure, and providing up-to-the-minute information on contemporary culture. It was a guide that encouraged independent travellers to find the best of Greece, and was a great success, getting shortlisted for the Thomas Cook travel guide award, and encouraging Mark, along with three friends, to expand the series.

The Rough Guide list grew rapidly and the letters flooded in, indicating a much broader readership than had been anticipated, but one which uniformly appreciated the Rough Guide mix of practical detail and humour, irreverence and enthusiasm. Things haven't changed. The same four friends who began the series are still the caretakers of the Rough Guide mission today: to provide the most reliable, up-to-date and entertaining information to independent-minded travellers of all ages, on all budgets.

We now publish more than 150 titles and have offices in London and New York. The travel guides are written and researched by a dedicated team of more than 100 authors, based in Britain, Europe, the USA and Australia. We have also created a unique series of phrasebooks to accompany the travel series, along with an acclaimed series of music guides, and a best-selling pocket guide to the Internet and World Wide Web. We also publish comprehensive travel information on our Web site: **www.roughguides.com**

Help us update

We've gone to a lot of effort to ensure that this second edition of *The Rough Guide to New Orleans* is as up to date and accurate as possible. However, things do change, and any suggestions, comments and corrections are much appreciated. We'll send a copy of the next edition (or any other *Rough Guide* if you prefer) for the best letters.

Please mark letters "**Rough Guide New Orleans Update**" and send to:

Rough Guides, 62–70 Shorts Gardens, London WC2H 9AH, or Rough Guides, 4th Floor, 345 Hudson St, New York NY 10014.

Or send email to: mail@roughguides.co.uk
Online updates about this book can be found on Rough Guides' Web site (see opposite)

The author

Samantha Cook first visited New Orleans in 1990, fell in love with the place and has returned every year since. She has been involved with Rough Guides for more than ten years, starting out as an author on the USA guide, and contributing to many other titles. For several years she worked in the office as an editor and managing editor, but has since returned to full-time writing. She is currently compiling the forthcoming *Rough Guide to Online Travel*.

Acknowledgements

In New Orleans, thanks again to Christine de Cuir, Sal Impastato, Paul Gustings, Larone Hudson, Rob Faust, Constantine Georges, Mark McGrain and Cheryl Gerber. And to new friends Leroy Jones, Miki Fujii, Henri Smith and Java Hudson. Then there's the old friends who came along and loved it too: Mark Owen, Maria Mercedes, Ally "Spooky" Scott and Matt "Heat Miser" Anstee. (Kisses to godson George Ventris, who'll come along as soon as he's old enough.) Cheers to the Rough Guides team, especially

Yuki, for her professionalism and charm, but also Melissa Baker, Rachel Holmes and Derek Wilde. Finally, love and more love to Greg Ward for the music piece, the fascinating Normandy snippets and the sheer fun of it all; to inspirational travellers Jim Cook and Ulli Sieglohr, to Bev Thomas and Albyn Hall, and to Pam Cook, who I hope will join me for a drink in the *Napoleon House* one day soon.

And finally, a sad farewell to Ernie K-Doe. The city will be a poorer place without him.

CONTENTS

MAP LIST

Introduction

As it enters its fourth century, **New Orleans** remains proudly apart from the rest of the United States. Intoxicating and addictive, the product of a dizzying jumble of cultures, peoples and influences, it's a place where people dance at funerals and hold parties during hurricanes, where some of the world's finest musicians make ends meet busking on street corners, and fabulous Creole cuisine is dished up in hole-in-the-wall dives. There's a wistfulness, too, in the peeling, ice-cream–toned facades of the old French Quarter – site of the original settlement – in the filigree cast-iron balconies overgrown with lush ferns and fragrant jasmine, and in the cemeteries, or "Cities of the Dead", lined with crumbling above-ground tombs. Doubtless New Orleans' melancholy air – and perhaps its *joie de vivre*, too – is due to the city's perilous geography. Set largely below sea level, and exposed to the devastating storms that career through the Gulf of Mexico, the city could be washed or blasted away in an instant.

Founded by the French in 1718 on the swampy flood plain of the lower Mississippi River, and today spreading back as far as the enormous Lake Pontchartrain, New Orleans is almost entirely surrounded by water, which since its earliest days has both isolated it from the interior and connected it to the outside world. By the time the

Americans bought it, in the Louisiana Purchase of 1803, New Orleans was a cosmopolitan city whose ethnically diverse population had mingled to create a distinctive Creole culture. In the nineteenth century its importance as a port made the city the haunt of smugglers, gamblers, prostitutes and pirates, who gave it the decadent "sin city" notoriety that it still has today. Ever since then more and more visitors, among them an inordinate number of artists, writers and sundry bohemians, have poured in to see what the fuss was about; many found themselves staying, unable to shake the place out of their system.

Given its allure New Orleans is a surprisingly small town, with its million or so residents spread across a patchwork of neighborhoods. Its compact size makes it a dream to visit; simple to get around and easy to get to know, it's one of the best places in the United States to kick back and unwind for a few days. Above all, New Orleans is less a city of major sights than of sensual pleasures. With its subtropical climate, Latin-influenced architecture and black majority population, its voodoo worshippers and its long-held carnival traditions, it is often called the northernmost Caribbean city. The pace of life is slow here, while the sybaritic vices are relished – no more so than during the many festivals, especially, of course, the world-famous carnival of Mardi Gras, when real life is put on hold as businessmen and busboys alike are swept along by an increasingly frenzied season of parties, street parades and masquerade balls. Whatever time of year you come, you'll slip easily into the indolent way of life, rejecting an itinerary of museum-hopping in favor of a stroll around the French Quarter, where the vibrant street life and decaying buildings provide endless feasts for the eye; a leisurely steamboat cruise on the Mississippi; or simply a long cool drink in a hidden courtyard. Perhaps the most taxing thing you'll do is head out on the slow-moving old streetcar to the residential Garden

District, where dark green shrubs weighed down by fat magnolia blossoms squat in the shadow of centuries-old live oaks tangled with ragged gray streamers of Spanish moss.

Though many of the city's most lingering pleasures come after dark, when the streets fill with people eating in the hundreds of superb restaurants, drinking at its many characterful bars and enjoying a live-music scene to rival any in the world, there's a whole lot more to New Orleans – the "Big Easy", the "city that care forgot" – than its fame as a nonstop party town. Ravaged by the Civil War and since then trailing in the wake of its more dynamic Southern rivals, today New Orleans depends heavily upon the cash brought by the millions of tourists seduced by the allure of authentic jazz, fine food and free-flowing alcohol. While having enormous amounts of fun here, you're always liable to be pulled up short by the divisions between rich and poor (and, more explicitly between white and black). Just footsteps away from the feted French Quarter and Garden District – themselves touched by decrepitude and decay – lie woefully neglected housing projects and poverty-scarred neighborhoods.

Perversely, New Orleans' second-league status, in commercial terms, has protected it from the modernization that has ripped out the old hearts of wealthier cities, and allowed it to hold on to its distinctive character. And this sense of historic continuity is not limited to architecture. From the devout celebration of Catholic saints' days and the offerings left at voodoo shrines, to the local street parades, in which umbrella-twirling dancers and blasting brass bands lead crowds of thousands through poor black neighborhoods just as they have done for several centuries, much of the city's vitality and its sheer panache comes from a heartfelt belief that what has gone before is worth keeping. The melange of cultures and races that built New Orleans still gives it its heart: not "easy", exactly, but quite unlike anywhere else in the States – or in the world.

WHEN TO VISIT

New Orleans has a subtropical **climate**, with warm temperatures, high humidity and heavy rainfall. Thanks to its busy convention calendar, swarming weekend tourist traffic and a seemingly endless stream of festivals, the city stays pretty full year-round, but the peak **tourist seasons** are Mardi Gras – which starts on Twelfth Night and builds up in intensity until Mardi Gras itself, the day before Ash Wednesday – and Jazz Fest, which spreads across a fortnight at the end of April and the start of May. Both, along with the increasingly popular French Quarter festival, occur in **spring**, which is a pleasant, sunny time to visit. However, the humidity is already building up by then, and Jazz Fest especially can be plagued by heavy rain.

The torpid months between May and September, when the blistering heat and intense humidity prove debilitating in the extreme, count as **off-season**; prices may be lower and crowds thinner at this time, but for good reason. From May to November the city is at risk from the **hurricanes** that sweep through the Gulf of Mexico. Even if it doesn't get a direct hit, New Orleans can be seriously affected by a tropical storm landing anywhere along the coast.

Climate-wise, **fall** is one of the best times to visit: October especially tends to be sunny, warm and relatively dry, though the nights can be chilly. Even in **winter** the days don't usually get too cold; the nights, however, are another matter, cursed by the bone-bitingly damp air that creeps in from the river.

Plagued by heavy pollination, humidity and pollution, New Orleans is a year-round nightmare for **allergy** sufferers, and can bring on miserable symptoms even for those who have never experienced them before. Bring your own medication, or stock up when you arrive.

| | F° | | C° | | RAINFALL | |
| | AVERAGE DAILY | | AVERAGE DAILY | | AVERAGE MONTHLY | |
	MAX	MIN	MAX	MIN	IN	MM
Jan	69	43	20	6	4.97	126
Feb	65	45	18	7	5.23	133
March	71	52	21	11	4.73	120
April	79	59	26	15	4.50	114
May	85	65	29	18	5.07	129
June	90	71	32	21	4.63	118
July	91	74	33	23	6.73	171
Aug	90	73	32	22	6.02	153
Sept	87	70	30	21	5.87	149
Oct	79	59	26	15	2.66	67
Nov	70	50	21	10	4.06	103
Dec	64	45	17	7	5.27	134

THE GUIDE

Introducing the city

One of New Orleans' many nicknames is "the Crescent City", because of the way it nestles between the southern shore of Lake Pontchartrain and a dramatic horseshoe bend in the Mississippi River. This unique location makes the city's layout confusing, with streets curving to follow the river and shooting off at odd angles to head inland. In the face of such dizzying geography, compass points are of little use – locals refer instead to lakeside (toward the lake) and riverside (toward the river), and, using Canal Street as the dividing line, uptown (or upriver) and downtown (downriver).

In a sense, everything begins at **Canal Street**, the broad commercial thoroughfare that sweeps from the river to the lake. Streets crossing Canal, which in the 1800s divided the old Creole city from the new American suburbs, change their names on either side of it – thus Royal Street in the French Quarter becomes St Charles uptown, Bourbon becomes Carondelet and so on, while downriver of Canal Street any street name prefixed with "North" simply swaps it for "South" uptown. **Building numbers** also restart at 100 on either side of Canal.

The telephone area code for New Orleans is ⊕504.

STAYING SAFE IN NEW ORLEANS

Though statistics show that it is gradually dropping, New Orleans' high crime rate should still be taken very seriously. Widespread poverty and attendant drug problems mean that simply crossing the street can take you from a familiar environment into a bleak, potentially threatening neighborhood, where tourists tripping around with cameras and wallets full of dollars are easy prey. That said, visitors who use a modicum of common sense will probably be faced with nothing more threatening than the gangs of young street hustlers who accost tourists in the French Quarter (see p.33).

However, you do need to keep your wits about you. While it's safe enough to walk around the French Quarter during the day, you should be on your guard after dark in the quieter streets above Bourbon Street. You're approaching Rampart Street here, the border with the underprivileged neighborhood of Tremé – though you're not necessarily in any danger, it can feel intimidating until you get your bearings. The Garden District, also, is safe enough during the day, though at night – when in any case there's little reason to be wandering around – you should be on your guard. Parts of the Lower Garden District, including some run-down stretches on and around lower Magazine Street, can feel menacing at any time.

Wherever you are, if you feel nervous, trust your instincts, turn back, or call a taxi. Above all, *always* take a cab when traveling any distance outside the Quarter at night.

Most tourists head first for the battered old **French Quarter** (or Vieux Carré), the compact, thirteen-block-wide site of the original grid settlement. Centering on lively Jackson Square, a stone's throw from the Mississippi, the Quarter's combination of Creole architecture, fabulous restaurants and eccentric street life proves irresistible. Downriver, oak-shaded Esplanade Avenue, lined with crumbling Italianate mansions, separates the Quarter from the funky **Faubourg Marigny**, a low-rent district of ramshackle Creole cottages. Though predominantly residential, the Faubourg, as it is known, features a handful of excellent bars, clubs and restaurants, especially along Frenchmen Street, which shoots off at an angle from Esplanade. There's another rash of good bars and restaurants beyond the Faubourg, across Elysian Fields – deliciously named, but not a place to linger – in the **Bywater**. A residential area of brightly painted shotguns, warehouses and storage lots, there's little to actually see here, but as the focus of an extremely hip arts scene, it's a prime place to hang out. The Quarter's lakeside boundary, Rampart Street, separates it from the historic African-American neighborhood of **Tremé**. Here, Louis Armstrong Park embraces Congo Square, site of Sunday slave gatherings in the 1700s, while the city's best brass bands play in small neighborhood bars. A terrific music festival, and a couple of low-key museums are attracting a trickle of tourists to what has always been a culturally vibrant area.

On the other side of the Quarter, across **Canal Street**, the **CBD** (Central Business District), bounded by the river and I-10 (Claiborne Ave), spreads upriver to the elevated Pontchartrain Expressway. This was the early "American sector", settled by Anglo-Americans after the Louisiana Purchase in 1803. Today, dominated by offices, hotels and banks, it also incorporates the revitalizing **Warehouse District** and, toward the lake, the gargantuan **Superdome**. A short ferry ride across the river from the foot of Canal Street takes you from downtown to the suburban west bank, where old **Algiers**, set on a dramatic bend in the Mississippi, features a Mardi Gras museum and some photogenic vernacular architecture.

Back on the east bank, it's an easy journey upriver from the CBD to the rarefied **Garden District**, an area of gorgeous old mansions – some highly restored, others derelict –

covering the thirteen or so blocks between Jackson and Louisiana avenues. Don't confuse it with the **Lower Garden District**; creeping between the expressway and Jackson, this is quite a different creature, its run-down old houses filling with the many artists and musicians who can no longer afford to live in the French Quarter. The best way to get to the Garden District is on the historic streetcar, which clangs its way along swanky **St Charles Avenue**, the district's lakeside boundary; you can also approach it from **Magazine Street**, a six-mile stretch of galleries, restaurants and antique stores that runs parallel to St Charles riverside. Entering the Garden District you're officially in **uptown**, which spreads upriver to encompass **Audubon Park and Zoo**, Loyola and Tulane **universities**, and, where the streetcar takes a sharp turn inland, the studenty **Riverbend** district.

If you're here for Jazz Fest, you'll be spending a lot of time in **Mid-City**, the huge sweep of land fanning out beyond Tremé and the CBD up to Lake Pontchartrain. In addition to the Fair Grounds racetrack, site of the annual festival, Mid-City incorporates **Esplanade Ridge**, where Victorian houses and a handful of good restaurants hug both sides of Esplanade Avenue. Esplanade slices through the heart of the district, ending up at **City Park** with its impressive Museum of Art.

ARRIVAL

By air

New Orleans International Airport (MSY), some eighteen miles northwest of downtown on I-10, is relatively small and easy to handle. The **information booth** (daily 8am–9pm) in the baggage claim area has leaflets and maps. For a list of **airlines** that use MSY, see p.287.

The best way to get into town is by **taxi**. Flat-rate fares to downtown – a twenty- to thirty-minute journey – are $24 for up to two people, or $10 each for three or more. Simply join the line outside baggage claim and wait for the controller to usher you into a cab. If you're traveling alone, it's cheaper to take the **airport shuttle** (every 10min; $10 to downtown hotels; ☎592-0555), but because it stops frequently to drop people off, the journey can take as long as an hour. Tickets are available from 24-hour desks in the baggage claim area or from the driver.

There's also a **public bus** from the airport to Tulane Avenue in the CBD (daily 6am–6.30pm; every 15–25min; $1.50), but it holds carry-on luggage only.

By car

New Orleans is traversed by **I-10**, which runs east–west between Florida and California. You can get onto it from I-59 (east of the city) and I-55 (west). Taking I-12, which runs east–west north of the lake, hooks you up with the **Lake Pontchartrain Causeway** – at 23 miles, the longest bridge in the world – which enters the city from the northwest and connects with I-10.

Approaching from either direction on I-10 you're confronted with the usual bewildering choice of lanes and lack of signs: make sure not to stray onto I-610, which bypasses downtown altogether. For the **CBD** take exit 234C, following signs for the Superdome; for the **French Quarter** take 235B, following signs for Vieux Carré, and for the **Garden District** take the St Charles Street exit.

By bus or train

Amtrak trains (☎1-800/872-7245), from LA, Miami, New York and Chicago, and **Greyhound** buses (☎1-800/ 231-2222) stop at the Union Passenger Terminal, Loyola

ARRIVAL

Avenue, near the Superdome (☎528-1610). This area, beneath the Pontchartrain Expressway, is dangerous at night; call a cab (see p.13) to collect you.

INFORMATION AND MAPS

Before you leave home it's worth contacting the **New Orleans CVB** (☎1-800/672-6124 or 504/566-5011,

NEW ORLEANS ON THE INTERNET

Ⓦ*www.annerice.com*
Author Anne Rice's official site has more than one hundred pages, including transcripts of her regular voicemail messages (☎522-8634; see p.95), all the scoop on her latest projects and an ordering service for a range of Rice-related merchandise.

Ⓦ*www.eccentricneworleans.com*
A fond celebration of New Orleans' many oddballs. Read about local legends past and present, from Ruthie the Duck Lady and Evangeline the Oyster Girl to cool cats Quintron and Miss Pussycat, darlings of the performance art scene.

Ⓦ*www.k-doe.com*
As camp, colorful and off the wall as the R&B legend himself, Ernie K-Doe's memorial site features a photo gallery, details of his Mother-in-Law Lounge, and snippets of homespun wisdom from the "Emperor of the World" himself.

Ⓦ*www.mardigrasindians.com*
Detailed, well-written and illustrated history of New Orleans' extraordinary black Indians (see p.310), produced under the aegis of the Mardi Gras Indian council.

Ⓦ*www.neworleanscvb.com*), whose Web site features a stack of downloadable discount coupons. Once you've arrived, for detailed information, including a choice of self-guided walking tours, drop by the **State Tourism Information Center**, in the French Quarter at 529 St Ann St, on Jackson Square (daily 9am–5pm; Ⓣ566-5031). Their free **maps** are adequate, but for more detail – and if you're driving – you'd do better to buy the Dolph Street Map of New Orleans, which is widely available.

Ⓦ*www.mardigrasneworleans.com*
Compiled by a fifth-generation New Orleanian, this is the best site for anyone interested in the history of Mardi Gras, along with tips on how to get the most out of carnival, with broadcasts, videos and useful links.

Ⓦ*www.neworleansonline.com*
Searchable resource with copious links. Features include a directory of restaurants and hotels, a detailed Mardi Gras section, well-researched articles, and essays on culture, music and activities. Offers internet-only accommodation deals and downloadable discount coupons.

Ⓦ*www.satchmo.com*
Probably the best all-round music site, featuring listings, features, interviews, music news, messageboards and a CD- and video-ordering service, and links to local music-related homepages.

See also overleaf for the online versions of the *Times-Picayune Gambit*, *Offbeat* and WWOZ.

INFORMATION AND MAPS

NEWSPAPERS AND MAGAZINES

Though New Orleans' **media** can be astonishingly parochial, there's no better way to get a sense of what drives this quirky city than by reading its papers. The **news daily** is the *Times-Picayune* (a *picayune* being the Creole term for a small coin), which costs 50¢, $1.50 on Sunday. Heavily geared toward local stories, it has some strong columnists, and on Friday it includes an **entertainment supplement**, *Lagniappe* (another Creole term, meaning a little extra, a treat) – though the music listings, arranged first by venue and then by date, aren't user-friendly. Literary events are listed in the books pages of the Sunday edition. There's an **online version** of the *Times-Picayune* at ⓦ*www.nolalive.com*

New Orleans also has a host of good **free papers**, available from cafés, bars and stores. The excellent **weekly** *Gambit* (ⓦ*www.bestofneworleans.com*), published on Tuesdays, leans slightly more to the left than the *Times-Picayune*, with lively editorials and local news. Its *Calendar* pages are a good source of **entertainment information**, and foodies will appreciate the dining supplement. A sister publication, the glossy monthly *Best of New Orleans*, is geared toward tourists who want to discover the "real New Orleans". Unfortunately, it doesn't reveal quite as many insiders' tips as it likes to imply: reviews are simply lifted straight from *Gambit*.

Star among the city's publications, however, has to be *Offbeat* (ⓦ*www.offbeat.com*), a splendid **music monthly** filled with news, reviews and extensive listings. Though it's essential for anyone interested in the live music scene, by the end of the month the **listings** can be less reliable, so call venues to check – the bi-hourly schedules announced on WWOZ (see opposite) are simply drawn from *Offbeat*. Newer on the scene, the monthly *Where y'at*, though in nowhere near the same class as *Offbeat*, is worth a look for features and record reviews.

For gay publications and Web sites, see p.264.

TELEVISION AND RADIO

You're not likely to be spending much time in front of the TV in New Orleans, but if you're near one on a Thursday evening at 10.30pm, it's worth checking cable channel Cox 10 for the live music show **Louisiana Jukebox**. Repeated throughout the week, it features performances by big-name and up-and-coming local stars, interviews and music news.

There's more New Orleans music on Sunday evenings, when local **radio station** WWNO (89.9FM) airs *American Routes*, which covers the history of American music from a local angle. By far the best of the radio stations, however, is the fabulous, nonprofit **WWOZ** (90.7FM). Playing roots New Orleans music – R&B, blues, brass, jazz, funk, gospel – along with world music, Cajun and old-time country, it also features jam sessions, interviews, poetry, and ticket competitions. You can hear it **online** at Ⓦ*www.wwoz.org*

CITY TRANSPORT

It's just as well that New Orleans' most visited neighborhoods are a dream to **walk** around – the French Quarter and Garden District, in particular, are best enjoyed by a leisurely stroll – because, other than the obligatory jaunt on the **St Charles streetcar**, you'll get little mileage out of the city's limited **public transport** system. To make the most of your time, budget for quite a few **taxi** rides, and always count on taking a cab if you're traveling beyond the French Quarter at night.

TELEVISION AND RADIO • CITY TRANSPORT

Buses and streetcars

The Regional Transit Authority (RTA; 24hr **information**
℡248-3900) runs a network of **buses** across the city ($1.25,
exact fare required). **Routes** are numbered and named; the
most useful include "Magazine" (#11), which runs along
Magazine Street from Canal Street to Audubon Park, and
"Esplanade" (#48), which will take you from the Quarter
up to City Park. The streetcar that so inspired Tennessee
Williams is sadly defunct, but you will still see a bus named
"**Desire**" (#82) along Canal, Rampart and Decatur.
There's little reason to jump on, but its illuminated sign can
be a startling vision at night as it sweeps towards you
through the dark.

VisiTour passes, available from the tourist office (see p.9)
and most major hotels, give unlimited travel on all streetcars
and buses ($5 per day, $12 for three consecutive days).

You're far more likely to use the handsome **St Charles
streetcar** (a National Historic Monument, dating back
around one hundred years) that rumbles a thirteen-mile
loop from Canal Street, along the "neutral ground" (median) of St Charles Avenue in the Garden District, past
Audubon Park and the Riverbend, to Carrollton ($1.25
each way; exact fare; 25¢ for transfers). The cars trundle
along at an average speed of 9mph; it takes about 45 minutes for a full one-way trip. Services taper off after dark,
when you're better off taking a cab than hanging around in
an unfamiliar neighborhood. For more on the **history** of
the streetcar, see p.91.

There's a newer, tourist-targeted, streetcar line along the
riverfront, where red trolleys make ten stops between the
Convention Center and Esplanade Avenue (Mon–Fri
6am–11pm, Sat & Sun 7am–11pm; every 15min; $1.50;

exact fare). It's a total trip of less than two miles, and though the views of the water are pretty, you're not likely to need it unless you have trouble walking.

Though it is legal to drink a cocktail on the streets of New Orleans (see p.208), you can't carry it – or any drink – onto the bus or streetcar. Nor can you eat or smoke on board.

The only public transport within the French Quarter are the **Vieux Carré** shuttles (Mon–Fri 5am–7pm, Sat & Sun 8am–6pm; $1.25; exact fare) – little green buses done up to look like trolleys.

Taxis

The most convenient way of traveling any distance in New Orleans, especially after dark, is by **taxi**. **United** is by far the best firm, with the most reliable drivers and the safest cars. You can call them (☎522-9771), hail them from the street (try along Canal or Decatur), or pick them up in the French Quarter outside the *Omni Royal Orleans Hotel* on St Louis Street at Royal, or the *Bourbon-Orleans* on Orleans Street.

Driving

It's not a particularly good idea to **drive** in New Orleans, especially around the French Quarter, where sections of the narrow, one-way streets are regularly closed off to create pedestrianized enclaves, plodding mule-drawn buggies cause traffic snarl-ups and parking is all but impossible. Citywide, the brutal **parking** restrictions are something of a local joke, with a host of impenetrable regulations that lead to regular impoundments and steep fines. Meters are expensive and invariably in use, while public parking lots will charge you as much as $20 for a couple of hours. If you've arrived by car, your best bet is to stick it in the hotel parking lot – most French Quarter hotels charge for the privilege – and forget about it.

You may, however, want to **rent a car** to head out of the city; though all the major chains have booths at the airport, it may be cheaper to arrange rental from a downtown branch. See p.287 for a list of toll-free numbers, and be aware that rates vary widely according to season, the day of the week and special deals.

SIGHTSEEING TOURS

There is a bewildering variety of **tours** of New Orleans, from whistle-stop jaunts in air-conditioned buses to preposterous moonlit ghost-hunts. **Walking tours** are especially popular – notwithstanding the possibility of showers and, especially in summer, debilitating heat and humidity. The list opposite includes the best; the tourist office (see p.9) has racks of leaflets detailing many others.

Many visitors, especially first-timers or those with kids in tow, take a narrated trot through the Quarter in one of the **mule-drawn carriages** that wait in line behind Jackson Square on Decatur. These can be fun, though in most cases you should take the "historic" running commentary with a pinch of salt – and the sight of the mules, decked out in funny hats and sunglasses, puts some people off. Rates are generally negotiable; expect to pay around $10–12 per person for thirty to forty-five minutes.

One romantic way to while away a few hours on a steamy afternoon is to take a narrated **cruise** along the Mississippi. For details of the *Natchez* steamboat, and the *John James Audubon* riverboat, which travels between the aquarium and the zoo, see p.106.

Some of the tour operators listed below can also take you to the River Road plantations, which are reviewed in the "Out of the city" chapter (see p.134).

Walking tours

Bienville Foundation

Ⓣ945-6789. 2hr–2hr 30min; $18–20; schedules vary with the season.
Superb "alternative" French Quarter walking tours, emphasizing literary sites, women's history, jazz, the city's multicultural legacy and its gay heritage.

Friends of the Cabildo

Ⓣ523-3939. Mon 1.30pm, Tues–Sun 10am & 1.30pm; 2hr; $10; no reservations required.
Reliable historical overviews, concentrating on the French Quarter. Tours set off from the 1850 House, 523 St Ann St on Jackson Square.

Jean Lafitte National Historica Historical Park Service

Ⓣ589-2636. Daily 9.30am, 11.30am, 1.30pm & 3pm; 30–45min.

Led by Park rangers, these free daily tours include a history jaunt (10.30am; 1hr 30min) covering the French Quarter and giving an overview of the city. You should collect a pass, available from the NHPS visitor center, 419 Decatur St, after 9am on the day to make sure of getting a place. It's also worth checking their cultural programs. For more on this exemplary visitor center, see p.36.

Le Monde Creole

Ⓣ568-1801. Mon–Sat 10.30am & 2.30pm, Sun 10am & 2.30pm; 2hr–2hr 30min; $17.50; reservations advised.
Run by the same people as the Laura plantation on the River Road (see p.139), these lively French Quarter walking tours stop at sites that played a part in the true-life saga of a wealthy Creole family – including, on

the morning tours, a local cemetery. The fee also gets you free entry to the Pharmacy Museum (see p.43). Tours set off from their store, Le Monde Creole, 624 Royal St.

Save Our Cemeteries

℡525-3377. Layfayette Cemetery No. 1: Mon, Wed & Fri 10.30am, $6, 1hr; St Louis Cemetery No. 1: Sun 10am, $12, 1hr 30min.

Non-profit organization that leads fascinating, scholarly tours of Lafayette Cemetery and St Louis No 1 Cemeteries. Call (by 4pm on Friday for the St Louis No. 1 tours) for meeting points and to reserve.

Bus tours

Gray Line

℡569-1401 or 1-800/535-7786. Reliable bus tours of the city

(2hr; $23), plantations (4hr–7hr 30min; $33–45), "haunted" sites (2hr; $18) and swamps (3hr 15min; $38), along with walking tours of the French Quarter (2hr; $15) and Garden District (2hr 15min; $18). All tours leave from the Toulouse Street wharf; reservations are essential.

New Orleans Tours

℡592-0560 or 1-800/543-6332. Similar to Gray Line, though fractionally cheaper, with a choice of van tours, walking tours and river cruises.

Roots of New Orleans

℡596-6889.

African-American heritage tours ($35–65), including a 5hr "Roots 'n' the church" deal that includes a gospel mass and brunch. Call for schedules and to reserve.

"Haunted" tours

In recent years the choice of tours promising magic, voodoo, vampires and **ghosts** has become dizzying. Among the high-camp, the overpriced and the just plain silly, there are a few actually worth checking out.

Historic New Orleans Walking Tours

☎947-2120.

Run by respected local historian Robert Florence, these lively tours give heaps of informed detail while foregoing the spooky costumes and to-go beers. The "Cemetery & Voodoo" tour covers St Louis No. 1, Congo Square, priestess Marie Laveau's home and a voodoo temple; meet at *Café Beignet*, 334 Royal St (Mon–Sat 10am & 1pm, Sun 10am; 2hr; $15). The anecdotal "Garden District & Cemetery" tour also emphasizes architecture and plant life; meet at the Garden District Bookshop in The Rink mall at Washington and Prytania (daily 11am & 1.45pm; 2hr; $14). No reservations; arrive 15min early.

New Orleans Ghost & Vampire Tour

☎524-0708.

If you're out less for authenticity than to whoop it up, consider the tours – featuring magic tricks and "psychic demonstrations" – led by Englishman Thomas Duran and his team. Ghost tours leave from Washington Artillery Park, across Decatur from Jackson Square (daily 8pm; around 2hr; $15). For the cemeteries, meet at *CC's Coffee House* on Royal and St Philip in the Quarter (Mon–Sat noon, Sun 10.30am; around 2hr; $15). No reservations.

New Orleans Historic Voodoo Museum Tours

☎523-7685.

Cemetery and voodoo tours of the Quarter (Mon–Sat 1pm; 2hr 30min; $19), "undead" tours (nightly 8pm; 2hr 30min; $15), a "mourning tour" of St Louis No. 1 (daily 10.30am; 2hr; $15), plus voodoo ceremonies and van trips to haunted swamps and plantations. Prices include reduced museum admission (see p.56). Reservations required.

Veronica Powers

☎947-6302.

Witty and informative tours led by a voodooist; she'll take

SIGHTSEEING TOURS

17

you through the cemeteries and to a voodoo temple, gearing tours around your interests. Call for schedules and meet at the Little Shop of Fantasy, 523 Dumaine St in the Quarter. Reservations essential; $13.

Swamp tours

The popular fantasy of the misty, mysterious **Louisiana swamp** as an eerie place, flickering with ghostly gray Spanish moss, is not so very far from the truth. New Orleans' local swamps – many of them protected wilderness areas just thirty minutes' drive from downtown – are otherworldly enclaves, brought to life by informed guides eager to share their knowledge of local flora and fauna.

When taking a tour it's important to remember that although the swamp ecosystem supports a wide range of **wildlife**, including bald eagles, deer, snapping turtles, bears, alligators and bobcats, what you actually get to see will depend upon the season, how hungry the animals are and sheer luck. Your best chances of seeing an **alligator** are in the summer, when they bask sleepily in the sun. Whatever time of the year you come, bring a hat, sunscreen and – most importantly – bug repellent.

Note that you can also take swamp tours with Gray Line (see p.16) or the Voodoo Museum (p.17). And if you prefer to explore the swamps **independently**, turn to the account of the Barataria Preserve in "Out of the city", p.146.

Dr Wagner's Honey Island Swamp Tours

☎504/641-1769. Daily; 2hr; without transport from New Orleans $20, under-12s $10; with transport $40/$20. No credit cards.

Based some ten miles outside suburban Slidell, north of Lake Pontchartrain, ecologist Dr Paul Wagner offers the most informative swamp tours available. Twelve-seater boats venture onto the delta of the lower Pearl River, a pristine wilderness inhabited by raccoons, nutrias, bobcats, wild pigs, black bears and alligators, as well as ibis, great blue herons and snowy egrets.

Louisiana Swamp Tours

Ⓣ504/689-3599. Barataria swamps Nov–Feb 9am, noon & 2pm; March–Oct also 4.15pm; without transport $20.50, children $16.50; with transport $38/$20. Plantation-swamp combination daily 8.30am & 10.30am; with transport only, $50/$30.

Daily boat tours through the Barataria swamps. They also offer a plantation-swamp combination. They're on Hwy-301, south of the Lafitte National Park visitor center (see p.148).

New Orleans Swamp Tours

Ⓣ504/592-0560. Barataria swamps daily 10am & 2pm; 1hr 45min; with transport only, $38, children $23. Bayou Sauvage wildlife sanctuary daily 10am, noon & 2pm; 1hr 45min; with transport only, $20/$10.

Large boats, holding forty to sixty passengers, ply the Barataria swamps and the nearby Bayou Sauvage wildlife sanctuary.

Voyageur Swamp Tour

Ⓣ504/643-4839. 2hr; without transport $20, children $12; with transport $40/$32.

"Eco" tours that use quiet, six-person boats – everyone helps to paddle – to reach stretches of the Honey Island swamp inaccessible to motorized vehicles. They're at 55344 Hwy-90E in Slidell.

SIGHTSEEING TOURS

The French Quarter

The heartbreakingly beautiful **French Quarter** – or Vieux Carré ("old square") – is where New Orleans all began. Today, battered and bohemian, decaying and vibrant, it's the spiritual core of the city, its fanciful cast-iron balconies, hidden courtyards and time-stained stucco buildings exerting a haunting fascination that has long caught the imagination of artists and writers. Though most of the buildings of the French city burned in two major fires in 1788 and 1794, the culture of the Vieux Carré remained predominantly French-Creole right up to the Civil War; these days it has more of the feel of a seductive Caribbean port than a European metropolis.

The area covered by this chapter is shown in detail on color map 4 at the back of this book.

The Quarter covers a compact **grid** – unchanged since it was laid out by military engineer Adrien de Pauger in 1721 – bounded by the Mississippi River, Rampart Street, Canal Street and Esplanade Avenue. Its hub is Europeanate **Jackson Square**, facing the river. Upriver, the **Upper Quarter** sees most of the **commercial activity**, concentrated in the blocks between brash Decatur and Bourbon streets. Here, as in the days of the Creole city, the gorgeous old buildings hold offices, shops, galleries, restaurants and bars on the lower floors, with apartments on the upper stories. In the streets beyond Bourbon, up toward Rampart Street, and in those of the **Lower Quarter**, downriver from Jackson Square, things become more peaceful – these are quiet, predominantly **residential** neighborhoods, home to much of the Quarter's **gay** community.

While there's no shortage of formal **attractions** – the Presbytère, Cabildo and Historic New Orleans Collection museums, to name but a handful – you could easily spend an entire week simply wandering the streets, absorbing the Quarter's melange of sounds, sights and smells. Early morning, when the city is washed in pearly light from the river, is a good time to explore, as sleepy locals wake themselves up with strong coffee in neighborhood patisseries, stores crank open their shutters and streetwise brass bands set up to blast the roofs off Jackson Square.

Walking tours of the Quarter are reviewed on pp.15–16.

Some history

Despite inauspicious beginnings as a miserable colonial outpost built on an unprepossessing swamp, the French – then Spanish – city thrived thanks to its location near the mouth of the Mississippi River. Well into the nineteenth century, when, following the Louisiana Purchase, the new, Anglo-American Faubourg St Mary mushroomed around it, the Vieux Carré held its own, becoming the **first municipality** of a divided city (see p.301). Though New Orleans' **antebellum** "golden era" marked the ascendancy of the American sector, planters, bankers and lawyers continued to build homes in the old Creole quarter, entertaining in its famed theaters and ballrooms. During this period a third of the French Quarter was owned by **free people of color**, wealthy francophones – many of them slave-owners from the West Indies – a significant number of whom sent their children to Paris to be educated.

For more on the history of New Orleans, see p.293.

After the **Civil War**, the district took a downturn, its old buildings used as tenements to house poor Italian and black families, or torn down to make room for new developments along the river and behind Canal Street. Things improved in the 1920s, however, when a colony of **artists**, including writers Sherwood Anderson and William Faulkner, drifted to the Quarter; it was partly their fascination with its architecture and rich cultural history that led in the 1930s to the formation of the **Vieux Carré Commission** – whose remit was to preserve the district's "quaint and distinctive character" – and a restoration program undertaken by Roosevelt's Works Progress Administration. Since then, the Quarter has been both a refuge for bohemians and something of a battleground for preservationists – the hardest fight yet being against a 1946 proposal to build a highway right through it, which was only definitively defeated in the 1970s. However, as the mounting number of themed restaurants, condo developments and fast-food outlets reveals, the Commission's authority does not extend to vetting either what buildings are used for, or what is done to their interiors. There is genuine concern that as skyrocketing rents squeeze out longtime locals and pump in well-heeled out-of-towners – those who can afford to pay premium rates for a bijou condo with a cast-iron balcony – this historically evolving, vibrant neighborhood could well transmogrify into a lifeless theme park.

For now, however, and against all the odds, the Quarter battles on, as vital and full of heart as ever. Its lopsided buildings, many of them buckling and rotting in the perpetual damp, still emanate a ghostly beauty, accentuated by the

THE FRENCH QUARTER

tiny aesthetic details – a string of Christmas-tree lights, a little cast-iron chair, voluptuous green ferns – added by residents too besotted by the place to let it die.

French Quarter accommodation is reviewed on pp.157–162, restaurants on pp.176–189, bars on p.208–212, and music venues on pp.221–224 & 228–230.

JACKSON SQUARE

Map 4, F5–G5.

Ever since its earliest incarnation as the Place d'Armes, a dusty parade ground used for public meetings and executions, **Jackson Square** has been at the heart of the French Quarter. Its spruce appearance today owes much to the **Baroness Pontalba,** who in 1851 revamped the drill ground into a landscaped park and renamed it for Andrew Jackson, hero of the Battle of New Orleans (see p.112), who went on to become the US president.

A welcome open space in the congested French Quarter, the square is bathed in the light from the river, "a worldly sort of light", as Mark Twain put it, that still today renders it "brilliant". And with its iron benches, neat lawns and blaze of flowerbeds, it somehow manages to stay tranquil, despite the streams of photo-snapping tourists, overexcited school groups, waiters on their breaks and the odd crashed-out casualty. Presiding over them all, an **equestrian statue** – the first in the nation, constructed by Clark Mills in 1856 – shows Jackson in uncharacteristically jaunty mode, waving his hat. It's a sculptural masterpiece, with the mighty horse, rearing on its hind legs, perfectly balanced on the plinth. The hectoring inscription, "The Union Must and Shall be Preserved", was pointedly added by General "Beast" Butler (see p.84) during the Civil War occupation.

JACKSON SQUARE

THE BARONESS

Jackson Square, and the smart red buildings that flank it, are the result of a melodrama of murder and money starring the willful Baroness Pontalba, known in New Orleans simply as "the Baroness". Born Micaëla Almonester in 1795, she was the daughter of Don Andrés Almonester, who came to New Orleans in 1769 as a clerk and went on to become one of the city's richest and most influential philanthropists. At the age of 16 she was married in St Louis Cathedral to Célestin Pontalba, a distant cousin. The couple moved to Paris, where Micaëla, whose considerable inheritance included all the real estate fringing the Place d'Armes, became convinced that her father-in-law, the Baron Pontalba, had engineered the wedding in order to get at her wealth. After a decade of bitter wrangling over money, Micaëla eventually left Célestin, taking their three children, upon which her father-in-law promptly disinherited them. In 1834, during a violent row, the baron shot her four times in the chest, and proceeded to kill himself. Micaëla miraculously survived, though she lost two fingers defending herself. Four years later, by then a baroness, she divorced Célestin, and in 1849 – with Europe in revolutionary turmoil – returned to New Orleans.

Back in the city, the baroness set about recreating the elegance she had so admired in the French capital. By all accounts she was a harsh taskmistress, supervising construction to the last detail and refusing to pay for the many changes she demanded. In 1851 the Pontalba Buildings were completed, at a cost of $300,000, and renovations began on the square; the baroness, however, returned to Paris for a reconciliation with Célestin. Seriously ill, he handed over his affairs to Micaëla, who, in an ironic twist, succeeded in adding all his property to her own.

St Peter, Chartres and St Ann streets are pedestrianized where they border the square. In this enclave you'll find some of the city's major sights: the chic **Pontalba Buildings**, their street-level rooms taken up by shops and restaurants; **St Louis Cathedral**; and, flanking the cathedral like stout bodyguards, the **Cabildo** and **Presbytère** museums. During the day, everyone passes by at some time or another, weaving their way through the tangle of artists, Lucky Dog vendors, rainbow-clad palmists, magicians, shambolic jazz bands and blues musicians. At night it's more peaceful, with just a few waifs and strays lingering in the shadows cast by the stately, floodlit buildings.

Pick up free maps, leaflets and self-guided walking tours at the State Tourism Information Center (see p.9), 529 St Ann St in the lower Pontalba Buildings.

St Louis Cathedral

Map 4, F5. Daily 7am–6.30pm; tours Mon–Sat 9am–5pm, Sun 1–5pm except during services; free.

A postcard-perfect backdrop for the Andrew Jackson statue, **St Louis Cathedral**, commanding the square across Chartres Street, is the oldest continuously active cathedral in the United States, and the third church on this spot. Its construction in 1794 – the second church had been destroyed by the fire of 1788 – was funded, along with the Cabildo and the overhaul of the Presbytère, by the philanthropist Don Almonester; in 1850, while Almonester's daughter was busy sprucing up the square around it (see box opposite), it was enlarged and remodeled by eminent architect J.N.B. de Pouilly. Dominated by three tall slate steeples, the dove-gray facade, which marries a Greek Revival symmetry with copious French arches, is oddly two-dimensional, like some elaborate stage prop for the lively street theater below.

Though the cathedral has always been central to the life of this very Catholic city – Andrew Jackson laid his sword on the altar in thanks for victory at the Battle of New Orleans; voodoo queen Marie Laveau (see p.58) was baptized and married here – the modest interior, an unexceptional assemblage of murals, sculpture and stained glass, presents little to get excited about. Highlights include Don Almonester's marble tomb, inscribed with a list of his many bequests, and an overblown tabernacle brimming with cherubs.

The view of the cathedral from Washington Artillery Park (see p.107), across Decatur Street, makes a great photo opportunity.

Flanking the cathedral, two narrow flagstoned lanes link Jackson Square to Royal Street. Downriver, **Père Antoine Alley** is named for the beloved Capuchin priest Antonio de Sedella, who came to New Orleans in 1779. He was promptly banished by the Spanish authorities – they'd discovered that he had been sent to enforce the Inquisition – only to return a few years later to become rector of the cathedral. Adored by his parishioners for his many kindnesses, he is still fondly remembered as a hero in a city that boasts many. On the other side of the cathedral, photogenic **Pirate's Alley**, supposedly where Jean Lafitte met Andrew Jackson to plan the Battle of New Orleans in 1815 (highly unlikely, since the alley wasn't built until the 1830s), is lined with vibrantly colored town houses. At no. 624, Faulkner House Books (see p.250) occupies a ground-floor room in the sunshine-yellow building where the author wrote his first novel, *Soldier's Pay*, in 1927.

Behind the cathedral, on a patch of land that was the scene of numerous duels in the 1800s, the pretty, iron-fenced **St Anthony's Garden** is sandwiched between the two alleys. In the center, in front of the huge marble statue of the Sacred Heart of Jesus – which casts an eerie shadow across the cathedral at night – is an obelisk commemorating the crew of a French ship who in 1857 all died of yellow fever in the Gulf of Mexico.

The Cabildo

Map 4, F5. Tues–Sun 9am–5pm; $5 (20 percent discount with admission to any other museum in the State Museum group; see box overleaf).

On the upriver side of the cathedral, the Hispanic **Cabildo** was built as the Casa Capitular, seat of the Spanish colonial government (the "Very Illustrious Cabildo"). Today, it is home to one of the best history museums you'll find anywhere. The building – which cuts an impressive dash with its columned arcade, fan windows and fine wrought-iron balconies – is another legacy of the philanthropist Don Almonester, who, after the original building burned in the fire of 1788, offered funds to remodel it in the grand style of the home country. Historically, the Cabildo is hugely significant – not least for being where, in 1803, the Spanish colony was transferred back to France, and three weeks later, under the terms of the **Louisiana Purchase**, was sold to the United States (see p.298).

This outstanding **museum** ably picks its way through the complex tangle of cultures, classes and races that binds together Louisiana's history. Crammed with well-captioned artifacts, it sets off with the Native Americans and winds up with the demise of Reconstruction – rather than attempting to see the whole place, it's best to concentrate on a few sections that particularly interest you. It certainly pulls no punches – in keeping with the city's uncommon fascination with matters morbid, there's a gloomy section devoted to

THE CABILDO

CHAPTER TWO

THE LOUISIANA STATE MUSEUM

The Cabildo – along with the Presbytère (see opposite), 1850 House (p.33), Old US Mint (p.39) and Madame John's Legacy (p.51) – is part of the Louisiana State Museum. Each site is open from Tuesday to Sunday from 9am to 5pm; buying a ticket to two or more gets you a discount of twenty percent, good for three consecutive days.

disease, death and mourning, while another displays the venom with which the White League-dominated Mardi Gras krewes (secret carnival clubs) resisted Reconstruction, barely masking their fury in racist, themed parades. A series of designs shows Union generals portrayed as insects and vermin and newly liberated slaves as simian fools. Black history is well represented throughout the museum, with as much emphasis on the free people of color as on the city's role as the major slave-trading center of the South. Bills of sale show slaves priced for as much as $1350 each, while a worn-smooth auction block stands in front of a mural depicting the markets held in the old St Louis Hotel (see p.48).

On the second floor you can see the bronze **death mask of Napoleon**, made and brought to New Orleans by the exiled emperor's doctor, Francesco Antommarchi, who displayed it in his office on Royal Street for thirteen years before donating it to the city in 1834. Also upstairs is the reconstructed **Sala Capitular**, where the Louisiana Purchase was signed in 1803, and where in 1892 the historic *Plessy vs Ferguson* case (see p.304), which legalized segregation throughout the South, was first argued.

If you've got time, head back to the lobby and nip through the side door into the old **Arsenal**. On the first floor is a room devoted to the **Mississippi**, where model ships and navigational equipment are outshone by the scores of prints, paintings and photographs cataloguing a

THE CABILDO

series of watery disasters – floods, hefty ice floes, steamboat explosions – as well as happier times on those opulent "floating palaces" that plied the river in the nineteenth century. Downstairs, the exhibit on the **coffee trade**, long a mainstay of the city's economy, provides a compelling overview of the changing fortunes of the port. Take time to check out the cases of rare coffee cups, where you'll see, among others, gorgeous specimens of Newcomb pottery, Limoges porcelain, Korean jade and Mexican onyx.

Tennessee Williams wrote much of *A Streetcar Named Desire* in the winter of 1946/47 while living at 632 St Peter St, footsteps away from the Cabildo.

The Presbytère Mardi Gras Museum

Map 4, G5. Tues–Sun 9am–5pm; $5 (20 percent discount with admission to any other museum in the State Museum group; see box opposite).

Forming a matching pair with the Cabildo, the **Presbytère**, on the downriver side of the cathedral, was designed in 1791 as a rectory. It was never used as such, however; the death of Don Almonester, its chief benefactor, put construction on hold, and it was not completed until 1813, when it went on to serve as a courthouse. Today it's an exceptionally good interactive **Mardi Gras museum**, which by covering carnival from every conceivable angle offers a penetrating look into the culture and history of the city, and, even better, a sense of what makes the place tick.

For a history of Mardi Gras, see p.306; if you're planning on coming to the city for carnival, turn to p.269.

Upon entering, you're heralded by a jubilant soundtrack into a darkened room where noisy videos of parades and street revels share space with seemingly incongruous objects – a decorated coconut, a toy coin, a stepladder – that give a taste of what's to come. Beyond the next section, which deals with **carnival's roots** in Europe and Africa and is illustrated with European carnival posters and vintage masks, much of the ground floor is concerned with **official carnival**. Here you can see close-up the extraordinary **costumes** worn at private balls and in the formal parades – jewel-encrusted sceptres, crowns and gauntlets, velvet and ermine cloaks heavy with gems and beads, and plumed, sparkling headgear fit for a fairytale king. Some of the most dazzling exhibits date from the 1870s to 1890s, the golden age of **carnival artistry**, when old-line krewes Comus, Rex, Proteus and Momus dominated the scene: as much creativity went into the invitations, with their arcane wording and bizarre imagery, as into the designs for parade floats and costumes – even the cue sheets for the elaborate *tableaux vivants* staged at the private balls are works of art. A glass case displays the popular newspaper illustrations that recreated these formal extravaganzas for the commoners, while a video offers a privileged glimpse into today's private balls, from old-krewe debs, graciously waving diamond-studded sceptres at their court, to tuxedoed businessmen in weird masks waltzing with ballgowned beauties.

On the second floor, **unofficial carnival** is covered in equal detail, with lots of good stuff on the **Mardi Gras Indians**, including a video of a Sunday evening Indian practice, and fine examples of the flamboyant costumes that are painstakingly hand-sewn by the tribes' friends and family for a full year. In these you can trace various trends in designs and styles: loosely, the downtown "gangs" prefer abstract African designs, sequins and big, sculptural elements, while those from uptown tend towards intricate beadwork, rhinestones and Wild West motifs.

For more on the Mardi Gras Indians, see p.310.

Another case holds costumes worn by lesser-known black carnival groups. The scary **Skeletons** originated in the 1930s, painting bones on tatty black suits and wearing massive papier-mâché skulls; their descendants, known as "bone gangs", occasionally parade with the Indians in Tremé. The **Baby Dolls**, on the other hand, are all but extinct – sassy groups of black prostitutes who, starting around 1912, would flounce through uptown on Mardi Gras day in big pink bonnets, short skirts and bloomers, turning tricks in bars. The section on **gay** Mardi Gras – a cornucopia of fantastic outfits – climaxes in a video of the notorious Bourbon Street awards, where gaggles of glamorous drag queens stagger under colossal get-ups as they compete for the prestigious best costume prize.

The room on **Cajun Mardi Gras** is one of the liveliest in the museum, revealing the celebrations of rural Louisiana to be just as stylized, if not more so, than their urban counterparts. Among the artifacts, photos and videos, highlights include the vaguely disturbing Cajun Mardi Gras costumes, with their tall conical hats, Spanish-moss wigs and impassive full-face masks. Watch out for the startling life-sized video screen disguised as a porch door, behind which mischievous, costumed figures jump out at you begging and taunting – an experience as unnerving and disorientating as carnival itself can be.

It would take several days to see this fantastic museum in its entirety – there are exhibits on "throws" (see p.274), trash collection, float building, music and so on – but be sure you leave time to play **dress-up**: there's a jumble of satiny clown outfits by the exit that you can try on, and a

THE PRESBYTÈRE MARDI GRAS MUSEUM

photo-booth if you want to pose for a souvenir snap. You exit the museum through the gift shop, which though mostly pretty tacky is worth a look for its quirky and vintage carnival **postcards**.

The Pontalba Buildings

Map 4, F5 & G5.

The elegant, three-story **Pontalba Buildings**, which line St Peter and St Ann streets where they border Jackson Square, were commissioned in 1850 by the formidable Baroness Pontalba (see p.24). Having returned from France in 1849 to find her real estate palling in comparison to the American sector across Canal Street, she sought to replace the shabby buildings around the Place d'Armes with elegant colonnaded structures resembling those she'd seen in Paris. The original **architect**, James Gallier Sr – whom the baroness eventually sacked because of their endless squabbling – was responsible for many of the buildings' Greek Revival elements, but the large courtyards at the back, and the arrangement of commercial units on the ground floor with living spaces above, are typically Creole. These were not, as is commonly claimed, the first apartment buildings in the United States, but they were innovative in their use of mass-produced materials and, in particular, of **cast iron** – the iron was cast in New York, the red brick pressed in Baltimore, and the plate glass and slate roof tiles came from England. The stunning visual effect of the wide galleries and balconies, their decorative curlicues centering on cartouches inscribed with the initials A&P – Almonester and Pontalba – sparked off a citywide fad for lacy cast iron, which came to replace the plainer, hand-wrought iron fashioned locally by African slaves.

As the Quarter declined after the Civil War, the apartments lost their exclusivity, and by the end of the nineteenth century they had become tenements. During one of the city's many yellow fever epidemics, health officials reported finding a cow living in one of the rooms. In the 1930s, however, restored by the WPA, they regained their former prestige and are now some of the city's most desirable places to live, with stores and restaurants, along with the **State Tourism Information Center** (see p.9), on the ground floors.

While exploring the Quarter, watch out for the young boys taking advantage of the crowds out to have a good time, spend cash and get drunk. They'll bet that they can tell you where you got your shoes, or some such challenge – the answer, of course, is that you got your shoes on your feet . . .

1850 House

In 1850, when New Orleans was one of the largest cities in the nation, riding on the wealth of its booming port, the Pontalba Buildings were the height of fashion among the prosperous middle class. The cordoned-off rooms of the **1850 House** (Tues–Sun 9am–5pm; $3, 20 percent discount with admission to any other museum in the State Museum group; see p.28), in the lower Pontalba Buildings at 523 St Ann St, recreate the tastes of a well-to-do Creole family from that era. Drawing attention to every piece of rococo revival furniture, Vieux Paris china and fine crystal, but leaving you with little sense of how the family might have lived, it is, in fact, the least interesting of the state museums to anyone but the most passionate fan of decorative arts.

For a good view of the Mississippi, leave the square and cross Decatur Street to the Moonwalk, a promenade where sidewalk musicians serenade you as freighters negotiate the river's perilous current. For more on the river, see p.103.

THE PONTALBA BUILDINGS

FRENCH QUARTER ARCHITECTURE

While the French Quarter streets are as straight as a die, its architecture is a fabulous jumble of shapes and sizes, colors, styles and states of repair. Little exists from before the two great fires of 1788 and 1794, after which Spanish Governor Carondelet ordained that all new buildings should be made of brick, plaster and stucco, with tiled roofs. That said, the streetscape is far from purely Spanish. Most structures marry French and Spanish colonial elements, and many reveal Caribbean influences. Others, most of them dating from the antebellum era, meld Anglo-American and Creole styles.

Many of the vernacular buildings are one-story Creole cottages, and multistory Creole townhouses, both of which are built about a foot off the ground, above a closed ventilated area known as a "crawl space", and with a high gabled roof. The interiors were designed without a hall, with four rooms in a checkerboard square; doors, indistinguishable from the outside from the shuttered ceiling-to-floor windows, open straight from the street into the living quarters. Outside areas held slave quarters, kitchens, outhouses and garconnières, where the sons of the house would take up residence after reaching adolescence. Planters from the West Indies brought the notion of building houses on pillars, protecting them from waterlogging, and added porches – known as galleries – to shield against the sun and rain. The ground floor was used for storage, with living space above and, during good weather, out on the gallery. Hot air inside the house could rise and escape through tall dormer windows, set in steep pitched roofs.

Under the Spanish, louvered shutters replaced heavier battened ones, and fine iron balconies were wrought by African craftsmen. Though they rarely stood higher than two stories, the public buildings especially became heavier-looking and more obviously Mediterranean in style. Courtyards were designed now as extra living areas, where residents cultivated lush tropical plants, along with potent flowers, spices and herbs to mask the odors from the street.

As the nineteenth century drew on, the Anglo-Americans tended to settle on the other side of Canal Street in what is now the CBD, but their influence was still felt in the Quarter, where a number of buildings were designed in simply elegant Federal or Greek Revival styles. With a concern for privacy alien to the Creoles, Americans built their homes with enclosed hallways and indoor toilets.

The ornate cast iron so associated with the Quarter didn't come in till the 1840s, when improved communications and technologies meant that it could be bought in bulk from the industrializing north. Inspired by Baroness Pontalba's apartment buildings on Jackson Square (see p.32), a fad developed for filigree balconies and fences, curly brackets and fluted columns, which were added to old buildings and incorporated into new ones. At the same time, large two- or three-story galleries were tacked onto the front of buildings, supported by narrow pillars, or colonettes. Extending over the sidewalk, the galleries provided shade and shelter for pedestrians and more living space for residents. In the late 1800s, shotgun houses emerged in force: composed of a single row of rooms opening onto each other, they're supposedly named for the fact that you could, in theory, shoot a bullet from the front door to the back without it hitting anything. Long, narrow clapboard structures, the shotguns are most notable for the decorative wooden gingerbread details that early owners ordered from catalogs and stuck to the fronts.

FRENCH QUARTER ARCHITECTURE

DECATUR STREET

Map 4, A6–N6.

When the French Quarter was laid out in 1721, **Decatur Street** (pronounced "deKAYter"), then known as Levee Street, abutted the Mississippi. Today, the land that separates it from the water – four whole blocks of it at Canal Street – has all been dumped by the dramatically shifting river. A broad thoroughfare, noisy with traffic and lined with cheap-and-cheerful tourist shops, bars and restaurants, Decatur becomes more countercultural as you head down-river, where, beyond the touristy **French Market**, a string of dive bars and thrift stores leads you toward the funky **Faubourg Marigny**.

Jean Lafitte National Historical Park Visitor Center

Map 4, D5. Daily 9am–5pm; free.

Something of an anomaly among Upper Decatur's brassy T-shirt shops and theme restaurants, the **Jean Lafitte National Historical Park Visitor Center**, 419 Decatur St, is easy to miss; the entrance is around the back, beyond a broad carriageway and large courtyard. This is a shame: quite apart from being a starting point for excellent **walking tours** (see p.15), as a free introduction to Louisiana's delta region and to the city itself the place can't be bettered.

- -

The Jean Lafitte National Historical Park, which preserves natural and historic sites of interest in the Mississippi Delta, is scattered throughout southern Louisiana. Other sites include the Chalmette Battlefield (see p.112) and the Barataria Preserve (see p.146).

- -

Illustrated panels and detailed time lines cover the walls on subjects as varied as music, cuisine, religions, wildlife and legends of this unique region. Once you've feasted your eyes on these, you can skip the twelve-minute movie with its overblown commentary and head instead for the **listening stations**, where Louisiana natives expound, in a variety of accents, on unique local phrases such as gumbo, *fais-do-do* and, in the words of the song, *Iko Iko*. **Touch-screen monitors** nearby show videos on jazz, brass bands, gospel, R&B, Cajun and zydeco, with classic footage of Louis Armstrong, Mahalia Jackson and Professor Longhair, among others.

Try to time your visit to coincide with one of the center's daily **cultural programs** (9.30am, 11.30am, 1.30pm & 3pm; 30–45min). Whatever you get – a walking tour, a talk, a film, a slide show – is sure to be good, covering one of a hundred different subjects as varied as the modern port, women in New Orleans or cast and wrought iron.

There's also a small **bookshop**, particularly strong on titles dealing with the early history of the city.

The French Market and Farmers Market

Spanning the three riverside blocks downriver from Jackson Square, the low, red **French Market** buildings (Map 4, G6–I6) are said to stand on the site of a Native American trading area. There has certainly been an active market here, in one form or another, since the 1720s; nineteenth-century visitors marveled at the exotic, chaotic jumble of Native Americans, Africans, farmers and fishermen, fast-talking in every language imaginable, trading fragrant herbs, mysterious wild birds and even alligators. Naturalist John James Audubon, shopping in 1821 for fowl to use as studies for his *Birds of America*, called it "the dirtiest place in all the cities of the United States". The

DECATUR STREET

37

colonnaded arcades – much reworked and restored since the first was built in 1813 – are more sanitized now, their specialty stores teeming with tourists snapping up T-shirts, cookbooks and pralines, while musicians play jazz outside the overpriced cafés. The 24-hour **Café du Monde**, traditionally *the* place to snack on *beignets* and café au lait (see p.200), is one place you won't want to miss. Come very early, or very late, and you can almost imagine yourself back at the old French Market coffee stands, where dockers, farmers, businessmen and society ladies would gather at the marble-topped tables to drink steaming, strong coffee before hurrying on with their affairs.

For market stalls, you'll need to head for the **Farmers Market** (Map 4, J6–K6), just off Decatur on N Peters Street, where fresh produce, spices, hot sauce and the like are sold around the clock; the **flea market**, next to it, is full of oddities, as are the quirky thrift and rummage stores opposite on Decatur.

For more on shopping in the French Market
and along Decatur Street, see p.240.

French Market Place, the innocuous alley that runs alongside the Farmers Market, was known in the second half of the nineteenth century as **Gallatin Street**, the dingiest, deadliest block in New Orleans. Blind-drunk sailors and swaggering young blades would enter this cesspit of brothels, barrel houses and dark gambling dens at their peril, many of them never to be seen again. Even police-men refused to set foot near the place, fearing encounters with garroters, murderous prostitutes and knife-wielding pimps. There's little to show for all this derring-do today: just the market stalls on one side and the shabby back end of the Decatur shops on the other.

building, a rust-colored Greek Revival hulk dating from 1835, was saved in the 1850s from sinking into the soggy earth by General Pierre Beauregard's engineering flair.

Most people, however, are here for the **Jazz Museum**, which traces the history of the music that New Orleans calls its own through a wealth of photographs, sheet music, posters, advertising images and old letters – look out for the pencil-written fan mail from a ten-year-old Harry Connick Jr to pianist Armand Hug ("When I saw you play my eyes almost fell out!"). The highlights are, of course, the **musical instruments**, whose battered, well-worn contours are enough to bring tears to the eyes of any jazz buff. There are some real treasures here: among them a cornet and bugle played by the young **Louis Armstrong** while learning his craft at the Waif's Home; Kid Ory's trombone; Sidney Bechet's soprano sax; and a beautifully engraved horn played by Bix Beiderbecke. Look out, too, for the very early brass instruments, including an elegant valveless French horn played in the orchestra of New Orleans' nineteenth-century French Opera House, and a rare B-flat baritone horn, made in 1866. You'll find plenty of quirky humor alongside the reverence, from the "Lose Weight the Satchmo Way" brochure ("A laxative at least once a week is very nice!") to the customized tin-can drum kit made by street musician Cocomo Joe.

Overall, however, despite the celebration, the genuine adulation and enthusiasm that has gone into putting this terrific collection together, small things, like a clumsily typed letter from jazz great Willie "Bunk" Johnson, bring a certain melancholy to the place. Poverty-stricken in his fading years, Johnson was reduced to writing to his old employer, begging him for a bicycle for his 68th birthday so that he would be able to get to the shops. We can only guess what band leader Eddie Edwards would have made of Johnson's plight: in 1929, on a letter from a club manager who agreed to pay his ten-piece Original Dixieland Jazz Band a measly $185 for an eight-hour gig, Edwards scrawled, "In future don't work. Tis better than to do so for nothing."

On the top floor, the Mint also hosts long-term exhibits of **decorative arts** from the state museum collection: you might see anything from **oil paintings** of nineteenth-century Creole nobility through **Newcomb pottery** – Louisiana's glorious contribution to the international arts and crafts movement – to a fascinating selection of **folk art**.

For more on the history of jazz in New Orleans, see p.322.

Esplanade Avenue and the Faubourg

The downriver boundary of the Quarter, **Esplanade Avenue** (Map 4, L7–L1) is a ravishing, if somewhat down-at-heel boulevard, lined with huge, twisted live oaks and decaying Italianate mansions. At the end of the nineteenth century this was the grandest residential street in the declining Creole city; these days its faded glamor is part of its charm. Crossing Esplanade from the Quarter brings you to **Faubourg Marigny** (Map 4), a hip, low-rent area of Creole cottages and shotguns populated by artists, musicians and sundry bohemians. The Faubourg, as it's known, is named for the Creole Bernard de Marigny, a millionaire roué, expert duelist and hopeless gambler who in 1808, aged 18 and in drastic debt, divided his vast plantation into lots and sold them off. Many were bought by the planters, among them numerous free people of color, who flooded the city in 1809 after the slave rebellions in Saint-Domingue (now Haiti). By the 1820s, much of Esplanade and the Faubourg was populated by the free women of color, who, under the semi-institutionalized system of **plaçage** (see p.56), lived with

DECATUR STREET

41

their children in houses bought for them by their white "husbands".

Though the Faubourg is slowly gentrifying, and its bars, coffee shops and restaurants are expanding further and further beyond the Quarter, it's best **not to wander** too far beyond the blocks around Decatur and Frenchmen, the district's main drag. Even Elysian Fields – the street where Stanley and Stella lived in Tennessee Williams' *A Streetcar Named Desire* – can feel distinctly dodgy, despite its heavenly name.

The Faubourg's accommodation is reviewed on pp.162–164, its restaurants on pp.189–190, bars on pp.212–213, and music venues on pp.224–225 & 230.

CHARTRES STREET

Map 4, A5–N6.

Chopped in half by Jackson Square, **Chartres Street** (pronounced "Charders") is quieter and more characterful than Decatur, its appealing mix of bars, patisseries and offbeat shops geared as much to locals as to tourists. It was here, in the building on the riverside corner opposite *Keuffer's Bar* (see p.209), that the **great fire** of Good Friday 1788 broke out, after a candle in a small household shrine set light to a curtain. The family, along with most of the city's population, was at church, leaving the conflagration to rage unabated and 856 buildings, including the cathedral, to be destroyed in its wake.

The Napoleon House

Map 4, D5.

Now a hugely atmospheric bar and restaurant (see p.210), the **Napoleon House**, 500 Chartres St, is in fact made up of two houses. The original, 1797 building is a two-story structure on St Louis; the elegant three-story building on Chartres was added in 1814. With its weatherbeaten stucco walls, heavy wooden shutters and cupola, it's one of the loveliest buildings in the Quarter, and even more so inside – make sure to spend time in its historic, shadowy bar or lush courtyard, sipping a Pimm's Cup and snacking on fine muffulettas (see p.173).

The main house was built for Mayor Nicholas Girod, who, so the story goes, volunteered to host the exiled French emperor in the New World. Sometimes the story goes even further, claiming that, with the help of pirates Jean Lafitte and Dominique You, Girod sent a boat, the *Seraphin*, to rescue Napoleon from the island of St Helena – unaware that he had died three days before it set sail.

Historical Pharmacy Museum

Map 4, E5. Tues–Sun 10am–5pm; $2 (free with a Le Monde Creole walking tour; see p.15).

The quirky **Historical Pharmacy Museum**, 514 Chartres St, offers fascinating insights into the history of medicine. Linging the walls of the 1820s apothecary – in a Creole-American townhouse designed by J.N.B. de Pouilly, who also remodeled St Louis Cathedral – rosewood cabinets are filled with dusty glass jars crammed with herbs, froufrou china containers advertising Creole miracle cures, old medical books and ledgers, and terrifying surgical implements. Indeed, the whole place delights in dwelling on the gorier side of medical history. There's lots of gruesome detail on the **epidemics** that ravaged the city in the nineteenth century, particularly yellow fever, or "black vomit", for which the purging, bleeding and blistering tried by the doctors did nothing to prevent it felling one tenth of the population in one year alone.

CHARTRES STREET

Look out for the 1850s **trephination drill**, a savage saw-toothed corkscrew that was bored into the skull in the belief that it might cure a headache, and the scary-looking **scarefier**, a nineteenth-century blood-letting apparatus with twelve razor-sharp blades. Perhaps worst of all is the present-day **leech mobile home**, a jar of water filled with fat, lurking slugs, just waiting to suck on the tissue of cosmetic or reconstructive surgery patients.

The fragrance in the courtyard of the Pharmacy Museum comes from its sweet olive tree, cultivated in many New Orleans gardens; you can buy it in perfume form at Hové Parfumeur (see p.261).

Climbing the winding stairs past the pretty courtyard brings you to the **entresol**. This shallow storage area, invisible from the outside of the building, is a typical feature of Creole townhouses, sandwiched between the ground-floor commercial area and the private living space above. Upstairs, the museum is mostly devoted to **women's medicine**, with jars of herbs and roots (complete with details of their dismal side effects), barbaric gynecological speculums and a recreated nineteenth-century home-birthing area. Potted histories chart the course of common drugs like morphine and opium – used in the 1800s by 65 percent of women aged 25 to 55 to cure everything from PMS to "hysteria". There's also an account of Lily the Pink, one Lydia Pinkham, whose wildly popular cure for female weakness (which, in the words of the song, did indeed prove to be "most efficacious, in every case") was found in 1906 to be made almost entirely of pure alcohol.

The Beauregard-Keyes House

Map 4, J5. Tours on the hour Mon–Sat 10am–3pm; $5.

The **Beauregard-Keyes House**, a raised 1826 Creole cottage at 1113 Chartres St, owes the first part of its name to Confederate **General Pierre Beauregard**, who ordered the first shot of the Civil War at Fort Sumter and remained a hero in the South long after the war was lost. He rented a room in the house for a couple of years during Reconstruction. In the 1940s, the house was bought by popular novelist **Frances Parkinson Keyes**, who wrote many of her New Orleans-based titles here. Perhaps unsurprisingly, tour guides tend to skim over the years in between, when the French Quarter had declined into a slum, populated mostly by the poor Italians who came to the city in the 1890s. In the early 1900s the house was home to one Corrado Giacona, a Sicilian who sold liquor from the downstairs rooms and refused to pay off the local mob. When four men broke in, intending to make him an offer he couldn't refuse, Giacona was armed and ready; he killed three and critically injured the fourth. Just a typical night in the pre-Vieux Carré Commission French Quarter – or Latin Quarter, as it was then known.

Nothing remains from Gicacona's inauspicious residence in the house, which today is at pains to present itself as an eminently genteel place. It works best as a museum of **decorative arts**, showcasing a wide range of fine old furniture, from Beauregard's rosewood armoires to Keyes' New England-made pieces. Oil paintings include a likeness of the general's daughter Laurie, wearing a bracelet of brass buttons that he sent her from battle. The back rooms look much as they did in Keyes' day, when she set up a study in the old slave quarters and, in keeping with American custom, moved the bathroom and kitchen into the main building. While traveling around the world as editor of *Good Housekeeping* magazine, Keyes accumulated an extensive **doll collection**, some of which is on display in the carriage house, along with decorative porcelain *veilleuses* (nightlights) from Europe.

CHARTRES STREET

It's no coincidence that tours draw to a close in the **gift shop**, which stocks secondhand copies of Keyes' titles (now out of print), including *Dinner at Antoine's*, which sold more than two million, and *Madame Castel's Lodger*, a romance about the house's Beauregard period; you can get them more cheaply, however, in local used bookstores. Before you leave, make sure to stop by the tranquil walled **garden**.

The Old Ursuline Convent

Map 4, J5. Tours Tues–Fri 10am, 11am, 1pm, 2pm & 3pm, Sat & Sun 11.15am, 1pm & 2pm; $5.

Built between 1745 and 1750, the tranquil **Old Ursuline Convent**, 1114 Chartres St, is the only intact French colonial structure in the city, and quite possibly the oldest building in the Mississippi valley. The Ursuline nuns arrived in town from France in 1727, invited by Sieur de Bienville to establish a hospital for his soldiers. Their importance to the early settlement was incalculable: in 1729 they established an orphanage for the children of colonists killed in the Indian rebellion at Fort Rosalie (now Natchez, Mississippi); they also taught (segregated) classes for young Creole, African and Native American girls. Since 1824, when the nuns moved to a new site, the imposing, dove-gray building – typically French-Canadian, with its tall casement windows and steeply pitched roof – has served variously as a school, the seat of the state legislature, and the archbishopric. It's said to be haunted by ghosts of the French **casket girls**, respectable white virgins shipped over in the early days of the colony, who were kept here by the nuns before being sold off as wives – an attempt by Bienville to discourage his French soldiers from coupling with Indian or African women.

Inside, the mishmash of religious paraphernalia includes brightly colored bishops' slippers (red for martyrdom, green for hope) and a gold-embroidered red velvet canopy. Look out for the heavy wooden "Doorway to Heaven", a table on which bishops lay in state in St Louis Cathedral. In the 1846 **St Mary's chapel** next door, a Baroque marble altar displays an overwrought scene of the Revelation and the Virgin Mary, who pops up again on the stained-glass windows; to the right of the altar, she's shown above a foggy view of the Battle of New Orleans.

ROYAL STREET

Map 4, A4–N5.

Elegant **Royal Street** was the main commercial thoroughfare of the Creole city, inhabited by the wealthiest sugar planters and lined with the finest shops. Despite being one of the most touristed routes through the Quarter, it's still a dignified old place, lined with landmark buildings, antique stores and small, chic art galleries. Its fabulous cast-iron **balconies**, the cream of the Quarter's crop, create a stunning streetscape familiar from countless movies, coffee-table books and postcards.

Exchange Alley

Map 4, A4–C4.

Exchange Alley, the pedestrianized lane running parallel to Royal Street between Canal and Conti, was originally intended to lead all the way to the Cabildo. It never got further than the St Louis Hotel, however – making a convenient conduit from the American sector straight into the hotel's slave exchange (see p.49).

In the 1800s this was the "street of the **fencing masters**", inhabited almost exclusively by skilled teachers who trained young men in the art of dueling. Duels, or *affaires d'honneur*, had long been part of the fabric of the

French and Spanish colony, fought with rapiers by proud young Creoles and settled at "first blood"; in the nineteenth century, however, as the city Americanized and rifles became the weapons of choice, the duels became contests to the death.

Exchange Alley cuts across **Bienville** and **Iberville streets**, parallel to Canal. The Vieux Carré Commission has no responsibility for these two streets, and despite the occasional new development, the sleazy, pre-preservation Quarter is revealed in all its dingy glory in the shabby buildings and lots, 1950s neon and dim, dank girlie bars.

The Supreme Court Building

Map 4, D4.

In 1910, when the Quarter was at its most run-down and the Vieux Carré Commission was barely dreamed of, an entire block, bounded by Royal, St Louis, Chartres and Conti, was demolished to make way for a colossal new courthouse. Abandoned in the 1950s in favor of more modern premises in the CBD, the Beaux Arts behemoth is now being restored to house the **Louisiana Supreme Court**. Though the sheer scale of the place makes it an incongruous sight in the narrow streets of the Quarter, its glossy veined marble facade, gleaming behind huge green palms, makes it an undeniably handsome one.

Omni Royal Orleans Hotel

Map 4, D4.

At the corner of Royal and St Louis, the swanky **Omni Royal Orleans Hotel** stands on the site of the famed **St Louis Hotel**, designed in 1838 by J.N.B. de Pouilly. With its copper dome, colossal spiral staircase and opulent frescoes, the St Louis was at the heart of Creole high society, hosting the grandest balls and, in its columned, marble rotunda, holding the city's largest **slave exchange**. To encourage traders to stay the full three hours between noon and 3pm, when auctioneering took place, management offered them a free lunch at the bar – a canny promotion that spread like wildfire through taverns around the nation until the onset of Prohibition.

The hotel's **demise** began with the Civil War. During the city's shambolic Reconstruction period it housed the State Capitol, but was abandoned in 1898 and left to decay for years. Visitors could pay a small fee to tour the ruins – in 1912, British author John Galsworthy was struck by his encounter with a wounded horse, stumbling alone through the broken marble. A hurricane blasted off the roof in 1915, and the wrecked building was finally demolished a year later, to be replaced in 1960 with the swanky *Omni Royal*. At the back of the hotel, on Chartres Street, you can still make out the shadow of the word "exchange", painted on blocks of stone taken from the original building.

Historic New Orleans Collection

Map 4, E4. Tues–Sat 10am–4.30pm; tours 10am, 11am, 2pm & 3pm; $4.

The bulk of the superb **Historic New Orleans Collection** is displayed in the 1792 **Merieult House**, 533 Royal St. In 1938, General Kemper and Mrs Leila Williams, wealthy plantation owners who struck oil on their property, bought and restored the building – one of the few survivors of the 1794 fire – along with a neighboring structure around the corner on Toulouse Street. Entry to the excellent **temporary exhibitions** in the street-front room of the Merieult House is free (past exhibits have covered Mardi Gras, maps, the cotton trade and jazz), but to see the best of the collection, you'll need to take a **guided**

ROYAL STREET

49

tour, which might cover the galleries upstairs, or the **Williams House** on Toulouse, depending on the preferences of the group.

The Historic New Orleans Collection gift shop
sells books, old prints and maps, and
a good range of unusual postcards, see p.248.

The extensive **main collection**, spread across the top floor of the Merieult House, is a fascinating treasure-trove of old maps, drawings, architectural plans, documents relating to the Louisiana Purchase, furniture and paintings. Galleries, organized chronologically, span the years from French settlement to the end of the nineteenth century, with additional themed rooms covering the plantations and the river. Though there is far more to see than can be taken in on one 45-minute tour, **highlights** include the only known portrait of Bienville painted from life and two revealing portraits of Andrew Jackson – furrow-browed and quizzical in 1819, and far more world-weary 21 years later, after his stint as the seventh US president. Look out, too, for the 1720 engraving that portrays the colony as a land of milk and honey peopled with beaming natives – an early publicity poster put out by John Law's Company of the West (see p.294) to attract settlers from Europe. In contrast, an 1803 engraving showing the view from Bernard de Marigny's plantation (today's Faubourg Marigny; see p.41) reveals a vast expanse of open lots and unpromising swamp. Among artifacts from the antebellum era you can see decorative broadsheets from the Creole Salle d'Orleans ballroom and the St Charles Theater, its equivalent in the American sector; a brace of dueling pistols; and designs for elaborate Mardi Gras floats.

For anyone interested in design and decorative arts, the 1889 **Williams House**, 718 Toulouse St (reached via

Merieult House), is a must. The Williamses were prominent citizens – as a young deb during Mardi Gras 1936 Leila reigned as Comus' Queen, while Kemper was Comus in 1953 – and a widely traveled pair, who filled their house with unusual, exotic objects. Treasures include a stool fashioned out of a column from a demolished plantation, lamps made from samovars and antique Chinese burial art, and a host of antique maps.

La Branche House

Map 4, F4.

The **La Branche House**, 700 Royal St, encapsulates all that people imagine the French Quarter to be. Its gorgeous cast-iron balconies and galleries, added a decade after the house was built, form a fanciful, filigree cage around the relatively plain, Greek Revival structure – the apotheosis of the style that the city went mad for in the 1850s. The building is now home to the *Royal Café* (see p.188), which dishes up good Creole food.

Incidentally, the La Branche family originally came from Germany; in New Orleans their name, Zweig, meaning "twig", was Gallicized, a common fate for many non-French surnames.

Madame John's Legacy

Map 4, H4. Tues–Sun 9am–5pm; $3 (20 percent discount with admission to any other museum in the State Museum group; see p.28).

A rare example of the French Quarter's early, West Indies-style architecture (see p.34), **Madame John's Legacy**, just off Royal at 628 Dumaine St, was rebuilt after the fire of 1788 as an exact replica of the 1730 house that had previously stood on the site. It was constructed using the *briquete* *entre poteaux* technique, in which soft red brick is set between steadying, hand-hewn cypress beams, and raised off the ground on stucco-covered brick pillars. The deep wraparound gallery provided extra living space, cooler and airier than the indoor rooms.

Today it stands flush with the street; in the days of the French colony it would have been surrounded by far more land. Gates at the side open onto the wide carriageway that leads around the back, past the kitchen and *garconnière*. Inside, a **museum** displays Southern folk art, and an interpretative exhibition details the house's various inhabitants and changes in fortune.

There never was a real Madame John – the name was given to the house by nineteenth-century author George Washington Cable (see p.314) in his tragic short story *'Tite Poulette*, and it simply stuck.

Look out for the cast-iron fence fronting the *Cornstalk Hotel*, 915 Royal St (see p.158). Bought from a catalog in the 1850s, at the peak of the city's craze for cast iron, the elaborate tangle of brightly painted cornstalks entwined with morning glories has a twin in the Garden District (see p.98).

Gallier House

Map 4, J4. Mon–Fri tours every half-hour 10am–3.30pm; $6, $10 with Hermann-Grima House (see p.55).

The handsome 1857 **Gallier House**, 1132 Royal St – reputedly Anne Rice's inspiration for Louis and Lestat's dwelling in her novel *Interview with the Vampire* – was built for himself and his family by James Gallier Jr, a leading architect like his father before him. Though it's in many ways a typical Creole structure, with a large carriageway leading to a courtyard, Gallier also incorporated a number of American elements, such as the enclosed hall and indoor bathroom. Innovations included a cooling system and a flushing toilet, while the filigree cast-iron galleries would have been the last word in chic.

Tours of the house, focusing on social history rather than fine furniture, are some of the liveliest in the Quarter. The place is set up to recreate the cluttered style of the antebellum era, when the citywide fashion for fancy decoration had to be balanced with the practicalities of living in a swampy climate: fine oil paintings and hand-carved closets stand tilted away from the walls, to avoid being blighted by mildew. In summer – when wealthy Quarterites would have fled the unbearably hot, disease-ridden city for their plantations, or Europe – the house adopts "summer dress": the furniture is swathed in gauze, and the carpets replaced with straw matting.

Though city slaves – valets, repairmen, cooks and nannies – were regarded as being better off than field laborers, who did the back-breaking work of the plantations, life was by no means easy, as a quick wander around the **slave quarters** reveals. These small rooms were minimally furnished with old or broken furniture from the main house, and because slave skins were thought to be "tough", were free of mosquito netting.

The LaLaurie Home

Map 4, J4. Not open to the public.

The most famous **haunted house** in New Orleans, the French Empire **LaLaurie Home**, lurks at 1140 Royal St on the corner with Gov Nicholls. In the nineteenth century this gloomy gray and black pile, now an apartment block, belonged to the LaLauries, a doctor and his socialite wife Delphine, who, although seen wielding a whip as she chased a slave girl through the house to the roof, was merely fined when the child fell to her death. Whispers about the couple's cruelty were horribly verified when neighbors rushed in after a fire in 1834 – believed to have been started intentionally by the shackled cook – to find seven emaciated slaves locked in the attic. There they saw men, women and children choked by neck braces, some with broken limbs; one had a worm-filled hole gouged out of his cheek. The doctor's protestation that this torture chamber was, in fact, an "experiment" was met with vitriol; the next day the pair escaped the baying mob outside their home and fled to France. Since then, many claim to have heard ghostly moans from the building at night; some say they have seen a girl stumble across the balcony.

During Reconstruction the building housed a desegregated girls' school, a hopeful venture that ended in December 1874 when the **White League** militia (see p.72) stormed in and evicted by force any of the pupils they believed to have African blood.

BOURBON STREET

Map 4, A3–M3.

Though you'd never guess it from the hype, there are two faces to world-renowned **Bourbon Street**. The tawdry, touristy, booze-swilled stretch spans the seven blocks from Canal to St Ann: a frat-pack cacophony of daiquiri stalls, novelty shops and tired girlie bars offering "French style" entertainment. This self-contained enclave is best experienced after dark, when a couple – though by no means all – of its **bars** and **clubs** are worth a look, and the sheer mayhem takes on a bacchanalian life of its own. When the attraction of fighting your way through the crowds of weekending drunks starts to pall, however, it's easy to dip out again into the quieter parallel streets to regain some sort of sanity. If you manage to make it as far as St Ann, you come to a kind of crossroads, marked by the gay dance clubs *Oz* and *Parade* (see pp.266 & 267). Beyond here, Bourbon transforms into an appealing, predominantly gay, residential area, scattered with neighborhood bars, corner laundromats and local restaurants.

Incidentally, the **name** has nothing to do with booze. One of the first streets laid out by Pauger in 1721, Bourbon was named for the royal family of France, and only took on its current character during World War II, when a rash of strip clubs and bars opened to cater to soldiers passing through the port.

Hermann-Grima House

Map 4, D3. Mon–Fri tours every half-hour 10am–3.30pm; $6, $10 with the Gallier House (see p.52).

Half a block above Bourbon Street at 820 St Louis, the 1832 **Hermann-Grima House** illustrates the lifestyle of two middle-class Creole families in antebellum New Orleans. Though in many ways a typically elegant, Federal mansion, with a number of characteristic American features – including the central hall – the house's loggia and outside kitchen whisper of a lingering Creole sensibility. It was built for Samuel Hermann, a German-Jewish cotton and slave trader, who, following nationwide economic panic in 1837 was forced to sell it in 1844 to Judge Felix Grima. The Grimas lived here until the 1920s, after which it became a women's hostel.

Creole cookery demonstrations are held in the Hermann-Grima House kitchen every Thursday from October to May.

Though **tours** skimp on contextual detail to dwell reverentially on replica antiques, they do at least give you time to wander around the rooms rather than trooping you past a

BOURBON STREET

succession of cordoned-off set pieces. Much of the furniture was made by prominent local craftsman Prudent Mallard; note especially the ornate bed with its characteristic egg motif, a visual pun on his surname.

Bourbon-Orleans Hotel

Map 4, G3.

The **Bourbon-Orleans Hotel**, on the corner of those two streets, stands on the site of the old **Salle d'Orleans** ballroom, which in the antebellum era was the grandest venue for the much mythologized **quadroon balls**. Usually romanticized as glittering occasions where dashing white men had their hearts stolen by beautiful, dusky quadroon girls (one-quarter black, usually born to a white father and mulatto mother), the reality of the balls was less glamorous: put simply, these were dances where wealthy white planters and merchants were able to consort with poorer, mixed-race girls chaperoned by their mothers. Little would usually come of the encounters, but occasionally, under a formalized system known as **plaçage**, arrangements would be made whereby the girls would be taken as mistresses, supported by their white men. A lucky few were set up in homes of their own, raising the children of their paramour, who would usually also be supporting a "respectable" white family. The Salle d'Orleans closed at the onset of the Civil War, was reborn as a convent, and finally became a flash hotel in the 1960s.

The Historic Voodoo Museum

Map 4, H4. Daily 10am–8pm; $7.

A mesmerizing, if muffled, soundtrack of drumming and chanting introduces the **Historic Voodoo Museum**, between Bourbon and Royal at 724 Dumaine St. A ragbag collection of ceremonial objects, paintings and gris-gris (spells or potions), the museum aims to debunk the myths that surround this misunderstood syncretic religion – an intention undermined somewhat by the self-consciously spooky atmosphere, not to mention its resident twelve-foot python, crumbling rat heads and desiccated bats. The gift shop sells gris-gris and voodoo dolls, while the gallery features folk art. Ask about their readings, rituals, weddings and city tours (see p.17), and see overleaf for more on the **history of voodoo** in New Orleans.

Lafitte's Blacksmith Shop

Map 4, I3.

The alarmingly tumbledown **Lafitte's Blacksmith Shop**, 941 Bourbon St at St Philip – now a great little bar (see p.209) – is one of the oldest buildings in the Quarter. Built around 1781, it's a typical early cottage, with a steeply pitched roof (the dormers were a later addition), and blotches of stucco on the walls have crumbled off to reveal its *briquete entre poteaux* construction (see p.52).

According to legend, the shop was used as a cover for pirate brothers Jean and Pierre **Lafitte**, leaders of the "Baratarians", a thousand-strong band of smugglers who hid out in the Barataria swamps at the mouth of the Mississippi. Though the importation of slaves was outlawed in 1804, there was such a high demand for labor in the thriving colony that illegal slave smuggling was a lucrative racket, and it was in murky little cottages like these that plans were hatched and raids were plotted.

For an account of the Barataria swamps, turn to p.146 in the "Out of the city" chapter.

BOURBON STREET

VOODOO

Voodoo, today practiced by around fifteen percent of the city's population, was brought to New Orleans by African slaves from the Caribbean, where tribal beliefs had been mixed with Catholicism, the official religion of the French colonies, to create a new cult based on spirit-worship. French and, later, Spanish authorities tried to suppress the religion (voodoo-worshippers had played an active role in organizing the slave revolts in Haiti), but it continued to flourish among the city's black population, especially after 1809 when the ban was lifted on importation of slaves from the Caribbean. Under American rule, the weekly slave gatherings at Congo Square (see p.63), which included ritual ceremonies, turned into a tourist attraction for whites, fueled by sensationalized reports of hypnotized white women dancing naked to the throbbing drum music.

Unlike the Caribbean, where the religion was dominated by priests, New Orleans had many voodoo priestesses. The most famous was Marie Laveau, a hairdresser of African, white and Native American blood. Using shrewd marketing sense and inside knowledge of the lives of her clients, she prepared gris-gris –spells– for wealthy Creoles and Americans, as well as Africans. Laveau died in 1881, after which another Marie, believed to be her daughter, continued to practice under her name. The legend of both Maries lives on, and their crumbling tombs are popular tourist attractions (see pp.127 & 130).

Nowadays voodoo is big business in New Orleans, with countless gift shops selling ersatz gris-gris. If you've got a serious interest in the religion, head instead for the Voodoo Spiritual Temple, 828 N Rampart St (daily 10am–8pm; ☎522-9627; Map 4, G1), which holds an open service on Thursday evenings and offers tours and consultations.

VOODOO

NORTH OF BOURBON STREET

Beyond Bourbon Street, the French Quarter becomes markedly more peaceful and residential, the tourists outnumbered by locals dog-walking, jogging, picking up provisions in corner groceries, or chatting on stoops. These quiet streets are fringed by some of the Quarter's finest **vernacular architecture**: narrow shotguns and Creole cottages, the hues of hand-tinted antique photos, standing flush with the sidewalk. Small courtyards are tended lovingly, with myrtle and magnolia blossoms tangling over cast-iron fences and fountains tinkling at the heart of hidden patios.

The streets above Bourbon can be eerily **isolated** after dark; if you feel at all nervous, restrict your explorations to the daylight hours.

Musée Conti Wax Museum

Map 4, D2. Mon–Sat 10am–5.30pm, Sun noon–5pm; $7.

The **Musée Conti Wax Museum**, 917 Conti St, tells the story of New Orleans through a series of lurid tableaux that includes the Battle of New Orleans, the arrival of the casket girls – portrayed here by a gaggle of department store mannequins with groovy 1960s make-up – Napoleon proclaiming in his bathtub, wild-eyed voodoo dancers and a hard-faced, whip-wielding Madame LaLaurie (see p.53). The grand finale, apropos of nothing, comes in the Haunted Dungeon, where encounters with Dracula, Frankenstein and sundry ghouls are backed by recorded shrieking and wailing.

Rampart Street and Tremé

Just footsteps from the French Quarter, the residential neighborhood of **Tremé** – bounded by Canal, Rampart, Broad and St Bernard streets (Map 4, A1–N1) – is the oldest African-American community in the United States. Many of New Orleans' most enduring cultural and artistic forms – **jazz** music, jazz funerals, Second Line **parades** – were born here at the end of the nineteenth century, and Tremé is still home to a star-studded roster of musicians who play loose sets to crowds of friends and family in numerous neighborhood bars. Until recently, however, Tremé was a no-go enclave for visitors. For decades, **North Rampart Street**, the run-down strip that separates the neighborhood from the French Quarter, was depicted – by locals and guidebooks alike – as a barrier not to be crossed. Much of the drug crime that marked New Orleans as the nation's murder capital in the 1980s and 1990s was concentrated in the blighted Tremé projects that lie just above Rampart; unwitting tourists who expected the Quarter street party to continue as they headed across the road were prime targets for muggings, or worse.

More recently, as the city as a whole has grown more financially stable, and crime rates have fallen, Tremé has started to shed its dismal image, and most tourists will at least encounter Rampart Street at some time during their stay. Though it can still feel dodgy at night, the presence of a couple of very popular **clubs** (*Donna's* and *Funky Butt*; see p.221 and 222) and a handful of good-value hotels – along with the gradual revitalization of **Louis Armstrong Park** as a place to hear music – have helped matters considerably. As for Tremé proper, visitors who approach with common sense will be well rewarded by the wealth of cultural experiences awaiting them. Chief among these is Tremé's brace of African-American heritage **museums**; in addition, the local **festival** (see p.285), held every fall since 1997, is easily the equal of the higher-profile French Quarter Fest for superb live music (R&B, jazz, blues, brass, African, gospel, zydeco), food stalls and crafts. Meanwhile, the **Second Line parades** continue as they have done for more than a century. Every fall, Social Aid and Pleasure Clubs, with names like the Jolly Bunch, the Black Men of Labor or the Sidewalk Steppers, strut through the streets in their flamboyant matching shoes, hats and umbrellas, to jubilant brass band music, gathering hundreds of spectators with them as they go.

Tremé still has some way to go before it feels entirely safe, and caution should be taken, especially at night – take a cab when visiting clubs, no matter how close they are to your hotel.

Some history

It is commonly accepted that **jazz** evolved in Tremé, born from the Sunday slave gatherings in **Congo Square** and developed in the "sporting houses" of **Storyville**, the area's long-defunct red-light district (see p.64). Many of the free craftsmen, artists and laborers who built New Orleans in the second half of the nineteenth century were born and owned property here, along with hundreds of its most famous jazzmen; after Reconstruction, however, when the free people of color found themselves stripped of the rights they'd had before the Civil War, the district took a downturn. In the 1890s, the blacks of Tremé began to form benevolent – or mutual aid – societies, paying dues to cover funeral- and health-related expenses. Known as **Social Aid and Pleasure Clubs**, these societies also staged street parades, their members dancing and high-stepping – "**Second Lining**" – behind noisy brass bands. The Second Liners also paraded with the local **jazz funerals**, singing and dancing behind the musicians to mark the passing of the deceased's spirit into heaven.

For more on jazz funerals, see p.128.

Tremé's financial decline continued as the twentieth century progressed, and by the 1970s the area was seriously neglected. Matters weren't helped by the construction of the I-10 overpass, which hacked the community in half at Claiborne Avenue and razed entire city blocks. A decade later, local **drug wars** had become so savage that the famed jazz funerals had degenerated into often violent "crack funerals". Things shifted in the early 2000s, however, as skyrocketing property prices in the Quarter tempted many residents to decamp for cheaper neighborhoods like Tremé. This **gentrification**, only really thus far apparent in the few blocks above Rampart, has been met with mixed feelings by residents, who fear for the future of the long-established families who currently rent the old shotguns and Creole cottages that their ancestors once owned.

LOUIS ARMSTRONG PARK AND CONGO SQUARE

Map 4, F1–H1.

The entrance to **Louis Armstrong Park**, a huge twinkling arch clearly visible the length of St Ann Street, promises more than the park itself delivers. Unprepossessing and windblown, it's a desolate patch, little improved by the lumpen Mahalia Jackson Theater of the Performing Arts or the Municipal Auditorium.

Though the park is open every day – don't even dream of venturing here after dark – it is liveliest during its occasional weekend **music festivals**, many of which are held in **Congo Square**, the small paved area to the left of the entrance arch. In colonial times this was the Place des Nègres, where every Sunday slaves taken from all over West Africa would meet in their thousands to trade, perform religious rituals, make music and dance the **bamboula**, named after the large drums that beat the rhythm. At 9pm sharp a policeman would fire a cannon to signal the end of the proceedings – the penalty for breaking the curfew was twenty lashes. In the American era, the gatherings quickly became tourist attractions, thronging with vendors and sideshows, from which fascinated white visitors would return with shocked tales of weird **voodoo rituals** and depravity. The slave gatherings were banned between 1834 and 1845, while in 1851, when the transformation of the Place d'Armes into Jackson Square left the soldiers without a parade ground, this open area was chosen as a replacement.

After the Civil War, however, Congo Square resumed its central role in the **political** life of black New Orleanians. In 1867, local blacks staged a mass sit-in protesting against segregation on the mule-drawn streetcars, demanding that as emancipated citizens they be accorded the same civil rights as whites. Almost immediately the streetcars were integrated, and stayed so until 1902, after the Supreme

STORYVILLE

Much to the dismay of many tourists, there is nothing left of New Orleans' notorious red-light district, Storyville, long since torn down to make room for housing projects. In 1897, in an attempt to control the prostitution that had been rampant in the city since its earliest days, an ordinance was passed confining the brothels to a fixed area enclosed by Basin, Iberville, North Robertson and St Louis streets. Rather than legalizing prostitution within these boundaries, the law simply decreed it to be illegal *outside* them; nonetheless, the trade continued to exist throughout the city and Storyville – nicknamed for the alderman who passed the ordinance, and more commonly known at the time as "the district" – simply became its most famous locale.

The district soon developed into a tourist attraction, with newspapers reporting the movements of its various stars, among them "Mayor" Tom Anderson, state legislator and oil company president, who owned many of the most notorious saloons. Anderson also produced the famed blue book, which advertised the "palaces" of landladies (they never called themselves madams) such as brawling Josie Arlington, who prided herself on her exotic continental girls, Emma Johnson, who staged lewd circuses in her "House of All Nations", and, Queen of Storyville, the diamond-bedecked Lulu White – Mae West's inspiration in her 1934 movie *Belle of the Nineties*. Though jazz was not, as is often claimed, invented in Storyville, it did evolve here, and many of the "professors" who played rumbustious piano to entertain the clients went on to become well-known musicians.

In 1917, the Secretary of the Navy decreed that red-light areas were bad for wartime morale, and Storyville was closed down. Its denizens, however, are immortalized in the extraordinary, humane portraits taken by E.J. Bellocq, the hydrocephalic photographer adopted by the prostitutes as their official recorder.

Court Plessy-Ferguson ruling had effectively retracted the civil rights won by blacks during Reconstruction (see p.304). In 1994, a group of Mardi Gras Indians and Native Americans blessed Congo Square as sacred ground, and three years later it was placed on the National Register of Historic Places.

OUR LADY OF GUADALUPE

Map 4, D1.

Our Lady of Guadalupe, 411 N Rampart St, was built following a yellow fever epidemic in 1826 as a catholic mortuary chapel for the neighboring St Louis No. 1 cemetery. In those days both were outside the city limits, protecting the population from what were believed to be poisonous miasmas that emanated from the mountains of corpses and from the back-to-back funeral processions. The church's statue of the unknown "St Expedite", mysteriously delivered here, so the legend goes, in a crate simply stamped *expedite*, is said to be worshipped by the city's voodooists.

St Louis No. 1 Cemetery is covered on p.127,
in the chapter devoted to New Orleans' Cities of the Dead.

BACKSTREET CULTURAL MUSEUM

Map 1, F6. Tues–Sat 10am–5pm; $3 donation.

Walking around the fascinating **Backstreet Cultural Museum**, just one block above Rampart Street at 1116 St Claude at Gov Nicholls, you feel as though you've been invited into someone's home and allowed to rummage through their personal possessions. Your host and guide is Sylvester Francis, an enthusiastic local who has spent the last twenty years attempting to preserve and celebrate local black street culture. Not only has he filmed and photographed scores of **jazz funerals**, but he also set up this little museum to display the kind of indigenous works of art that might otherwise be left to rot in a cellar. As befits its location in an old funeral home, much of the collection revolves around **urban mourning customs**, often to very moving effect: among the church programs, news clippings and scrapbooks is a case of T-shirts, screenprinted with blurred photos of recently deceased loved ones – many of them boys killed by "lead poisoning", as locals call gun wounds – and inscribed with dates of the victim's "Sunrise" and "Sunset". Francis, who used to parade with the Gentlemen of Leisure Social Aid and Pleasure Club, will also show and talk about his natty marching regalia, frilly Second Line umbrellas, and magnificent **Mardi Gras Indian suits**, emblazoned with feathers and sequins.

To read more about the Mardi Gras Indians,
see p.310; for more on jazz funerals turn to p.128.

ST AUGUSTINE'S CHURCH

Map 4, J1.

Directly across the road from the Backstreet Museum, the imposing catholic church **St Augustine's**, 1210 Gov Nicholls, has been active since 1842. It was designed by J.N.B. de Pouilly – who eight years later went on to remodel St Louis Cathedral in the French Quarter – and built with contributions from local blacks, freed and enslaved. Though anyone is welcome to attend services, held by the dynamic Father LeDoux, the church is fullest on the occasional Sundays when a guest singer or musician joins the choir for mass and the pews are packed with tourists. Its spruce interior, lined with tall white columns and illuminated by stained-glass porthole windows portraying French saints, also features bright, jazzy paintings and flags fluttering from the ceiling printed with affirmations – Purpose, Self-Determination, Unity, Creativity – in English and Swahili.

Every fall the St Augustine churchyard is home to the fabulous Tremé Festival; for details, see p.285.

TREMÉ VILLA MEILLEUR—NEW ORLEANS AFRICAN-AMERICAN MUSEUM

Map 1, F6. Mon–Sat 9am–5pm; $4.

Two blocks above St Augustine's at 1418 Gov Nicholls, the **Tremé Villa Meilleur–New Orleans African-American Museum** – more commonly known as the African-American Museum – is spread across three properties set in flower-filled courtyards. The bulk of the collection is in the Meilleur House, a Caribbean-style plantation home built in 1828, whose airy, high ceilinged-rooms make a great space for rotating exhibitions of art from Africa and the diaspora. Works by local black artists, from ceramics to textiles to photography, are displayed in a smaller, double-shotgun cottage and a three-room single shotgun on the grounds.

The CBD and Warehouse District

Neither as visually stunning nor as immediately appealing as the neighboring French Quarter, New Orleans' Central Business District, or **CBD**, is of more interest to visitors for its hotels and restaurants than for its sightseeing potential. Historically, however, its significance can't be overstressed: this was where American New Orleans started, created by vigorous Anglo newcomers who, after the Louisiana Purchase in 1803, built a new city of exchanges, insurance companies, banks and shops – along with grand theaters and hotels – as they set about making themselves rich. Rivaling their equivalents in the Creole city, the developments marked the onset of New Orleans' **Americanization**, an era of phenomenal change and economic growth that lasted until the Civil War.

The area covered by this chapter is shown in detail on color map 3 at the back of this book.

Upriver from the Quarter, across Canal Street, the CBD's sweep of offices, old bank buildings and fancy hotels stretches west as far as the Pontchartrain Expressway, bounded riverside by the Mississippi and, lakeside, by I-10 (Claiborne Avenue). Apart from the gargantuan **Superdome**, which lies at the lakeside edge of the CBD, most of what there is to see is in the **Warehouse District**, a revitalizing area of low-rent studios and pricey loft apartments, loosely bounded by Poydras Street, the Expressway, Convention Center Boulevard and St Charles Avenue. In the last decade, a number of the neglected warehouses and old factory buildings have been given over to galleries, restaurants and bars, with a spirited arts community thriving on and around **Julia Street**. But while these and the slick new **National D-Day Museum** and **Ogden Museum of Southern Art** are raising the cultural profile of the district, there's still some way left to go, and assurances that the area's many run-down, abandoned-looking buildings are, in fact, hives of creativity don't necessarily make the Warehouse District a great place to walk around at night.

Some history

In the eighteenth century, much of the area now covered by the CBD was a vast sugar plantation belonging to **Bertrand Gravier**. Following the devastating fire of 1788, which destroyed most of the French Quarter, Gravier sold off parcels of his land to allow settlement along the river. The emergent suburb, **Faubourg Ste Marie**, named after his wife, remained sparsely populated until the Louisiana Purchase in 1803. Within fifteen years or so of annexation, however, the faubourg – its name now Americanized to St Mary – expanded rapidly, populated by the factors, brokers, bankers and planters who flooded into New Orleans eager to exploit its booming port. The city's center of commerce swiftly shifted away from the French Quarter to the "**American sector**", as

St Mary was referred to, and eventually in 1836 New Orleans was carved into **municipalities**, each with its own council – a state of affairs which lasted until 1852. **Canal Street** was the dividing line between the first (Creole) and second (American) municipalities, and gradually took over from Royal Street in the French Quarter as the city's chief commercial thoroughfare. The Americans also built fine Federal-style townhouses for themselves, on and around **Julia Street**, while huge warehouses backed the bustling wharves.

After Reconstruction, as the French Quarter fell into decline, the CBD struggled on, keeping its head above water on the back of continuing cotton wealth; the warehouses, meanwhile, were turned over to wholesalers and meat packers. During the 1970s **oil boom**, many of the old banks and exchanges were torn down to make way for corporate towers (though building anything too high has always been a problem on this soggy soil – today the tallest building reaches just 51 stories), parking lots, business hotels and the landmark hulk of the Superdome.

Hotels in the CBD are reviewed on pp.164–165; restaurants on pp.191–193.

During the 1980s, when the boom went **bust** as suddenly as it had hit, the CBD experienced a mass exodus and eventually turned to tourism for its salvation. Since then, many of the older buildings, capitalizing on their proximity to the French Quarter, have been converted into boutique hotels and ritzy restaurants. The Warehouse District, meanwhile, which had disintegrated into a forgotten wasteland, was reawakened by the 1984 **World's Fair**, held in restored buildings along the wharves. Since then it has flourished, not least in the development of its world-respected **art galleries**.

CANAL STREET

Map 3, N6–N1.

The widest main street (170ft) in America, and on the parade route for all the super krewes at Mardi Gras (see p.312), the once glorious **Canal Street**, which runs from the river to Lake Pontchartrain, is looking rather down at heel. It is still the backbone of the city, however, literally dividing downtown (downriver) from uptown (upriver).

There never was a **canal** here, though one was planned in the early 1800s, and you'll see a phantom waterway marked on many early maps. The street started as a rough ditch cut along the ramparts of the city, separating it from the plantations – and later the American suburb – beyond. It was eventually filled to become the town commons, and as the Faubourg St Mary grew, settlers built homes along its muddy expanse. When New Orleans was divided into municipalities, this was the "**neutral ground**" in the middle, and many traders set up here in order to get business from both sides of the city. By the 1850s, all the homes had been replaced by department stores and opulent theaters.

- -

For a superb view of New Orleans, from the Mississippi to the lake, head for the World Trade Center, a woefully drab 1960s tower at the foot of Canal. There's a viewing platform on the 31st floor and a revolving cocktail bar two floors above (see p.215).

- -

Though the grand old **department stores** that gave Canal Street so much of its character are slowly disappearing, the gorgeous **storefronts**, decorated in Beaux Arts, Italianate and Art Deco styles, for the most part remain, safe from the demolition that richer cities would have inflicted upon them. Today the lovely old buildings are filled with chain hotels, tacky T-shirt and souvenir stores, fast-food outlets and none-too-reputable electrical shops.

THE BATTLE OF LIBERTY PLACE

The riverside end of Canal Street, opposite the Custom House, was the site of one of the most significant battles in the city's bitter Reconstruction era (see p.303). On September 13, 1874, the Metropolitan police force, which included many freed slaves, seized a boat-load of arms destined for the White League – a militia formed by ex-Confederates committed to bringing down the radical Republican government and stamping out what they called the "Africanization" of their city. Claiming that the action of the police was an infringement of their constitutional right to bear arms, the League placed an advertisement in the *Times-Picayune*, calling for a mass demonstration in protest.

On September 14, some five thousand whites met at the Henry Clay statue, which stood at the heart of the city on Canal Street where it crossed St Charles and Royal. After a morning of rabble-rousing, during which the call was made to depose the hated Republican Governor Kellogg, the White Leaguers armed themselves and marched down Canal Street to the river, where they met a defensive line made up of the Metropolitan police and the black militia. A twenty-minute conflict ensued, which resulted in the police being chased back to Jackson Square in the French Quarter, where Kellogg was overthrown. Though just five days later President Grant sent in troops to reinstate him, the Battle of Liberty Place, which left eleven policemen – six of them white – and sixteen rioters dead, was seen by the White League as a victory for freedom, a blow against the Reconstruction government and – despite lame public assurances that their motives weren't racist – an assertion of white supremacy. The League was formally disbanded two years later, when, Reconstruction over, Louisiana returned to home rule.

The ramifications of the battle did not end there, however. In 1891, the Liberty Monument, inscribed with a list of the White League members who had died fighting, was erected on the median at the foot of Canal Street. Well into the 1930s, Confederate supporters gathered at the granite obelisk every September 14 – their insistence that to do so was a celebration of political liberty was undermined somewhat by the plaque added to the monument in 1932, the wording on which blatantly rejoiced at the demise of Reconstruction and the victory of "white supremacy".

In 1981, "Dutch" Morial, New Orleans' first black mayor, ordered that the monument should be surrounded by tall bushes, effectively hiding it from view. Under increasing pressure from civil rights groups, who demanded that, as a racist symbol, it should be torn down, and white reactionaries, who insisted it was part of the city's history, the city council vacillated for years, until eventually, in 1989, the monument was removed and put into storage. Spearheaded by David Duke, a former Grand Wizard of the Ku Klux Klan and candidate for Louisiana governor in 1991, a lawsuit was filed to return the monument to the street, and in 1993, amid violent demonstrations, the Liberty Monument was rededicated in an inconspicuous spot next to a parking lot behind the aquarium. Though its supremacist plaque was replaced by a list of the Metropolitan police killed in the battle, the new dedication: "In honour of those Americans on both sides of the conflict . . . A conflict of the past that should teach us lessons for the future . . ." is infuriatingly ambivalent, and the monument remains an ugly, graffitied testament to a century of vexed race relations.

THE BATTLE OF LIBERTY PLACE

The casino

Map 3, M5.

Splayed out at the foot of Canal Street, Harrah's **casino**, all postmodern turrets and baubles, stands as a hulking testament to a political saga of double-dealing and ineptitude in the great Louisiana tradition. In the early 1990s, political opposition to the very notion of legalizing gambling in New Orleans, on the grounds that to do so would siphon income away from the city's genuinely unique attractions, ensured that even when it did finally open, a decade later, the casino was more white elephant than cash cow. Forbidden to offer the themed attractions, hotel rooms and flash restaurants that you'd expect in, say, Las Vegas, Harrah's began as little more than an unprepossessing warehouse stuffed with slot machines. Tourists stayed away in droves, and in order to remain open Harrah's had to persuade state authorities to loosen their restrictions on accommodation and dining. It remains to be seen whether this will change the casino's fortunes, but for now the place remains pretty much devoid of interest.

The Custom House

Map 3, N4. Mon–Fri 8am–4.30pm; free.

Along with the Mint (see p.39), the gray granite **Custom House**, 423 Canal St, was a key player in New Orleans' grand antebellum building program. In order to handle the huge volume of commerce coming through the port, and to celebrate its value to the city, work started in 1848 on what was to be the largest federal building in the nation, larger even than the US capitol; rooting such a monster in the city's shifting, soggy soil proved difficult, however, and what with the break during the Civil War – when the half-finished building was used by Union General "Beast"

CANAL STREET

Butler (see p.84) as a prison for Confederate soldiers – the Custom House was only completed in 1881.

Mark Twain may have had a point when he dismissed the foreboding classical exterior as "inferior to a gasometer", but fans of Greek Revival architecture should head inside, where, on the second floor, a huge **marble hall**, illuminated by a 54-foot skylight, poignantly recalls the lofty aspirations and optimism of the city's Golden Age. Flanked by fourteen fat Corinthian columns of Italian marble, the room is brimful of images of wealth and success: the capitals feature heads of Mercury, the Greek god of commerce, and Luna, goddess of the moon (playing on New Orleans' status as the Crescent City), while bas-relief panels depict proud portraits of Bienville and Andrew Jackson.

TOWARD THE WAREHOUSE DISTRICT

Turning off Canal at Baronne Street – look for the wonderful old Walgreen's sign – brings you to the oddly Moorish **Church of the Immaculate Conception**, or Jesuit Church (Map 3, M3), worth a look for its flamboyant arches, cast-iron spiral columns and pews. Designed by local architect James Freret, the gilt bronze altar, with its trio of onion domes, won first prize at the Paris Exposition of 1867. Like so many of New Orleans' buildings, the original church, built in 1857, threatened to collapse under its own weight into the swampy earth; what you see today – a perfect replica – dates from the 1930s.

As you move upriver from the church and head down Common Street toward Carondelet, you come to the heart of the old CBD. Though it doesn't look like much today, the sober, eleven-story **Latter and Blum** building, 203 Carondelet (Map 3, M3), was New Orleans' first "skyscraper", designed in 1895 by eminent local architect Thomas Sully who, though he is most famous for his St

Charles Avenue mansions (see p.100), was inspired in this case by the Chicago School. Nearby, the 23-story **Hibernia National Bank**, 313 Carondelet (Map 3, M3), is another landmark. Built in 1921, it was the city's tallest building until 1962, and its circular belvedere can be seen from anywhere in the CBD. It's especially striking when floodlit at night, and positively ethereal during Mardi Gras, when bathed in the carnival colors of purple, green and gold.

Another block toward the river, at 201 St Charles Ave, the **First NBC building** (Map 3, M4) is built on the site of the old **St Charles Hotel**, designed in 1835 by **James Gallier Sr** – one of New Orleans' premier architects, propelled to fame by his work on the hotel – and Charles Dakin. The equivalent of the St Louis Hotel in the French Quarter, this was the American sector's grandest building, a columned Greek Revival showpiece that was originally topped with a huge dome (the dome was destroyed in a fire in 1851, after which the hotel was rebuilt without it). Featuring a major slave exchange, the St Charles was at the commercial heart of antebellum, Anglo-American New Orleans, and *the* place to stay – among the famous names who slept here was "Beast" Butler (see p.84), who, during the Civil War occupation, took over the entire place after he was refused the VIP suite. Following another fire in 1894, Thomas Sully redesigned the building in Beaux Arts style, and it remained one of the city's top hotels – particularly during the 1930s, when Lyle Saxon, a key player on the New Orleans literary scene, hosted wild salons in his fifth-floor suite – before being eventually demolished in 1974.

Lafayette Square

Map 3, L4.

Laid out in 1788, **Lafayette Square** was the political hub of the American sector. Surrounded by dreary court buildings and offices, it centers on a bronze **statue** of early nineteenth-century statesman **Henry Clay**. When the statue was dedicated in 1860, it stood at the heart of the city, on Canal Street where Royal met St Charles, and provided a focal point for countless public meetings – including the rally that led to the Battle of Liberty Place (see p.72). In 1901 it was moved to this less conspicuous spot to make room for increasing traffic along Canal.

On the lakeside of the square, another bronze statue portrays **John McDonogh**, an outspoken abolitionist and leading light in the American Colonization Society, which advocated the return of slaves to Africa. Regarded as a miser during his lifetime, upon his death in 1850 he left his considerable riches to be divided between New Orleans and his native Baltimore for the establishment of racially mixed public schools. Many of New Orleans' public schools are the result of that legacy; the statue, designed in 1898 at a cost of $7000, was funded by nickel donations from the city's schoolchildren.

Gallier Hall

The magnificent **Gallier Hall** (Map 3, L4), across from Lafayette Square on St Charles Avenue, is the grandest example of Greek Revival architecture in New Orleans. Fronted by an ornate ninety-foot facade with ten fluted white Ionic columns and a pediment featuring Justice, Liberty and Commerce, it was designed by James Gallier Sr as the City Hall for the second municipality (the first municipality had its own, the Cabildo, on the Place d'Armes). By the time it was dedicated in 1853, however, New Orleans had reunited; thus the building served as seat of government for the whole city right up to the 1950s, when the new City Hall was built on Poydras.

These days, Gallier Hall hosts civic events and receptions. Traditionally, too, it's the site of one of the premier **Mardi**

Gras parade-viewing platforms, packed with assorted bigwigs, including the mayor. The enormous floats stop for quite a while here, and experienced bead-beggars know to stake out the spot across the street.

For more on Mardi Gras parades, see p.272.

St Patrick's Church

Map 3, L5.

James Gallier Sr, though best known for his accomplished Greek Revival buildings, also had a hand in the neo-Gothic **St Patrick's Church**, near Lafayette Square at 710 Camp St. In 1838 Irish architects Charles and James Dakin set to work on rebuilding the small wooden church that had stood on this site since 1833 – the second municipality was thriving, and needed a Catholic place of worship to equal St Louis Cathedral, where services were held only in French. Work was completed by Gallier, who designed the interior with its fine stained glass, elaborate altar, sweeping vaulting and neo-Gothic tracery.

THE WAREHOUSE DISTRICT

Map 3, J6–M5.

During the antebellum era, the **Warehouse District** was a bustling area of vast factories and warehouses storing sugar, cotton, grain and tobacco ready to be loaded onto ocean-going ships, and coffee, luxuries and manufactured goods from overseas waiting to be transported upriver by steamboat. After Reconstruction, however, as the port went into decline, the district deteriorated into a dangerous no-go zone, only reviving a century or so later after it was chosen as the site of the 1984 **World's Fair**. The fair was the first

THE WAREHOUSE DISTRICT

in history to lose money, but it did bring visibility to the area's previously neglected lofts and factory buildings, and the die was cast for the Warehouse District. Loft-living was big business in the 1980s, and there was no shortage of eager developers hungry to make a profit.

The tourist literature pushes the Warehouse District as a thriving **arts community**, buzzing with workshops, cutting-edge galleries and designer stores. However, though it is certainly a desirable place to live – the spacious lofts and river views an agreeable alternative to the bohemian funkiness of the congested Quarter – and though it features a couple of the city's major **museums** and the best of its **private galleries**, the many empty lots and derelict buildings do little to make you want to wander around the streets for very long.

There's a lively farmers' market every Saturday morning on the 700 block of Magazine Street (8am–noon); see p.204.

That said, there's enough here to whet the appetite of anyone with an interest in **architecture**. Although many structures were demolished in the 1960s and 70s, a profusion of the original buildings – churches, factories and tall brick townhouses, as well as warehouses – remains, offering a counterpoint to the Creole flavor of the Quarter. Here, Federal, neoclassical and Greek Revival styles dominate, reflecting the very American nature of the antebellum Faubourg St Mary.

Julia Street and the galleries

Map 3, K5.

Though the low-rent buildings all over the Warehouse District are filling with studios and workshops, when people talk about the **Arts District** they're mainly referring to

Julia Street, especially the stretch from Commerce Street up to St Charles Avenue, which has a growing reputation for showcasing the best in regional and national contemporary art. While hopping between the hip private **galleries** along here – easily done on foot – is worth an afternoon of anyone's time, probably the best time to visit is on the first Saturday of every month from October to May, when the string of art openings pulls a mixed crowd of uptowners, art students and conventioneers, all nibbling cheese, sipping Chablis and checking out the art and each other.

Many of the Arts District galleries close for summer, and some shut up shop during the day on reception days; call to check, or consult the listings papers *Lagniappe* or *Gambit* (see p.10) before setting off.

The biggest shindig of all, *the* place for the local art world to see and be seen, is **Art for Art's Sake**, held on the first Saturday in October. In the evening the streets around Julia and Camp Street are closed off, and a shuttle bus runs between here and the galleries on Magazine Street. There's a street-party ambience, with stalls selling wine and beer, and nervous artists milling around; later the revels shift to the Contemporary Arts Center (see p.87). **Jammin' on Julia**, on the first Saturday in May (during Jazz Fest), is a similar, though smaller-scale event.

In addition to the galleries, Julia is a good place to check out the **architecture** that characterized the American sector. At no. 545 you'll see three of the district's earliest warehouses – simple, shuttered structures built in 1833; compare these with the larger, utilitarian building at no. 329, New Orleans' first reinforced concrete construction. In the block between St Charles and Camp stands a parade of renovated row houses known as the **Thirteen Sisters**. When they were built in

THE JULIA STREET GALLERIES

The following is a list of some of the most consistently interesting galleries on and around Julia Street. However, exhibitions rotate regularly, and it's a matter of taste as to which ones will appeal – for a full rundown check the listings papers.

Arthur Roger Gallery

No. 432 (Mon–Sat 10am–5pm; ☎522-1999).
Large, swish space for an eclectic and always fascinating range of cutting-edge art, sculpture and video. If you see only one Arts District gallery, make it this.

Galerie Simonne Stern

No. 518 (Mon noon–5pm, Tues–Sat 10am–5pm; ☎529-1118).
One of the first galleries to set up in the area, with strong shows of contemporary painting, photography and sculpture from Louisiana and nationwide.

LeMieux Galleries

No. 332 (Mon–Sat 10am–5.30pm; ☎522-5988).
Contemporary art, folk art and crafts from Louisiana and the Gulf Coast. Retrospectives have included the "Caribbean-Cubist" images of New Orleans by Paul Niñas, who painted the mural in the swanky *Sazerac Bar* (see p.214).

New Orleans School of Glassworks & Printmaking

Magazine St (Mon–Sat 10am–5pm; ☎529-7277).
Stunning, unusual handblown glass on display, and a chance to see the glassblowers in action.

Sylvia Schmidt

No. 400a (Tues–Sat 11am–4pm; ☎522-2000).
Arresting contemporary fine art and abstracts, photographs, prints, sculpture and drawings from local and international artists.

1833 these red-brick residences were the most desirable in the American sector, modeled in the Federal style favored in the northeastern states; just sixty years later they had declined into slums. Opposite, no. 603 houses the temporary home of the **Ogden Museum of Southern Art** (see p.85).

Louisiana Children's Museum

Map 3, L5. Sept–May Tues–Sat 9.30am–4.30pm, Sun noon–4.30pm; June–Aug Mon–Sat 9.30am–4.30pm, Sun noon–4.30pm; $5.

In a sturdy 1861 warehouse topped by an elaborate cornice, the **Louisiana Children's Museum**, 420 Julia St, is worth a trip only if you've got very bored kids in tow. Too often the exhibits don't work, and many are wearyingly earnest, geared toward school groups rather than fun-seeking visitors. However, there are enough things to wind up, push, pull and plunge to keep the younger ones diverted for an hour or so, and though the scope for role play is limited, few people – kids or adults – will be able to resist pretending to be a news anchor in the KidWatch TV studio.

Confederate Museum

Map 3, K5. Mon–Sat 10am–4pm; $5.

It can be all too easy to forget that easy-going New Orleans has its roots entrenched in the Deep South; anyone who needs reminding should take a trip to the **Confederate Museum**, 929 Camp St at Lee Circle. A gloomy Romanesque Revival hulk, purpose-designed by Thomas Sully in 1891 as a place for Confederate veterans to display their mementos, this so-called "Battle Abbey of the South" is a relic from a bygone age. Jefferson Davis, who died in New Orleans' Garden District in 1889 (see p.96), lay in state here briefly, and there remains a funereal air about the place, with its bittersweet remembrances of long-lost generals and their forgotten families. Its aim, more than a century after the event, remains to tell "the story of insult and oppression . . . pillage and ruin . . . want and suffering and humiliation and insult and punishment".

The Confederate Museum is just a stone's throw from Lee Circle, which centers on a bronze statue of the Confederate general atop a sixty-foot marble column, built in 1884. The statue faces north, of course.

Inside the church-like hall, glass cases are filled with flags, swords, mess-kits, uniforms and helmets. There are wordy accounts of battles and of generals, but very little background detail – when the museum was built the "lost cause" would have been fresh in visitors' minds – and certainly no attempt at hindsight or analysis. That said, the place has an undeniable pull. Along with affecting sepia photos – of the wealthy, muddy antebellum city, and sad-eyed youths awkward in uniform – oddities include a crown of thorns hand-woven by Pope Pius IX and sent to Jefferson as an encouraging gift. There's also an account of the **Confederate Native Guards**, free blacks who signed up but weren't allowed to fight by the other Confederate states because of the color of their skin.

The curators obviously feel that the exhibit on notorious Union **General "Beast" Butler** (see overleaf) needs no introduction, and concentrate instead on tales of his corruption and cruelty. The throwaway line at the end, "justice requires that it be stated that he did feed the poor, clean up the streets and prevent disease", strikes an odd note, as does the startling assertion that after the war he befriended the widow of William Mumford – the man he hanged for tearing down the Union flag – and secured her "a government position".

Reconstruction, too, is covered in the bitterest terms, charging that the US government deliberately kept the

"BEAST" BUTLER

Though he was in New Orleans for just nine months, Major Benjamin Butler, who commanded the military rule of the city after it fell to Union troops in 1862, is one of its most demonized figures. Dubbed "Beast" Butler by diehard Rebels, for what they saw as his cruelty and injustice – in June 1862 he hanged a man who had torn down a Union flag *before* the city was occupied – he has also been called "Spoons", a nickname that grew out of rumors that he pilfered his hosts' cutlery. The truth, however, is that during occupation families who refused to swear allegiance to the Union may have had property – including silver – confiscated. It is highly unlikely that "Spoons" pocketed the cutlery himself, though he may have personally profited from its sale.

So unpopular was the Beast that local beauties – who, it is said, had his likeness painted in their chamber pots – would retch loudly as Union soldiers walked by. After a month or so of this, in a fit of pique at the behavior of what he called "these she-adders", Butler announced the General Order 28, claiming "When any female shall by word, gesture, or movement, insult or show contempt for any officer of the United States, she shall be regarded and held liable to be treated as a woman of the town plying her vocation." The order, denounced by Jefferson Davis (who proclaimed that the general deserved to be hanged) and the British parliament (who saw it as terribly ungentlemanly), was recalled, as was Butler himself in December 1862.

THE WAREHOUSE DISTRICT

Southern states from recovery. Accounts of white supremacist groups, such as the **White League** (see p.72), are puffed up with patriotic outrage, couched in terms of individuals seeking political liberty in order to protect themselves from the "police state". That the Metropolitan police was composed of many Union sympathizers and freed slaves is seen as an affirmation of White League beliefs rather than a challenge to them.

For more on the Civil War in New Orleans,
see p.302; for Reconstruction see p.303.

Ogden Museum of Southern Art

Map 3, K5. Mon–Fri 10am–5pm; free.

The **Ogden Museum of Southern Art**, due to open next door to the Confederate Museum in 2002, is expected to make a huge splash. You can get a taste of the eclectic collection, which runs the gamut from rare eighteenth-century watercolours to contemporary collage, ceramics, photography and sculpture, in its temporary residence at 603 Julia St, but this small space represents just a drop in the ocean compared to the purpose-built, modern five-story gallery, linked to an 1889 neo-Romanesque library building, that it will soon call home.

National D-Day Museum

Map 3, K5. Daily 9am–5pm; $7.

Shaped by the vision of New Orleans-based historian Stephen E. Ambrose, the massive **National D-Day Museum,** 945 Magazine St, opened on June 6, 2000, the 56th anniversary of the Allied invasion of Europe. The museum's core collection concentrates on the events of that dramatic day, but emphasizes that the Normandy invasion was not the only D-Day in history. Considering any shoreline assault to be a D-Day – "D" stands simply for day, and as a military expression dates back as far as 1918 – the displays range across the endless island-hopping of the Pacific War too, and thus trace the entire history of US involvement of World War II. For all but diehard military buffs, the sheer quantity of the museum's hardware and uniforms may prove exhausting, but luckily there is enough film footage, background material, and, especially, oral testimony from both sides of the conflict to broaden the focus.

The amphibious craft that made the Normandy landings possible – the **LCVP**, or Landing Craft Vehicle, Personnel – was manufactured right here in New Orleans. In the 1930s, boatbuilder Andrew Jackson Higgins developed a flat-bottomed vessel for use in the Louisiana bayous; by 1945 his factories were turning out hundreds of boats per month for the war effort. An LCVP occupies pride of place in the museum foyer.

In theory, visits begin with a 48-minute film show, but you may as well head upstairs to the **galleries**. On the third floor, "Before The War" and "The Road To War" lead into a thorough exposition of the Normandy invasion. Oral testimonies juxtapose the experiences of the 1.5 million GIs who were stationed in Britain prior to the landings with those of the nervous German defenders of the Atlantic Wall, a network of fortifications that extended along Europe's northwestern seaboard. Eisenhower's nerve-wracking decision to launch "Operation Overlord" on June 6, 1944, is chronicled in detail through timelines, photographs and documents. In the event, nowhere in Normandy did the Atlantic Wall hold out even a day; on Utah Beach, it lasted barely five minutes. Harrowing photos show the full carnage of that tumultuous battle and of many others: in all, between June 6 and August 22, 124,400 US soldiers, together with 82,300 from the UK and Canada, died.

The rest of the museum is devoted to "**D-Day Invasions in the Pacific**". An animated map plus multimedia timeline plots the American advance toward Asia, while further displays sketch out what could have been the bloodiest test of all – the never-implemented plans for the invasion of Japan.

Actual footage of kamikaze attacks shows the potential ferocity of Japanese resistance; you're left in little doubt where your sympathies should lie regarding the moral debates that surrounded Truman's decision to drop the atomic bomb.

On the first floor, along with a welcome **PJ's café**, there's a store stocking facsimile wartime newspapers, model LCVPs, 1940s sewing patterns and the like.

The Contemporary Arts Center

Map 3, K5. Tues–Sun 11am–5pm; ground-floor galleries free; changing exhibitions $5; Ⓦ*www.cacno.org*

Housed in a restored nineteenth-century warehouse and ice-cream factory, the **Contemporary Arts Center** (**CAC**), 900 Camp St, is the city's premier modern art gallery. A kind of anchor for the Arts District, it's a beautifully designed space, and there's always something interesting going on, from the temporary shows on the ground floor to major exhibitions upstairs, with a lively program of cutting-edge performances, movies, lectures and workshops to boot. It also hosts a number of lively fundraisers, climaxing in October's **Art for Art's Sake** bash (see p.284), when you can wander the galleries with a beer and a gumbo, dance to live bands, or watch a fashion show.

The CAC café offers free internet access; see p.202.

THE SUPERDOME

Map 3, K1–2. Tours Mon, Wed & Fri 10.30am, noon & 1.30pm, except during special events; $6.

Dominating the tangle of busy gray highways at the lakeside edge of the CBD, the **Superdome** is the home of the New Orleans Saints football team. At 52 acres, 27 stories high and with a diameter of 680ft, this is one of the largest buildings in the world, completed in 1975 at a cost of nearly $200 million. The investment paid off: more **Superbowl** games have been held here than in any other US city, bringing in huge amounts of revenue – the next is scheduled for 2002. You can't really appreciate the sheer enormity of the place until you venture inside, either by seating yourself with 76,999 others to see a **Saints game** (Aug–Dec; $25–50) or, second-best, by joining a statistics-heavy guided tour.

The wildly popular intercollegiate football championship, the Sugarbowl, is held at the Superdome every New Year. For details on booking for this or any other Superdome event, see p.239.

The dome is also used for major gigs and special events – guides boast that it has hosted not only the largest-ever rock concert audience (for The Rolling Stones in 1981), but also the largest movie audience (the world premiere of Disney's *The Hunchback of Notre Dame* in 1996). It was also designed to function as a hurricane shelter, much needed in this storm-battered city – in September 1998, in the run-up to Hurricane Georges, it sheltered 14,000 people for two days before the hurricane veered sharply east at the last minute and bypassed the city altogether.

Tours lead you around the stalls and behind the scenes to the visiting team's locker room (the Saints' is out of bounds for security reasons) and the press box. Disappointingly, you can't walk, let alone kick a ball, on the astroturf (how the guides chortle when they tell you it's called "Mardi Grass").

The **New Orleans Arena**, tagging along beside the Superdome like a clingy kid brother, opened in 2000 as the home of the New Orleans Brass ice hockey team, and doubles as a downtown arena for big, tight-trousered rock bands. See p.237 for details.

THE SUPERDOME

The Garden District
and uptown

The grand, residential **Garden District**, around two miles upriver from the French Quarter, was created in the 1840s by the energetic breed of Anglo-Americans who, having outgrown the Faubourg St Mary (today's CBD, see p.69), announced their ever-accumulating wealth by building sumptuous mansions in huge, lush gardens. Shaded by jungles of subtropical foliage, the glorious houses – some of them spick-and-span showpieces, others in ruins – evoke a nostalgic vision of the Deep South in a profusion of galleries, columns and balconies. It's a ravishing spectacle, if somewhat Gothic – perfect for author **Anne Rice**, who was born nearby and has since bought and restored a number of local properties, as well as featuring several of them in her fiction.

The Garden District began in 1834 as the city of **Lafayette**, which remained separate from New Orleans until 1852. Development sped up with the arrival, in 1835, of the **New Orleans and Carrollton Railroad** – forerunner of today's streetcar – which ran along St Charles Avenue, the broad street bordering the suburb on its lakeside edge.

Lafayette's construction frenzy was brought to a halt by the Civil War, when occupying troops made themselves comfortable in the capacious homes; the turn of the next century, however, saw another spate of mansion-building, this time along **St Charles Avenue** and the crucial streetcar line, extending further and further upriver with each passing year. The august residences of the Garden District, meanwhile, remained in the hands of the monied elite, as they continue to do today.

The area covered by this chapter is shown in detail on color maps 2 & 3 at the back of this book.

The Garden District heralds the onset of **uptown** New Orleans, the big chunk of the city that extends from Jackson Avenue to Audubon Park. The **St Charles Avenue streetcar**, which follows the same route as the early railroad, is still by far the best way to get to and around the area, affording front-row views of "the avenue", as St Charles is known locally. Clanging its way from Canal Street, it courses through the low-rent **Lower Garden District** before arriving at the Garden District proper, beyond which it continues past increasingly opulent mansions. It eventually reaches peaceful **Audubon Park** and its **zoo**; a little farther, the track turns inland to the studenty **Riverbend** area, which has some great bars and restaurants.

Running parallel to St Charles, and forming the riverside boundary of the Garden District, **Magazine Street**, its shotgun houses filled with thrift stores, antique shops and designer studios, is the other main channel between Canal Street and uptown.

THE ST CHARLES STREETCAR

There can be few more romantic ways of passing an hour or so in New Orleans than planting yourself on a mahogany bench on the St Charles streetcar, catching the breeze from the open window, and watching as one of America's loveliest avenues unfolds in front of you.

The streetcar, now a National Historic Monument, began in 1835 as the New Orleans and Carrollton Railroad, a steam-powered train that took a whole day to cover the six and a half miles from Canal Street, via Lafayette and a string of small faubourgs, to the resort town of Carrollton. After the Civil War, the inefficient steam engines were replaced by mules – a cleaner, quieter form of transport – until overhead electricity was introduced in 1893.

The streetcar network spread quickly, with cars traveling three abreast along tracks crisscrossing Canal Street and the French Quarter. Though Tennessee Williams was said to be inspired by the clanging of the trolley bell beneath his French Quarter apartment to pen his 1947 play *A Streetcar Named Desire*, the service was already dwindling by then, faced with competition from motorbuses, and by 1964 only the St Charles line remained.

In the 1980s, a new streetcar line, geared primarily toward tourists, was developed along a two-mile stretch of the river-front (see p.12). Plans are now well under way to resurrect the Canal Street route, and, by 2003, to have linked all three tracks. For more on the practicalities of streetcar travel, see pp.12–13.

Hotels in the Garden District are reviewed on pp.166–168, restaurants on pp.193–195, bars on pp.215–216 and clubs on pp.226 & 232.

THE ST CHARLES STREETCAR

THE LOWER GARDEN DISTRICT

Map 3, G6–I6.

The **Lower Garden District** is a loose term for the area between the Warehouse District and the Garden District proper. Sprawling down through a cluster of unpronounceable streets named after the Greek muses, via gentrifying **Coliseum Square** to the river, it's a hip, racially mixed neighborhood, the once decorative, now decaying, nineteenth-century buildings housing a motley population of artists and poor families. While it's no great shakes for sightseeing, it does have a number of budget **hotels**, and lower **Magazine Street** – more countercultural here than along its uptown stretch – holds various alternative galleries, thrift stores and places to eat. This end of the street is studded with desolate, run-down blocks, however, so keep your wits about you if you decide to walk it. The #11 bus runs the length of the road, but services are sporadic.

THE GARDEN DISTRICT

Map 3, B4/5–F5/6.

Pride of uptown New Orleans, the **Garden District** drapes itself seductively across an area just thirteen blocks wide and five deep, bounded by Magazine Street and St Charles, Jackson and Louisiana avenues. Here some of the swankiest homes in the city – during Carnival season, many fly the official Mardi Gras banner, announcing that a resident has been honored as King or Queen of Rex – stand in the shadow of hauntingly derelict piles.

The mansions of Lafayette were built in a variety of **architectural styles**, each according to the whim of its owner. The earliest homes stood one to a block, situated on the corners and fronted by brick flagstones that came over as ballast on ships returning from Europe. As fortunes were made, tastes became more and more flamboyant, each nouveau-riche planter and merchant trying to outdo his neighbor. Today you'll see ordered, columned Greek Revival structures; romantic, Italianate villas; Moorish follies; Second Empire piles and fanciful Queen Anne mansions, plus a number of buildings that defy categorization, with motifs mixed up together to form transitional, or hybrid, styles.

It's no coincidence that so many gallery ceilings in the Garden District are painted sky-blue – it's a well-known ploy to deter dimwitted insects, who thrive in the copious foliage, from nesting there.

Though most visitors come here to gaze upon the houses, the neighborhood also lives up to its name with its fabulous **greenery**. Unlike the Creoles of the French Quarter, who were constrained by lack of space, the planters and traders who built in Lafayette reveled in its expansiveness, setting their mansions back from the street and surrounding them with lush gardens. Today, everywhere you turn, foliage threatens to overtake the place: huge, mossy live oaks form a canopy over the streets, while broad oleander trees and banana plants fight for space with vividly flowering azaleas, camellias and crepe myrtles. The air is scented by jasmine, sweet olive and waxy magnolia blossoms – originally planted, it is said, to mask the odors from the tanneries and slaughterhouses of the **Irish Channel**, the working-class district that spread out beneath Lafayette toward the river.

The Garden District's cemetery, Lafayette No. 1, is covered on p.126, in the chapter devoted to New Orleans' Cities of the Dead.

THE GARDEN DISTRICT

The Garden District mansions are only open to the public during New Orleans' Spring Fiesta (see p.282). The neighborhood is best explored on an official **walking tour** (see p.14) or one of the self-guided tours available from the State Tourism Information Center (see p.9). Other than a handful of fellow tourists, you'll see little human activity on these rarefied streets, where the uncanny hush is interrupted only by birdsong and the buzzing of distant lawnmowers – worlds away from the crash and clatter of the Quarter.

Toby's Corner and McGehee School

Map 3, E5.

The Greek Revival mansion known as **Toby's Corner**, 2340 Prytania at First, is the oldest surviving house in the Garden District. It was built in 1838, in unadorned plantation style, with a raised floor to prevent waterlogging. Thomas Toby himself, a native of Philadelphia, had made a fortune by inventing a revolutionary cotton hauler, then promptly lost most of it backing the doomed Texan revolution of 1835.

Covering the entire block opposite Toby's Corner, fronted by mighty Corinthian columns, the private **McGehee School**, 2434 Prytania at First, is housed in what was formerly the residence of Union sympathizer Bradish Johnson. Built during Reconstruction, the showy Second Empire trophy was the envy of every sugar planter in town, boasting not only an exquisite domed marble staircase, but also a newfangled elevator, a sure sign of wealth and distinction.

Joseph Morris House and the White House

Map 3, E6.

The **Joseph Morris House**, the lovely rose-pink villa on the corner of First Street and Coliseum, is a quintessential example of the dreamy Italiante style that swept through the Garden District in the 1860s. Its romantic aspect, enhanced by a web of cast-iron galleries, is set off perfectly by the orderly, straight-down-the-line Greek Revival **White House**, opposite at 1312 First St.

Anne Rice's house (Rosegate)

Map 3, E6.

A gorgeous Italiante-Greek Revival hybrid on the corner of Chestnut and First, **Anne Rice's residence** is also the fictional home of her Mayfair witches. Built in 1856, it was the first house on the block, and today its elaborate floriated iron fence encloses other, newer houses. Notice the Egyptian "keyhole" front door, flaring out at the base, and the sky-blue gallery ceilings so common in the Garden District (see p.93). Peering out from the first-story balcony, the bizarre fiberglass German Shepherd – representing the mastiff that befriends the vampire Lestat – is said to have been a gift to Rice from her vet. Or a gift from Anne Rice to her husband. Or a gift from an anonymous fan. It depends upon your tour guide. You'll usually see at least one of the author's stretch limos parked outside the house; she has three, with the registration plates Seraphim, Cherubim and Ophanim.

In recent years, Rice has sporadically allowed free tours of her home, usually for just a couple of hours a week. Anyone interested should log on to her Web site (see p.8) to check the latest situation.

Anne Rice leaves long voicemail messages,
which include her views on current affairs,
her favorite TV programs and books, and
updates on her state of mind, on ☎522-8634.

Payne-Strachan House

Map 3, E6.

One block south of Anne Rice's house, the relatively un-ostentatious, columned **Payne-Strachan House**, 1134 First St at Camp, is a prime specimen of antebellum Greek Revival styling. Built in 1849 for the pro-Union planter Jacob Payne, the house is most notable for being where Jefferson Davis, president of the Confederacy, died in 1889, while visiting Payne's son-in-law. A granite slab outside commemorates the event.

Musson House and Showboat House

Map 3, E5.

Back up on Coliseum Street and Third, the Italianate **Musson House**, a fanciful pink clapboard structure fronted with fabulous cast-iron balconies, was built in 1850 for Michel Musson, the Creole uncle of the French Impressionist painter **Edgar Degas**. After the Civil War, having lost much of his wealth, Musson abandoned the Anglo-dominated Garden District in favor of Esplanade Avenue, the Creole equivalent of St Charles Avenue. He went on to join the supremacist White League, and was a voluble presence at the rally that led to the Battle of Liberty Place (see p.72).

Michel Musson can be seen testing a cotton sample in the foreground of Degas' painting *A Cotton Office in New Orleans* (see p.118).

Opposite the Musson House, the gallery-swathed **Showboat House**, 1415 Third St, is one of the Garden District's most palatial mansions. An Italianate-Greek Revival structure built in 1860 by eminent architect Henry

Howard, it is best known, prosaically, for its early form of indoor plumbing, whereby the roof acted as a large vessel to collect rainwater that was then channeled down into the house.

Lonsdale-Rice House and Briggs House

Map 3, E5.

The enormous Italianate **Lonsdale-Rice House**, 2521 Prytania St at Third, was built by Henry Howard in 1856 for coffee magnate Henry Lonsdale, who, like so many of Lafayette's major players, lost his fortune in the Civil War. The house was later turned over to a religious order, who added a chapel, and, in 1996, Anne Rice – who had attended services here as a child – bought it outright.

On the other side of the road, the Garden District's only neo-Gothic mansion, the stern-looking **Briggs House**, 2605 Prytania at Third, was designed by James Gallier Sr in 1847. Though there are a couple of significant neo-Gothic buildings – also the work of Gallier – in the CBD, as a rule Southerners weren't that keen on the narrow windows and arches that characterized the style. This building, whose pared-down aspect does look a little out of place in the overblown Garden District, was built for an English insurance broker.

Colonel Short's Villa

Map 3, D5.

Yet another Henry Howard structure, the Italianate **Colonel Short's Villa**, 1448 Fourth St at Prytania, was built for $25,000 in 1859 – a relatively paltry sum, even then. Just a few years later, it was commandeered by Yankee forces, who enjoyed its facilities for the duration of the Civil War. While the building itself, with its columns and galleries, is undeniably striking, it's the cast-iron **cornstalk fence** that grabs your attention. A rural tangle of corn cobs and morning glories, it was picked, during the city's cast-iron craze, from the same catalog as its twin in the French Quarter (see p.52). You'll spot crumbly patches, where the fence is rusting away: cast iron, despite its decorative qualities, tends to be less durable than the simpler, hand-wrought iron favored in the early nineteenth century.

The turquoise Queen Anne building at 1403 Washington Ave is *Commander's Palace*, one of the finest Creole restaurants in the city (see p.194).

New Orleans Firefighting Museum

Map 3, D6. Mon–Fri 9am–4pm; free.

Housed in a nineteenth-century fire station, the **New Orleans Firefighting Museum**, 1135 Washington Ave, is a quiet little specialist museum where the sheer enthusiasm of the staff (many of them ex-firefighters) is bound to spark the interest of the most casual visitor. The highlight, among the vintage uniforms, photos and memorabilia, is the 1838 hand-pump engine, which looks like – and probably was – the brainchild of some crazy inventor.

ST CHARLES AVENUE

A stately, live oak-lined swathe sweeping its way from Canal Street upriver to Audubon Park, **St Charles Avenue** (Map 3, A3–N4) is uptown's showpiece boulevard. Most of its ostentatious homes were built in the late nineteenth and early twentieth centuries – after 1893, when the streetcar line was electrified, merchants flourishing in the post-Civil War South found that to live on "the avenue", as it is still called, was an ideal way to display their new wealth.

The **streetcar** (see p.91) is still by far the best way to see the avenue, which gets more magnificent the further uptown you go. **Lower St Charles** is a scrappy ragbag of empty lots and architectural nonentities; beyond the Garden District, however, the private mansions cut as impressive a dash as they did a century ago, their cut-glass doors sparkling like priceless crystal.

The atmospheric *Columns Hotel*, 3811 St Charles (on the lakeside of the avenue), is a fabulous place to stop off for a drink, either in the faded bar or on the avenue-side veranda, fronted by its stout Doric columns (see p.216).

St Elizabeth's Orphanage

Map 2, I6. Orphanage tours usually Mon–Fri 1pm, Sat 11am, 1pm & 3pm, but are often subject to change – call ☎899-6450 to check; $7; Stan Rice art gallery Wed–Sun 10am–4pm; free.

A couple of blocks south of St Charles, the red-brick Second Empire **St Elizabeth's Orphanage**, 1314 Napoleon Ave at Prytania, is another of Anne Rice's properties. As a little girl she once knocked on its doors in search of playmates; forty years later she bought the place and has since converted the massive structure, which covers the entire block, into a glorious palace. Today the huge, high-ceilinged rooms are filled with her personal effects, including ranks of overwrought Roman Catholic art and husband Stan's bright, quirky paintings. **Dolls** and mannequins from her prodigious collection pop up all over the place, casting a vaguely surreal spell. Rice hosts frequent charity events in the ballroom, while newlyweds can hold receptions in the white chapel, illuminated by vivid stained glass and bursting with religious icons.

ST CHARLES AVENUE

Houses on the avenue

St Charles Avenue's showy **mansions** display a variety of styles, from Italianate through Romanesque to Queen Anne. Many of them – including his own little Queen Anne gingerbread home at 4010 St Charles (riverside; Map 2, J6) – are the work of eminent architect **Thomas Sully**, also responsible for some of the most important buildings in the CBD.

You can hardly miss the **Brown House**, a limestone Romanesque monster at no. 4717; it's the largest mansion on the avenue (lakeside; Map 2, H6). Further along, at no. 5705, look out for the gleaming white 1941 replica of **Tara**, Scarlett's beloved home in *Gone with the Wind* (lakeside; Map 2, F5); close on its heels at no. 5809, the aptly nicknamed **Wedding Cake House** (lakeside; Map 2, E5) is an ostentatious Greek Revival building, frosted with a layer of balconies, balustrades, cornices and columns. Beyond, the handsome **university campuses** of Loyola and Tulane (lakeside; Map 2, D4 & E3) stand side by side facing Audubon Park.

Uptown hotels are reviewed on pp.168–169, its restaurants on pp.195–198, bars on pp.216–217, and clubs on p.233.

AUDUBON PARK

Map 2, B/C8–C/D4.

Built on plantation lands once belonging to Etienne de Boré – who in 1795 perfected the sugar granulation process, and went on to become the city's first mayor – Upper City Park was laid out in 1871. After hosting the 1884 Cotton Exposition, which, though it proved to be a financial flop, marked the onset of a nascent tourist industry in New Orleans, the park was redeveloped and renamed for Haitian naturalist John James Audubon, who stayed in the city in 1821 while compiling *Birds of America*. Today the 350-acre **Audubon Park** is a lovely, much-used space, dotted with lagoons and picnic areas, shaded by Spanish moss-swathed trees and looped by an extensive cycling and jogging path.

Audubon Zoo

Map 2, C7. Daily 9.30am–5pm; summer Mon–Fri 9.30am–5pm, Sat & Sun 9.30am–6pm; $9, children $4.75; zoo and aquarium (see p.110) $17.50, children $9.25.

The best thing about the **Audubon Zoo** – a fifteen-minute walk or short shuttle ride (every 20–30min) from the park's St Charles entrance – is its beautifully recreated **Louisiana swamp**, complete with Cajun houseboats, wallowing alligators and knobbly cypress knees poking out of the emerald green water. Animals here include raccoons, otters, bears, cougars and the broadhead skink, Louisiana's largest lizard. If the snakes and reptiles leave you cold, you can take refuge with the fluffy bobcat kittens in the cosy swamp nursery.

Star of the swamp, is, of course, the **alligator**, and you'll find anything and everything gator-related here, from monstrous prehistoric skulls to the tank of tiny hatchlings perched precariously on small logs. The main attraction is the mysterious blue-eyed **white alligator** – who suffers the woefully unmysterious name Mr Bingle – one of eighteen leucistic hatchlings discovered by a Cajun fisherman in a nearby swamp in 1987.

Throughout the swamp, a trail of panels puts the exhibits into historical and cultural context, while videos illustrate subjects ranging from Cajun dancing to cooking. At the barn-like **café**, you can eat gumbo and crawfish pie seated in a rocking chair on the veranda; look carefully and you'll see the enormous snapping turtles just beneath the water's surface.

Each October, Audubon Zoo hosts the splendid Swampfest, featuring the best in Cajun and zydeco music, food and crafts. See p.284 for details.

In stark contrast to the swamp, some of the zoo's other recreated habitats, despite their lush vegetation and pleasant boardwalks, are showing their age. Many of the enclosures are simply too small, their inhabitants hemmed in and dispirited. Best bets are the **African savannah** – where most visitors, underwhelmed by Monkey Hill, which at 28ft is proudly labeled as the highest natural point in the city, prefer instead to watch the hippos, leopards and giraffes – and **Jaguar Jungle**, where jaguars, sloths, anteaters and monkeys prowl, doze, snuffle and swing among mock Mayan ruins. Look out too for the komodo dragons, and, in the **Asian domain** the rare white tiger, who like the alligator is leucistic, with light blue eyes.

One appealing way to get to or from the zoo – perhaps combining it with a streetcar ride in the opposite direction – is to take a narrated cruise on the **John James Audubon riverboat**, which plies the Mississippi between the zoo and the aquarium. For details, see p.106.

The Mississippi River

A resonant, romantic and extraordinary physical presence, the **Mississippi River** is New Orleans' lifeblood and its *raison d'être*. Some half a mile wide, it writhes through the city like an out-of-control snake, swelling against the constraining, man-made levees as it courses toward the Gulf of Mexico. Nineteenth-century visitors marveled at this mighty highway into a still unexplored interior, writing long, lyrical accounts of its "vast and melancholy solitude", its power and its hazards; as the city's port grew, however, and river traffic increased, New Orleans gradually cut itself off from the water altogether, hemming the river in behind a string of warehouses and freight railroads.

More recently, as the importance of the port has diminished, a couple of downtown **parks**, plazas and riverside walks, accessible from the French Quarter and the CBD, have focused attention back onto the waterfront, capitalizing on its magnetic appeal. Most tourists combine a river walk with a **shopping** trip at the French Market, Jackson Brewery or Riverwalk malls (for more details on these, turn to the "Shopping" chapter, which starts on p.241) or a visit to the superb **Aquarium of the Americas**. The main draw, however, is the river itself, best seen from the **Moonwalk** or **Woldenberg Park**, or, even better, on a **cruise** aboard a restored steamboat or paddlewheeler. Some of these, which share river space with tugs and towboats, barges, naval tankers and darting water-taxis, take you as far as **Chalmette**, riverfront site of the 1815 Battle of New Orleans.

You can also get out onto the water on the free ferry from Canal Street, which struggles against the current to deliver you within minutes to the old shipbuilding community of **Algiers** on the west bank. Though taking the ferry is fun in itself, it's worth disembarking at the other end and strolling the Spanish moss-draped streets to the quirky **Mardi Gras museum**.

Some history

It took considerable persistence for the French-Canadian explorer Jean Baptiste le Moyne, **Sieur de Bienville**, to impose a city on the banks of a force of nature as powerful as the Mississippi River. His dream, however, of a mighty metropolis built on the back of lucrative river trade – a vision not shared by his critics, who could see only a soggy handful of cypress huts doomed by endless flooding – was eventually realized. By the nineteenth century, New Orleans' position, on a portage between the river and Lake Pontchartrain, which opened into the Gulf of Mexico, made it an ideal **entrepôt** – the meeting point for the riverboats carrying cotton, sugar, tobacco and lumber down from the interior, ocean-going ships hauling the goods out to the rest of the world, and foreign vessels bringing manufactured and luxury commodities from overseas. In 1803, as the United States began its inexorable sweep westward, the Americans snapped the city up, under the terms of the **Louisiana Purchase**, which ensured them control of the entire river. Within a year, tonnage using New Orleans' port had increased by fifty percent, and, for the next quarter century, the number of flatboats and keelboats docking at the end of Tchoupitoulas Street averaged around a thousand per year. The flatboats, which came from the interior but were unable to negotiate the current and return upstream, were sold for lumber or transformed into floating brothels and gambling dens, while the boatmen – a lawless, brawling breed known derisively by the Creoles as "**Kaintocks**" (many came from Kentucky) – would kick up hell in the city before making their way back into the interior by land. **Pirates** plied the Mississippi, too, ready to hijack the cumbersome vessels; most notorious among them were Jean and Pierre Lafitte and their band of **Baratarians** – named for their swampy hideout, around twenty miles downriver – who hatched countless dastardly plots in the coffeehouses and bars of New Orleans.

For an account of the Barataria swamps today, turn to p.146 in the "Out of the city" chapter.

In 1812 the **steamboat** exploded – sometimes literally – onto the scene. Though these "floating palaces", with their puffing chimneys, fancy galleries and enormous paddle-wheels, have become icons of the great days of river travel, the earliest packets, with their propensity to overheat and burst into flames, were seen as novelties only, and far too dangerous to carry passengers. By the 1840s, however, hundreds of them churned along the river, bringing goods, news, travelers and sharp-suited card sharks to the city, while their cousins, the flamboyant **showboats** – a common sight on the Mississippi well into the 1930s – staged vaudeville, circus, melodrama and Shakespeare for plantation owners, rough boatmen and straggling river communities.

RIVER CRUISES

Quite apart from the sheer delight of churning along one of the world's greatest rivers on a big old sternwheeler, a short cruise on the Mississippi offers a fascinating glimpse into the workings of the nation's most important waterway. If you're after a cruise plain and simple, the three-deck Natchez sternwheeler steamboat – heralded by its hauntingly off-key calliope tunes, which float through the French Quarter about thirty minutes before the boat sets off – is by far the best choice. It leaves twice a day from the Toulouse Street wharf behind Jackson Brewery and heads seven or so miles downriver, turning back near the Chalmette battlefield. You can sit on deck or lunch inside on fried chicken and red beans, with live Dixieland jazz accompaniment (daily 11.30am & 2.30pm; 2hr; $15.75, $21.75 with lunch; dinner jazz cruise 6pm; 3hr; $45.50 with food, $25.50 without; ☏586-8777).

Though less atmospheric than the historic Natchez, the John James Audubon riverboat is a great option if you want to combine a cruise with a trip to the aquarium (see p.110) or Audubon Zoo (p.101), or both. Cruises leave daily from the aquarium at 10am, noon, 2pm and 4pm, and from the zoo an hour later (1hr one way; $11.75 one way, $14.50 round trip; $22.50 with aquarium; $20.50 with zoo; $28.25 with both; children half-price; ☏586-8777).

The only boat that stops at Chalmette, site of the Battle of New Orleans, is the Creole Queen paddlewheeler (10.30am & 2pm; 2hr 30min; $16, $22 with lunch; dinner jazz cruise $45; ☏524-0814), which leaves from the Plaza d'España.

Tickets for all cruises are sold at riverside booths behind Jackson Brewery and the aquarium.

Today, though New Orleans' antebellum golden era as the world's biggest export **port** – when scores of steamboats, ocean-going sailing ships, keelboats and barges lined the waterfront for miles on end – is a distant memory, in terms of tonnage New Orleans is still one of the busiest ports in the world. The river, meanwhile, continues to bide its time behind the levee, as unpredictable and intractable as ever.

The Riverfront streetcar, which makes ten stops between Esplanade Avenue and the Convention Center, can be useful if you're footsore, and offers pretty views of the water. See p.12 for details.

WASHINGTON ARTILLERY PARK AND THE MOONWALK

Map 4, E6–J6.

Directly across Decatur Street from Jackson Square, **Washington Artillery Park** is a rather grand name for a small, elevated strip of concrete, reached by steps, that gives superb photo opportunities of the square and St Louis Cathedral, and, in the other direction, of the Mississippi. Street performers use the space below on Decatur as a stage, while spectators lounge on the steps.

Descending the steps on the river side, walking through the break in the concrete flood walls, over the Riverfront streetcar tracks, and up another flight of steps, brings you to the **Moonwalk**, a riverfront promenade named for "Moon" Landrieu, mayor of the city from 1970 to 1978. It's a great spot, especially at sunset, when its iron benches fill with tourists gazing at the panorama upriver to the Mississippi River Bridge and, downriver, to the wharves that begin at Governor Nicholls Street. Gulls dip and dive in front of you, in the vain hope of plucking catfish out of the whirling eddies, while ships battle against the current at **Algiers Point**, the sharpest bend in the entire river,

THE BIG MUDDY

*"You know, they straightened out the Mississippi in places,
to make room for houses and livable acreage. Occasionally
the river floods these places. 'Floods' is the word they
use, but in fact it is not flooding; it is remembering.
Remembering where it used to be . . . "*
– Toni Morrison, "The Site of Memory" in *Out There:
Marginalization and Contemporary Cultures*
(ed Russell Ferguson)

North America's principal waterway, the Mississippi – the
name comes from the Algonquin words for "big" and "river" –
is the third longest river in the world after the Nile and the
Amazon. Starting just ninety miles south of the Canadian border in Minnesota, it writhes its way 2348 miles to the mouth at
the Gulf of Mexico, 217 river miles (65 miles as the crow flies)
from New Orleans. On its way it takes in more than one hundred tributaries and drains 41 percent of continental America,
an area of more than a million square miles.

The Big Muddy – so nicknamed because it carries 2lb of
dirt for every 1000lb of water – is one of the busiest commercial rivers in the world and one of the least conventional.
Instead of widening toward its mouth, like most rivers, the
Mississippi grows narrower and deeper. Its "delta", near
Memphis, Tennessee, over three hundred miles upstream
from the river's mouth, is not a delta at all, but a fertile, allu-
vial flood plain. On the other hand, its estuary deposits,
which extend the land six miles out to sea every century, are
comparatively paltry: though enough mud is deposited at the
mouth of the river each year to cover the state of Connecticut
with a layer one inch thick, Gulf currents disperse the sedi-
ment before it has time to settle. The Mississippi is also, in
the words of Mark Twain, who spent four years as a riverboat

pilot, "the crookedest river in the world". As it weaves and curls its way extravagantly along its channel, it continually cuts through narrow necks of land to shape and reshape oxbow lakes, meander scars, cutoffs and marshy backwaters. Some engineers predict that eventually the river will desert its present channel altogether and find a shorter route to the sea, bypassing New Orleans entirely.

Another manifestation of the Mississippi's power is its propensity to flood – a particularly serious threat to low-lying New Orleans, which at its highest point reaches just 15ft above sea level. Although the city was settled on a natural levee, this was little safeguard against further flooding and wasn't enough to prevent the swollen Mississippi from sporadically wiping out sugar crops and entire cotton plantations. As the city developed, it became crucial to find effective ways to tame this destructive force, and in 1792 Governor Carondelet decreed that landowners should build and maintain artificial levees, imposing steep fines for non-compliance. The plan backfired somewhat, however, as landowners would send men out at night, under the guise of checking their own levees for crevasses (tiny cracks that could be caused by something as small as a crawfish), but in reality to force holes into the levees of their neighbors.

Since disastrous flooding in the 1920s wiped out entire communities throughout the Mississippi valley – which led to the Flood Control Act of 1928 – the federal government has been responsible for a wide range of protective measures all along the river. In New Orleans, the levee is backed by a series of flood walls. Recently these have been rendered less necessary with the building of the Spillway, which, when the river reaches dangerous levels, automatically drains into Lake Pontchartrain – to the dismay of conservationists, who claim that it pours polluted water into the lake.

THE BIG MUDDY

churned by a savage centrifugal force. Safe enough during the day – though you may have to contend with panhandlers, extrovert street punks and **hustlers** – the Moonwalk is best avoided late at night.

WOLDENBERG PARK TO THE RIVERWALK MALL

Map 4, E7–A9.

Long, thin **Woldenberg Park** curves upriver from the end of Toulouse Street in the French Quarter to the **Aquarium of the Americas**. Though in itself the park is nothing to get excited about, its riverside location makes it a good place to sprawl on the grass with a picnic, watching the traffic on the Mississippi, and the stream of tourists flowing to and from the aquarium or one of the river-cruise terminals. Beyond the aquarium, you have to cut through the ugly concrete **Canal Street wharf**, terminal for the free ferry to **Algiers**, to reach the **Plaza d'España** and the touristy **Riverwalk** shopping mall.

On Lundi Gras, the day before Mardi Gras, Zulu hosts a fantastic day-long party in Woldenberg Park; see p.275.

Aquarium of the Americas

Map 4, B8. Daily from 9.30am; closing hours vary; $13, children $6.50; IMAX $7.75/$5; aquarium and IMAX $17.25/$10.50; aquarium and Audubon Zoo (see p.101) $17.50/$9.25; ⊤581-4629 or 1-800/774-7394.

As you enter New Orleans' superb **aquarium**, through a clear **tunnel** where tropical fish, flapping rays and hawksbill turtles whirl above and around you, you know you're in for something very good indeed. It's a vast place, where different environments are recreated in lively detail – the steamy **Amazonian rainforest**, for example, demonstrates how monstrous fish, grown fat on the river's bounty, develop sensitive whiskers and an acute sense of hearing in order to make their way through the silty, muddy water. Rainbow macaws flap above you as you cross a tree-top pathway, while thumbnail-sized poisoned-dart frogs and bird-eating spiders lurk menacingly in glass enclosures. The **Mississippi delta**, meanwhile, complete with its own mossy cypress trees, features one of New Orleans' white alligators (see p.101), ancient paddlefish, and the unnerving giant flathead catfish, who feed on geese, ducks and dogs.

There are so many other things to see – including a **penguin** enclosure and a pair of hyperactive **otters** – that it can be a challenge to get around it all. Do, however, make time for the **sharks**, which range from weird-looking Australian wobbegongs to leathery nurse sharks – which you're encouraged to stroke – and the infinitesimal **jellyfish** that sparkle in the dark blue water like tiny Christmas-tree lights. And on *no* account miss the **sea horse** exhibit, where you'll find the leafy sea dragon, nonchalantly disguised as a tangle of foliage, and the strange **weedy sea dragon**, hovering in the kelp like some arthritic Dr Seuss creature. The five-story **IMAX** theater shows the usual overblown epics of mountaineering, space exploration and other derring-do.

For details of the narrated *John James Audubon* **riverboat cruise**, a great way of getting from the aquarium to uptown's Audubon Zoo, see p.106.

To enjoy an unmatched bird's-eye view of the river,
head for the 1960s World Trade Center (see p.71),
at the foot of Canal near the aquarium.

WOLDENBERG PARK TO THE RIVERWALK MALL

Plaza d'España and the Riverwalk Mall

Nudged in between the river and the World Trade Center, the sunken **Plaza d'España** (Map 4, A9), ringed with Spanish coats of arms and centering on a fountain, is most lively on Lundi Gras, when a free, touristy party, following the Zulu bash in Woldenberg Park (see p.275), celebrates the mayor handing over the city to Rex, King of Carnival.

From the plaza you can enter the half-mile-long **Riverwalk mall** (Map 3, M6–7), which is usually scuttling with big-spending weekenders and conference delegates scooping up suitcase-fulls of souvenirs as they rush between the convention center and the French Quarter. Even if you're not shopping, it's worth strolling along the mall's outdoor **promenade**, which is raised above river-level and dotted with illuminating historical plaques. It was here, in 1996, that a Chinese freighter, losing the battle against the current at Algiers Point, ploughed into the side of the mall in the middle of the afternoon, smashing much of the place up. For more on **shopping** in the Riverwalk mall, see p.243.

CHALMETTE BATTLEFIELD

Daily 9am–5pm; free.

About six miles downriver from the city, off Hwy-46, the **Chalmette Battlefield National Historical Park** was the site of the **Battle of New Orleans**, the final skirmish of the War of 1812. In 1814, having captured Washington DC, the British turned their sights to the Gulf, inviting the notorious Lafitte pirates to join them in the campaign against General Andrew Jackson. The double-crossing Lafittes, however, aligned themselves with Jackson and, though neither of them actually fought, furnished him with arms and troops, in exchange for which they were pardoned of all piracy charges.

On December 23, 1814, British General Edward Pakenham and his nine thousand Redcoats arrived five miles downriver of the city, to be met by Jackson's five-thousand-strong volunteer force of Creoles, Anglo-American adventurers, free men of color, Baratarian pirates and Native Americans. Though at first the British troops succeeded in pushing back the ragbag American army, on **January 8, 1815**, after a battle of minutes, Jackson's men routed their opponents. The death toll came to seven hundred Redcoats, including Pakenham, and just a dozen or so Americans. Ironically, the battle, from which Jackson went on to become a national hero – and eventually US president – was unnecessary. Soon after it was fought, the news reached the city that the Treaty of Ghent had already ended the war in December 1814.

Today the Battle of New Orleans is commemorated by a 110-foot **obelisk** and an **interpretive exhibit** – a source of delight to war buffs but probably too much of a good thing for casual visitors. Park rangers give short **talks** (11.15am & 2.45pm; 15min) for visitors who have arrived on the *Creole Queen* **river cruises** (see p.106); if you've come under your own steam you'll have more time to wander freely around the site (a loop of a mile and a half) and to watch the thirty-minute video that details the events leading up to the War of 1812.

ALGIERS

Map 1, G7.

A free **ferry ride** from the bottom of Canal Street brings you within five minutes or so – depending on the current – to the west bank and the quiet neighborhood of **Algiers**. Seen from the lofty heights of the World Trade Center (see p.71), the **ferry** looks tiny, swirling alarmingly with the river's flow – the Mississippi is at its deepest (nearly 200ft) here, and the current fierce, churning furiously around the extreme bend in the river. Even if you don't disembark, the views of both banks – especially at sunset – and the chance to see the river traffic up close make it well worth a ride in itself.

Ferries leave every 30min: from Canal Street between 6am and midnight, and from Algiers between 5.45am and 11.45pm. Pedestrians ride free; it's $1 each way for bikes and cars.

Settled a couple of years after New Orleans was established on the east bank, Algiers, a swathe of plantations originally belonging to Bienville, was entirely separate from the early city. The origins of its **name** are obscure, though one theory holds that, as a major eighteenth-century disembarkation point for the slave boats, it may have been named for the African slave port. In 1819 the first **shipyard** opened on the point, and settlement increased rapidly as a rash of dry docks, boat-builders and related industries spread along the river-front. The coming of the **railways** and the development of the **shipbuilding industry** during the Civil War led to further growth, and in 1870 the city was incorporated into New Orleans. Here, in the same way as across the river, the saloons – haunts of gamblers, dockers, seamen and prostitutes – spawned some of the earliest **jazz** music, often created by freed slaves who had played in brass bands on the local plantations. Practically the whole town had to be rebuilt after a devastating **fire** in 1895; most of the buildings you see today date from just after that time. Algiers fell into decline after the 1920s, and was touched little by the oil boom and subsequent modernizations that were inflicted on the east bank.

Though you're safe enough walking around Algiers during the day, it's best not to wander too far off the beaten track, especially if you're alone.

ALGIERS

Visitors to **Mardi Gras World**, the district's one real tourist attraction, are shuttled to and from the ferry landing; to pass the time before catching the ferry back you could take a stroll through quiet streets lined with a host of **architectural styles** and lovely subtropical gardens. Take time, too, to climb up onto the **levee**: the downtown skyline is at its most photogenic from here.

Blaine Kern's Mardi Gras World

Map I, F7. Daily 9.30am–4.30pm; $11.50.

The free bus waiting at the Algiers ferry terminal will whisk you off to the cavernous "dens" of **Blaine Kern's Mardi Gras World**, 223 Newton St at Brooklyn, where year-round (except during the fortnight or so before Mardi Gras itself) you can see artists preparing, constructing and painting the overblown papier-mâché floats used in the carnival parades. Kern's team makes floats for around forty or so of the krewes, including super krewe **Bacchus**, whose enormous King Kong family, Bacchawhoppa whale and Bacchagator – a leucistic alligator, like those in the city's zoo and aquarium – hibernate here for most of the year. It's a surreal experience wandering these paint-splattered warehouses, past piles of dusty, grimacing has-beens from parades gone by. Many of the figures – from limbless cartoon characters to giant caved-in crawfish, and from superstars to presidents – are recycled for future parades, so little is ever thrown away. In keeping with the carnival spirit, there are plenty of opportunities to dress up, fool about and take photos – you're encouraged to try on colossal Marilyn and Nixon papier-mâché heads, velvet cloaks and towering plumed headdresses – and each visitor gets free coffee and a slice of King cake before they go.

ALGIERS

For more on Mardi Gras, see p.269 and p.306.

Exploring Algiers

A block or so from the ferry landing, the turreted **Algiers Courthouse**, 225 Morgan Ave (Mon–Fri 8.30am–7pm), has piles of free self-guided walking tours of Algiers, concentrating either on architecture or the area's jazz history. Turning onto the 100 block of **Bermuda**, trimmed with gingerbread homes and cast-iron fences, then again onto the 300 block of **Delaronde** – more gingerbread, lovingly restored – brings you to a rare survivor of the 1895 fire, the **Seger-Rees-Donner House**, at no. 405: an austere Greek Revival home with Gothic-style iron railings, built in 1850. If you continue along Delaronde for a couple more blocks, you'll come to **Olivier Street**, the first few blocks of which feature some of Algiers' best-preserved architecture, a jumble of Creole cottages, Greek Revival, Italianate, Queen Anne and Edwardian styles. Turn right again onto Alix; a block away at Verret, the towering neo-Gothic **Holy Name of Mary Church**, built in 1929, retains the Carrara marble altars and stained-glass windows from a nineteenth-century church that stood on the same site.

Conveniently situated opposite the church, an ideal place to hang out before walking the few blocks back to the ferry landing, **News 'n' Brews**, 347 Verret St at Alix, is a laid-back hangout serving good **espresso**, bagels, muffins and cookies.

Mid-City and City Park

Predominantly residential **Mid-City**, the large stretch of land that fans up from Tremé toward Lake Pontchartrain, is of most interest to visitors for City Park and the eclectic **New Orleans Museum of Art**. Snaking down the eastern side of the park and a mile or so beyond, **Bayou St John**, once an important waterway, today flows placidly through a desirable residential area; nearby, the **Fair Grounds** racetrack hosts New Orleans' annual **Jazz Fest** (see p.279), when it bursts at the seams with tens of thousands of music fans from around the world.

You may well also venture into Mid-City for its **restaurants** (see pp.198–200). There's an especially good cluster along **Esplanade Ridge** – the "high" ground (about 4ft above sea level) that hugs either side of Esplanade Avenue. Beyond the ridge, however, it's not a good idea to wander around the poverty-scarred outskirts of **Tremé**; bus #48, which runs from the corner of Rampart in the French Quarter, along Esplanade all the way to City Park, is a safe way to travel during the day, but you should call a **taxi** (see p.13) after dark.

ESPLANADE AVENUE

Map 1, F6–E5.

In the antebellum era, wealthy Creoles turned their sights toward **Esplanade Avenue**, the broad, live oak-lined street that sweeps up from the Mississippi to City Park. Escaping the congested French Quarter, they lined the grand boulevard with large, fashionable homes, fronting them with voluminous cast-iron galleries. Today, many of the houses, though still hauntingly lovely, are decidedly run-down, and stretches of the road lie blighted and desolate. Restoration, monitored by a vocal preservation group, is gradually improving matters, and a handful of the homes have been converted into luxurious **B&Bs** (see pp.163–164).

Degas House

Map 1, F5. Mon–Fri 10am–3pm, Sat & Sun 9am–4pm; $10.

Art buffs shouldn't get too excited about the Italianate **Degas House**, 2306 Esplanade Ave at Tonti Street. Built in 1854, it was rented in the 1870s by the Mussons – Creole relatives of the French Impressionist painter Edgar Degas – who had been forced to sell their Garden District mansion following a downturn in their fortunes after the Civil War (see p.96). Degas lodged here for a while in 1872, and though he returned to Paris the next year, frustrated by the degenerative eye problem that prevented him from painting outdoors, he did produce at least one important work during his stay: *A Cotton Office in New Orleans*, a complex commercial scene that works just as well as a family portrait, showing Michel Musson, Degas' uncle, at work in his cotton exchange, along with sundry nephews and sons-in-law. The artist also made numerous portraits of his blind cousin Estelle, who was married to his brother René until he ran off with a neighbor. Today the house – which is, in fact, just half of the original building (the other half is now next door, standing a few feet away on the left) – is used as a pricey B&B. Tours, though anecdotal, have little to divulge about the building itself, which, lined with reproductions of the artist's work, rather overdoes the tenuous Degas connection.

BAYOU ST JOHN

Map 1, D2–5.

Were it not for **Bayou St John**, New Orleans might never have existed. Local Indians had long used the site of today's city as a portage: the alligator-filled bayou, an inlet of Lake Pontchartrain, provided a handy short-cut between the Mississippi and the Gulf of Mexico via the lake, bypassing the river's perilous lower reaches. As the city grew, the countryside around the bayou was carved into plantations worked by African slaves, and in the early 1800s it evolved into a popular gathering place for local **voodooists** (see p.58). Though it remained a key waterway until the 1920s, today Bayou St John flows through the heart of a well-heeled residential neighborhood – it's a favorite spot for fishing and dog-walking – with not an alligator to be seen.

St Louis No. 3 Cemetery, near Bayou St John on Esplanade Avenue, is covered in the chapter devoted to New Orleans' Cities of the Dead; see p.130.

Pitot House

Map 1, D5. Wed–Sat 10am–3pm; $5.

One of the prettiest houses in New Orleans, the **Pitot House**, 1440 Moss St, stands near the upper end of Esplanade on the banks of the bayou. It's the only remaining West Indies-style plantation home in the city, built in 1799 and named for its second owner, James Pitot, a French merchant who came to the United States fleeing the 1792 slave rebellions in Haiti. Pitot developed one of the city's first cotton presses, and succeeded Etienne de Boré as mayor in 1804. With its stucco-covered walls, ground-floor basement, airy galleries and double-pitched roof, it's a typical Caribbean-New Orleans structure (see p.34), and has been decorated in a simple, elegant style true to its period. From the front galleries you get lovely views out over the parterre garden to the bayou, while crops of cotton, indigo, ginger and bananas form a patchwork across the small back garden. **Tours**, a lively mix of anecdote, historical snippets and architectural detail, draw your attention to everything from the *briquete entre poteaux* (bricks between posts) construction of the building to the customized food cupboards, their legs planted in bowls of water to confound the ants. Look out, too, for the lush, apricot-colored sofa in the drawing room: the site of an orgy of blood-lust in the movie *Interview with the Vampire*, here it looks rather genteel.

CITY PARK

Map 1, D3–4.

City Park covers some 1500 acres between Bayou St John and Lake Pontchartrain. Crisscrossed with roads, and by no means as peaceful as Audubon Park uptown (see p.100), it's nonetheless an impressively landscaped space, streaked with lagoons and shaded by centuries-old **live oaks** draped in ragged gray beards of Spanish moss. Built in the 1860s, the park expanded in the 1920s, when the Beaux Arts Delgado Museum, now the **New Orleans Museum of Art**, established itself as the city's most important gallery.

Today the art museum remains the chief attraction, though visitors who've overdone it pounding the streets of the French Quarter might take solace in the atmospheric Art Deco **Botanical Garden** (Tues–Sun 10am–4.30pm; $3), filled with thousands of native plants, including blooming azaleas, magnolias and camellias. And anyone with young children in tow can head for the **Storyland** playground (Wed–Fri 10am–12.30pm, Sat & Sun 10am–4pm; $2), which, designed in the 1950s, is as dated as you'd expect, though not unpleasantly so. Kids also like the neighboring **carousel gardens**, where an indoor antique merry-go-round is joined by a miniature railroad, bumper cars, rollercoaster and a ferris wheel (Wed–Fri 10am–2.30pm, Sat & Sun 10am–4.30pm; $1, plus $1 per ride, $8 unlimited rides). Opening hours of all the park's attractions can vary; call ☎482-4888 before you set out.

To the left of the museum, the venerable **Dueling Oak**, with a diameter of more than 15ft, was a favorite spot for volatile young adversaries to settle the *affaires d'honneur* that felled so much of the male population of antebellum New Orleans.

New Orleans Museum of Art

Map 1, D4. Tues–Sun 10am–5pm; $6.

Near the Esplanade entrance to City Park, the **New Orleans Museum of Art** (**NOMA**) holds an impressive, wide-ranging collection and hosts major touring exhibitions, film shows and lectures. Some works suffer from poor or nonexistent captioning – **Art of the Americas**, for example, where Maya stelae, delicate Costa Rican jade and gold, Navajo kachinas and fabulous Plains Indians beadwork are sporadically labeled. Not so the **Asian galleries**, however, where everything from tiny eighth-century Jain bronzes to Zen ink paintings and elaborate suits of Edo armor is put into context. Similarly, the **African galleries** – a dizzying array of masks, beaded ceremonial costumes and fetishes – and the **Oceanic galleries** – which include wizened heads from Papua New Guinea and fierce eighteenth-century Hawaiian temple figures – plot admirably

CITY PARK

clear courses through their jaw-dropping treasures.

Of the **paintings**, French artists – naturally – are particularly well represented. Watch out for the symbolic portrait of Marie Antoinette by the young court painter **Élizabeth Louise Vigée-Lebrun**, and **Edgar Degas'** 1872 painting of his New Orleans cousin, Estelle Musson (see p.118) – a poignant image of an unseeing woman reaching out to a blazing red gladiola. **Claude Monet**'s *Snow at Giverny* (1893), painted when the artist's eyesight was at its poorest, shrouds his beloved French home in a lavender-white blur. You'll also see one or two minor works each from names such as Braque, Dufy, Dubuffet, Chagall, Modigliani, Miró, Picasso, Pollock, Giacometti and Warhol, while the museum's **sculpture garden** spreads remarkable pieces by such luminaries as Barbara Hepworth, Henry Moore, Isamu Noguchi and Alexander Calder across five landscaped acres.

Finally, under no circumstances miss NOMA's outstanding collection of **Fabergé eggs**, exquisite pieces of end-of-Empire decadence. Russian jeweler Peter Carl Fabergé, commissioned in the mid-1880s by Tsar Nicholas II to make a precious egg for his precious daughter, went on to design sixty ever more elaborate creations for the autocratic Russian court. That first piece, an extravagant take on traditional Russian stacking dolls, is among those on show: a silver egg containing a hinged jeweled chicken, holding a gold crown hiding an emerald ring. Fabergé also created fabulous fairytale flowers, some of which are displayed here: humble dandelions and lilies magically transformed with platinum pods, gold stems, translucent nephrite leaves and seeds made from infinitesimal diamonds.

The NOMA café (Tues–Sun 10.30am–4.30pm), whose big picture windows overlook City Park's trees and lagoons, serves good coffee, drinks and lunches.

The cemeteries

Though picking your way through a crumbling, overgrown graveyard may sound more like a nightmare than a dream vacation, New Orleans' above-ground **cemeteries**, scattered throughout the city, are fascinating places. They're known as "Cities of the Dead", and amid their tangled pathways, lopsided marble-fronted tombs and decaying monuments to long-forgotten families, the city's history and folklore, and its strange love affair with death, seem somehow to come alive.

New Orleans' **first settlers** buried their dead underground. This set-up wasn't ideal, however; so much of the city is at, or below, sea level that every time the city flooded waves of moldy coffins would float to the surface of the sodden earth. Meanwhile, as the colony grew, so did the **death rate**, reaching a peak in 1783 when a yellow fever epidemic wiped out fifty percent of the population. With dismal sanitation, infections brought by sailors arriving from the Caribbean and fever-carrying mosquitoes proliferating in stagnant swamps and cisterns, the hot, filthy city was a breeding ground for disease.

Believing that germs were carried in miasmas emitted by decaying bodies, New Orleanians began to build their cemeteries outside the city limits, where, in traditional Spanish style, bodies were stored in **above-ground** brick and stucco vaults, or in smaller vaults packed into the walls. Not only did this protect the coffins from flooding, but also it meant families could reuse tombs – a felony in other US states, but still legal in New Orleans.

By the **antebellum** period, New Orleans had the highest mortality rate in the country: in the summer of 1853 alone some 11,000 people – one tenth of the population – died from **yellow fever**. Meanwhile, a booming economy and a fad for French funerary design, as perfected in Père Lachaise cemetery in Paris, led to a demand for increasingly ornate resting places. The finest architects were commissioned to build tombs in various decorative styles, from Baroque and neo-Gothic to Italianate and neoclassical. Many were set in little gardens surrounded by cast-iron railings, with benches where families could greet friends on All Saints' Day (see p.126). Wide avenues, designed to accommodate grand funeral processions, divided the cemeteries into blocks.

Family tombs stood two or more stories high. The first coffin, placed on the top level, would remain there until the death of another family member, when it would be shifted down to the next level, and so on, until all levels were filled. After a year and a day, with the heat and humidity having sped up decomposition, the first body could be removed from its coffin, and the desiccated remains and ashes poked down into the damp pit at the base of the tomb. Eventually, the remains of numerous family members would be mixed together in this *caveau*, as the long lists of names on the tombs attest.

Bodies could also be stored in rented **wall vaults**, which followed the same "year and a day" principle but held only one coffin at a time. Jewish families built tombs in **copings** – elevated, walled frames containing soil, allowing the body to be buried in the earth, as the religion demands, and above ground, as geography insists. The largest, most ornate tombs, with dozens of vaults, belong to the city's many mutual **benevolent societies**.

Because the marble enclosure tablets needed to be kept clear for the long lists of names, epitaphs are rare – as if to compensate, there's an overload of **symbolism** throughout the cemeteries, with a profusion of broken columns (signifying a life cut short), winged hourglasses (the passage of time), roses with broken stems, or arrows pointing downwards (death), rosebuds (the death of a child, also represented by lambs), and waterlilies (death while pregnant or in childbirth).

Visiting and safety

Though part of the thrill of venturing into the Cities of the Dead is fueled by the vampires-and-witches tales of local horror author Anne Rice, many of which refer to specific cemetery locations, a real **danger** comes from a different source – the threat of being mugged, or worse. Though statistically the probability that you'll be attacked is slim, you should *never* venture into the cemeteries alone. Nearly all the city **tours** include a quick trip around at least one of them; if you're interested in more than an overview, contact Historic New Orleans Walking Tours (see p.17) or Save Our Cemeteries (see p.16).

The most touristed cemeteries are **Lafayette No. 1**, in the Garden District opposite *Commander's Palace* restaurant (see p.194), and **St Louis No. 1**, on the border of Tremé and the French Quarter. The nearby **St Louis No. 2**, surrounded by a run-down housing project, and **St Louis No. 3**, out in Mid-City near City Park, are less popular. The only cemetery that is safe to tour independently – by car – is ostentatious **Metairie**, upriver from City Park on the Pontchartrain Expressway.

ALL SAINTS' DAY

In New Orleans All Saints' Day, November 1, is traditionally when families come to whitewash and repaint their tombs, trim the grass and shrubbery, and add fresh flowers – especially the long-lasting and vibrant red coxcomb – to their plots. In the nineteenth century this was a lively social occasion, when old friends, settling down on the iron benches with picnics, would exchange news and gossip. Orphans and nuns sold pralines and fruit outside the gates, while stallholders hawked raisin-filled "funeral pies" and hard Italian cookies called *ossi de muerte*, or bones of the dead – you'll still find both in the city's bakeries at the end of October.

Nowadays, as many of the old families have died off and younger members have moved away, the All Saints' tradition is waning. People still tend their family tombs around this time, but not necessarily on the day itself, and while devout Catholics are sure to attend afternoon mass, said by priests who drive along the ceremonial alleys sprinkling holy water on the tombs, few make a day of it.

LAFAYETTE NO. 1

Map 3, D5. Mon–Fri 7.30am–2.30pm, Sat 7.30am–noon; free.

Lafayette Cemetery, in the heart of the Garden District at 1400 Washington Ave, was built in 1833 for the wealthy, Anglo-American population of Lafayette City (see p.89). The place was filled to capacity by 1852; in that year alone two thousand yellow fever victims were buried here.

Today, Lafayette No. 1 is an atmospheric place, its wide intersecting avenues swathed with overgrown foliage. Many of the tombs are sinking into the gunge below, and as the soft red brick cracks and the marble tablets buckle, some of them are slowly opening, revealing the *caveau* within. It's no surprise that all this decaying grandeur should capture the imagination of author **Anne Rice**, who has used the place in many of her novels – in 1995, she even staged a mock jazz funeral here to launch publication of *Memnoch the Devil*; the "corpse" was herself, dressed in an antique wedding dress, in an open coffin carried by pallbearers.

ST LOUIS NO. 1

Map 4, D1. Mon–Sat 9am–3pm, Sun 9am–noon; free.

St Louis No. 1, 400 Basin St between Conti and St Louis, is the oldest cemetery in the Mississippi valley. It was built in 1789, outside the city limits in an attempt to protect the population from the fatal fumes they believed emanated from corpses, and its tombs vary from early Spanish structures made of brick and plaster to later mausolea designed by eminent architects including Benjamin Latrobe and Jacques de Pouilly.

Its position on the lakeside fringe of the French Quarter makes the cemetery a regular stop on the tour-bus circuit. There is invariably a huddle of people by the simple tomb of "voodoo queen" **Marie Laveau** (see p.58), graffitied with countless brick-dust crosses. They're usually being told some tall tale about how, if you knock on the slab three times and mark a cross on her tomb, her spirit will grant you any favor. The family who own it have asked that this bogus, destructive tradition should stop, not least because people are taking chunks of brick from other tombs to make the crosses. Voodoo practitioners – responsible for the candles, plastic flowers, beads and rum bottles surrounding the plot – deplore the practice, too, regarding it as a desecration that chases Laveau's spirit away. Nearby, the enormous circular white marble structure, topped by a cross and angel, is the 1857 **Italian Benevolent Society** mausoleum, which has space for thousands of remains. This is

THE JAZZ FUNERAL

Rooted in the city's long tradition of military brass band parades, African processions and vibrant street culture, the jazz funeral is unique to New Orleans. Emerging in the late 1800s, organized by black benevolent societies for their members, "funerals with music" were led by brass bands who, after playing a dirge on the route from church to graveyard would then burst into a joyful tune to celebrate the prospect of eternal life. They were followed by a Second Line of mourners who danced and exulted with the music. Though the overall spirit was one of rejoicing, the Second Line were decorous, keeping a respectful distance from the band and covered hearse. Parades were led by a strutting Grand Marshall, whose formal dress included a stuffed white dove on one shoulder, to represent the soaring spirit of the deceased.

As the twentieth century progressed New Orleans' parade tradition dwindled. By the 1970s many older band players had died, and there were few young musicians emerging to take their place. The brass band renaissance was largely due to banjoist-composer Danny Barker, who returned to New Orleans in the mid-60s after thirty years in New York, and through a local church taught aspiring youngsters not only to play the music but also to honor the spirit of the old marching bands. As the music revived, so did the street culture, and parading came back in force.

In the late 1980s, however, a new kind of jazz funeral emerged. Faced with a staggering number of crack-related

where Peter Fonda and Dennis Hopper writhed and sobbed in their LSD-induced hell in the movie *Easy Rider*, local gossip has it that the tomb's headless statue of Charity was decapitated by a crazed Hopper during filming.

St Louis's other famous dead include the city's first

deaths, families in the projects began to call upon young bands like the ReBirth and the Soul Rebels to play at the funerals of their peers. The bands sometimes joined the funeral party for just a few blocks, leading the way to the victim's home, a corner where they used to hang out, or even the spot where they were killed. Unlike in earlier jazz funerals, the Second Line predominated, with noisy mourners spraying beer over the coffin, wielding guns and throwing bottles. The potential for **violence** was such that when Barker died in 1994 his family announced there would be no jazz funeral – though they were eventually persuaded to change their minds by the many musicians who wanted to pay homage to their teacher and mentor.

Today, the jazz funeral, widely recognized as an important cultural phenomenon, is subject to fierce debate among commentators, musicians and historians. To many, the legacy of the crack funerals, and the gradual loss of the dirges from the brass band repertoire represent the loss of a crucial spiritual element. Others argue that the funerals, like anything else, should be allowed to evolve. Meanwhile, while white New Orleans whoops it up at jolly mock-funerals – to mark divorces and liquidations, to promote book launches and conferences – on the streets of Tremé jazz funerals are still held for local musicians, Mardi Gras Indians and even Second Liners. As at any funeral, tourists are not welcome.

For more on the jazz funeral, visit Sylvester Francis' Backstreet Museum in Tremé (see p.65).

THE JAZZ FUNERAL

African-American mayor, **Ernest "Dutch" Morial**, and **Homer Plessy**, whose refusal in 1892 to move from the whites-only section of a train led to the historic *Plessy vs Ferguson* case. His defeat gave rise to the Supreme Court's "separate but equal" ruling, which effectively stripped blacks of the civil rights they had won during Reconstruction and established segregation in the South for another sixty years.

At the back of the cemetery, in the nonconsecrated **Protestant section**, a sinking tomb engraved with the words "For the virtuous there is a better world" was designed by Benjamin Latrobe for the wife and baby of **Governor Claiborne** – the city's first American governor – both of whom died of yellow fever. The Mrs Claiborne buried in the cemetery's Catholic section was his second wife.

ST LOUIS NO. 2

Map 1, E6. Mon–Sat 9am–3pm, Sun 9am–noon; free.

St Louis No. 2, 200 N Claiborne Ave between Iberville and St Louis, is one of the most desolate of the Cities of the Dead, hemmed in between Tremé's Iberville housing project and the interstate. Built in 1823, it's a prime example of local cemetery design, with a dead-straight center aisle, and many grandiose Greek Revival mausolea, designed by de Pouilly. A second **Marie Laveau**, believed to be the famed voodoo queen's daughter, has a tomb here – daubed with red-chalk crosses, like the original in St Louis No. 1 (see p.127) – as do Baratarian swashbuckler **Dominique You** and his friend **Mayor Nicholas Girod**, who plotted together to return Napoleon from exile (see p.43).

ST LOUIS NO. 3

Map 1, E4. Daily 10am–3pm; free.

Built in 1856 on the site of a leper colony, **St Louis No. 3**, in Mid-City at 3421 Esplanade Ave, is a peaceful burial ground used mostly by religious orders; all the **priests** of the diocese are buried here, and fragile angels balance on top of the tombs. It also holds the family tomb of **James**

Gallier Jr, designed by the architect himself, and that of photographer **E.J. Bellocq**, whose remarkable images of the Storyville prostitutes (see p.64) have become icons of a lost era. More recently, following a huge jazz funeral in 1999, Mardi Gras Indian **Donald Harrison Sr**, Chief of the Guardians of the Flame tribe, was entombed here. Harrison, whose son Donald Harrison Jr is the well-known jazz saxophonist, was one of the best loved and respected of the big chiefs, whose tireless work to earn recognition for the Indians took him from lecture tours in the public schools of New Orleans to the reservation of the Seneca tribe.

For more on New Orleans' Mardi Gras Indians, see p.310.

METAIRIE

Map 1, B4–C5. Daily 8.30am–4pm; free.

Metairie Cemetery, 5100 Pontchartrain Blvd, is quite different from the other Cities of the Dead, resembling a huge, formal park more than a haunted secret garden. Built after the Civil War on a racetrack, it covers 155 landscaped acres and is crisscrossed by wide, driveable streets. Though it may be less evocative than the older cemeteries, there's a certain fascination in the sheer hubris of these mighty granite tombs: every bombastic funerary style conceivable, from Egyptian and Moorish through neoclassical to Gothic, is employed to honor mayors, governors, Confederate generals, and countless Rexes, kings of Carnival. Metairie is **safe** to tour alone, but you'll need a **car** to get to and around the place. The funeral home at the gate can lend you a free **audio tour**, for which you should allow an hour.

Highlights include the overblown **Brunswig mausoleum** – a pyramid fronted by a marble sphinx – and the

METAIRIE

tomb of **David Hennessy**, topped with a 26-foot broken column covered by a pall, a police belt and baton. Police chief Hennessy was fatally shot in 1890 when New Orleans was in the grip of a wave of anti-Sicilian racism; his death provoked an international incident when eleven of the nineteen Sicilian immigrants charged with his murder were themselves killed by a thousands-strong lynch mob, and the Italian government demanded $25,000 compensation for the families of the victims. The cemetery's largest memorial, topped by a sixty-foot obelisk, was built in 1914 by wealthy Irishman **Daniel Moriarty** for his wife Mary, a woman twice his age, whose nouveau-riche brashness and advancing years meant that she was never quite accepted by the city's Anglo elite.

Until recently, notorious Storyville landlady **Josie Arlington** (see p.64) was also entombed in Metairie. Her cenotaph, fronted by a statue of a young woman reaching out to a closed door – symbolizing Arlington's boast that no virgins were allowed in her "palace" – became such a tourist attraction that eventually her descendants were forced to sell it and remove Arlington's remains to an unmarked tomb in a secret location.

Out of the city

By far the most popular side trip from New Orleans is the drive along the **River Road**, which hugs the banks of the Mississippi all the way to Baton Rouge, seventy miles upriver. A series of bridges and ferries allows you to crisscross the water, and you can stop off and tour several restored antebellum plantation homes along the way.

Alternatively, a thirty-minute drive south from New Orleans brings you to the remote fishing village of **Lafitte**, a trip which satisfies all sorts of adventurous urges: not only can you travel to the end of the road, which simply gives up the ghost in the face of encroaching swamps and bayous, but you can also take a stroll or canoe-ride through the **Barataria Preserve**, a tangle of hardwood forest, cypress swamp and marsh that eventually dissolves into the Gulf of Mexico. And for anyone traveling with kids, **Jazzland** amusement park, out in the suburbs northeast of downtown, is a good bet, offering all the usual thrill rides with a vaguely Louisianan twist.

The accommodation price codes used in this chapter and throughout the book are explained on p.156.

The River Road plantations

In the nineteenth century, the spectacular homes strung along the **Mississippi River Road** were the focal points of vast estates from where wealthy planters – or rather, their slaves – loaded cotton, sugar or indigo onto steamboats berthed virtually at their front doors, ready to be transported to the markets in the city. Most of the **plantations** that you can visit today grew **sugar**, which from the earliest days of the colony was vital to the economy, protected by tariffs that blocked imports from the Caribbean. Though some sugar farms still exist, the era of the sugar baron was over by the 1930s, when many of the houses, too expensive to maintain, were abandoned. At the same time, the construction of the levee – a response to catastrophic flooding throughout the Mississippi valley in the 1920s – enabled ocean-going tankers to ply the river as far as Baton Rouge and heralded the era of the **petrochemical** companies.

There's a color map of the River Road
at the back of this book.

Today, the levee runs the length of the banks, blocking the river from view, and though you'd never guess it from the tourist brochures – which romanticize the area as a magnolia-scented idyll swathed in azaleas and dreamy Spanish moss – it's the hulking chemical plants that dominate the River Road **landscape**. Almost as soon as you've crossed the soupy swamp that surrounds New Orleans you're confronted with a vista of grim refineries, whose colossal pipes, according to local environmental groups, annually spew out millions of pounds of toxins into the Mississippi. There *are* rural expanses, where wide sugarcane fields are interrupted only by vine-strewn, tumbledown shacks – the **prettiest stretches** are near the small town of Convent, on the east bank – but you'll more often find yourself driving through straggling communities of boarded-up lounge bars and laundromats, scarred by scrap piles, burnt-out cars and smokestacks.

In the last few decades, some – but by no means all – of the neglected **plantation houses** have been given a reprieve as wealthy individuals, hoping to combat the local dependence on chemical industries, or PR-savvy oil companies, looking to clean up their image, have set about restoring them as tourist attractions. Generally speaking – the superb **Laura** plantation is an exception – **tours**, more often than not led by guides in ballgowns, skimp on detail about the estates as a whole, which included huge mills and vast complexes of slave quarters, and concentrate instead on the big houses, presenting them as showcase museums filled with fine antiques. The cumulative effect of these endless evocations of a long-lost "gracious" era can be stultifying, to say the least, making it a bad idea to try to visit too many homes in one day. Pick out just one or two, and even better, reckon on spending the night, maybe taking in another one on the drive back to the city. Many of the houses have **B&B rooms**, which as well as being rather wonderful places to sleep, allow you to absorb more of the atmosphere of the plantations than is possible on the tours.

Incidentally, for anyone who prefers not to drive, a number of operators offer **bus trips** from New Orleans to the plantations; turn to p.14 for details.

PLANTATION PRACTICALITIES

To **drive to the River Road** from New Orleans, take I-10 west to exit 220, turn onto I-310 and follow it to Hwy-48 on the east bank (ie *above* the river on the map). It shortly becomes Hwy-44, or the River Road. For the west bank (*below* the river), cross Destrehan Bridge onto Hwy-18 rather than branching onto Hwy-48. Since signs for the plantations are poor, you should get hold of the detailed *Louisiana River Road Plantation* map, sold in bookstores around town (remember that the kinks in the river mean that distances are larger than they may appear). When timing your trip, it's best to get an early start, and certainly to avoid the last tours of the day – not only do they tend to be the most hurried, but also you'll be hitting rush hour on the River Road. **Tours** last between 45 minutes and an hour.

For **food**, give the plantation restaurants a miss. You'll do far better at *Hymel's* (Tues & Wed 11am–2.30pm, Thurs 11am–2.30pm & 5–9pm, Fri 11am–2.30pm & 5–10pm, Sat

DESTREHAN

Map 5, F6. Daily 9.30am–4pm; $8.

Destrehan, on the east bank, thirty minutes' drive from downtown New Orleans, is the oldest intact plantation house in the lower Mississippi valley, and a beautifully preserved example of Louisiana's early West Indies-style architecture (see p.34). Built in 1787, the house is named for Jean d'Estrehan, who, with his brother-in-law Etienne de Boré, invented the sugar granulation process that revolutionized New Orleans' nineteenth-century economy. D'Estrehan bought the house in 1792 and added two wings; it underwent further remodeling in the 1830s, when a number of Greek Revival features, including the eight thick Doric columns, were added.

DESTREHAN

11.30am–10pm, Sun 11.30am–8pm; ☎225/562-9910), on the east bank, four miles downriver of the Sunshine Bridge on Hwy-44. The long menu includes delicious seafood, and the jukebox is a treat, playing C&W and Cajun music to a crowd of regulars. Three-course lunch specials go for $5–10. If you'd rather have an alligator po-boy to go, head for the west bank and *B&C Seafood*, east of Laura in Vacherie (Mon–Thurs & Sat 9am–5.30pm, Fri 9am–6.30pm; ☎225/265-8356). Also on the west bank, but at the other end of the spectrum, *Lafitte's Landing*, in Donaldsonville (Tues–Sat 6–10pm, Sun 11am–3pm; ☎225/473-1232), is very good indeed; diners come from as far as New Orleans to taste chef John Folse's famed Cajun-Creole haute cuisine, and it makes sense to book.

If you want to stay overnight, Oak Alley (p.141), Tezcuco (p.142), Madewood (p.145) and Nottoway (p.146) offer accommodation. Each has its own style, but they all throw in a free house tour and a good breakfast.

In the 1970s the plantation was bought from oil giant Amoco by the nonprofit River Road Historical Society, whose restoration emphasizes the architectural features of the **main house**. Built using the *bouisallage entre poteaux* technique (horse hair and Spanish moss, providing insulation, packed between steadying cypress pillars), it is raised a story off the soggy ground to prevent flooding, and surrounded by double galleries to catch the breezes.

It was at Destrehan, after the **slave rebellion** in January 1811 (see p.300), that a tribunal sentenced twenty slaves to death, ordering their heads to be exhibited on spikes strung out along the River Road.

DESTREHAN

SAN FRANCISCO

Map 5, D5. Daily 10am–4.30pm; $8.

Some twenty miles west of Destrehan, on one of the most industrial stretches of the River Road, **San Francisco** was built in 1856 by Creole planter Edmond Marmillion. Its fantastic combination of Italianate, Gothic Revival and gingerbread style was dubbed "Steamboat Gothic" by novelist Frances Parkinson Keyes; painted in carousel shades of green, turquoise and peach, its rails, awnings, galleries and pillars recreate the ambience of a Mississippi showboat. San Francisco was a sugar estate until 1974, when the land was bought by a local oil company – their huge tanks now surround the place – which has funded its restoration.

Tours of San Francisco focus on the gorgeous **interior** of the main house. Designed in the old Creole style, which was already out of fashion when it was built, its rooms open directly onto each other, with no hallway. The main rooms were on the top story, decorated in bold colors and featuring cypress-paneled tongue-and-groove ceilings rather than plaster. Its exquisite ceilings, walls, blinds, moldings and doors, a riot of pastoral trompe l'oeils, floral motifs and Italian cherubs, were the result of a redecoration masterminded by Marmillion's Bavarian daughter-in-law.

The house used to stand in more than one thousand feet of **gardens**, over half of which were swallowed up when the levee was built in the 1930s.

The name San Francisco is a corruption of the Creole
"sans fruscin", or "without a penny" – a moniker coined
by Marmillion's son, due to the colossal sum that
went into decorating the place in 1860.

LAURA

Map 5, D6. Daily 9.30am–5pm (last tour 4pm); $8 admission includes $2 discount on Le Monde Creole French Quarter walking tours (see p.15).

A bridge at Gramercy/Lutcher, a few miles beyond San Francisco on the east bank, crosses the river to Vacherie, where **Laura** is causing something of a stir on the River Road scene. Rather than dwelling lovingly on priceless antiques, **tours** here, which draw upon a wealth of recently discovered historical documents – from slave accounts and photographs to private diaries – sketch a vivid picture of plantation life in multicultural Louisiana.

The earliest **inhabitants** of the Laura plantation were the local Colapissa tribe, who lived in huts behind the main house – built in 1804 by the slaves of a Frenchman, Guillaume DuParc – until around 1815. In the antebellum era, a multiracial mix of some five hundred people lived on the estate – two hundred of them slaves, whose quarters were strung along a three-mile road out into the fields.

DuParc died before the first sugar crop came in, and his wife Nanette ran the place for the next twenty years before handing it to her daughter, Elizabeth. The estate, which stretched eighteen miles inland from the river, was managed by the women of the family until 1891, when **Laura Locoul** – DuParc's great-granddaughter, for whom the plantation was renamed in 1874 – rejected the life carved out for her, sold the estate to the German Creole Waguespack family and moved to St Louis. It was bought in 1993 by a group of enthusiastic investors who embarked on an extensive restoration process that continues to this day.

The **house** looks largely as it did in 1905, during the Waguespacks' era: the original building would have been simpler, without the front door (Creoles believed front doors to be vulgar, used only by barn animals and

Americans) and double steps. Built long before the construction of the levee, it stands facing the river to get the best of the breezes but high off the ground in order to safeguard it from flooding; its columns, rooted 8ft into the silty earth, fan out underground to create a firm foundation. Guides chart the evolution of the building, emphasizing the craftsmanship of the slaves who built the place in just eleven days – after a full eleven months gathering the cypress and the bricks – and pointing out details such as the *demi-portes*, narrow doors which, designed to impede hoop-skirted women from entering, led to the men's privies. The facade, brightly colored in red, blue, green and yellow, gives the place a distinctly Caribbean feel and identifies it as a Creole structure: Anglo-American planters preferred their homes to be snowy white.

The Locoul saga is continued in Le Monde Creole's walking tours of the French Quarter (see p.15), where the family kept their city apartments.

Brimming with human-interest stories, tours of Laura reveal the hard-nosed realities of Creole **plantation management**. Traditionally, the business had to stay within the family – while the owner could hand it down to whichever child he or she wished, the recipient would have to have children themselves in order to inherit. Brutally, any family member not involved in the business had no right to live in the big house – even the doughty Nanette had to buy land from the estate in her declining years in order to build a home near her family, while in a climate of sibling squabbles and backbiting, the big house was subjected to a frenzy of wing-claiming and annex-building.

Laura also calls itself "the home of **Brer Rabbit**". Retold by the plantation's Senegalese slaves, the African folk tales of wily Compair Lapin were transcribed by a local

LAURA

Frenchman, Alcée Fortier, friend of author Joel Chandler Harris.

OAK ALLEY

Map 5, C6. Daily: March–Oct 9am–5.30pm; Nov–Feb 9am–5pm; $10.
The quintessential image of the antebellum plantation home, **Oak Alley** is set in a wide expanse of sugar fields some nine miles upriver from Laura on the west bank. Though the house dates from 1839, when, as the tourist brochure puts it, "Southern aristocracy ruled the land", the 28 monumental **live oaks** that form a magnificent canopy over the avenue from the front door to the river are 150 years older – and are expected to live another three hundred years.

Built on the site of an early Creole plantation, the Greek Revival house, surrounded by fluted Doric columns – 28 of them, mirroring the number of live oaks – was originally called Beau Séjour. Abandoned in 1917, in the 1920s it was bought by the Stewarts, whose meticulous restoration set a trend for rescuing the old homes along the river. Today, 25 acres of the original estate are open to the public, while the remaining one thousand acres are leased out to sugar planters.

Oak Alley's famous live oaks are bare of the Spanish moss that drapes the greenery elsewhere in the region: Mrs Stewart thought that the ghostly gray wraiths were creepy and had them removed.

Supremely photogenic Oak Alley is one of the most touristed of the River Road plantations. The anecdotal **tours**, led by crinoline-garbed guides, are lively enough, though their version of events is somewhat sanitized; they're most interesting when pointing out domestic objects long since abandoned, such as the "rolling pin" headboard, with a detachable wooden pole to smooth out the lumpy Spanish moss- and horsehair-filled mattress.

Oak Alley's **restaurant** (daily 9am–3pm) does decent, if scandalously overpriced, Creole standards, including gumbo, red beans and rice, and crawfish *étouffé*. You can also **stay** in pretty B&B cottages on the grounds (⊤504/265-2151 or 1-800/44-ALLEY; ➎).

TEZCUCO

Map 5, B5. Daily: March–Oct 9am–5pm; Nov–Feb 10am–4pm; $8.

Some 25 miles from San Francisco on the east bank, near the village of Burnside, **Tezcuco** – or "resting place", named for the lake in Mexico – is an antebellum raised cottage built in the Greek Revival style. **Tours**, led by guides dressed up as Southern belles, concentrate on the columned main house, which was constructed between 1855 and 1860 as a summer retreat. Though it is a three-story structure, the top floor, too hot for habitation, was used only for storage. To combat the debilitating heat, rooms were built with fifteen-foot ceilings and hinged doors that could be removed in the stuffiest months. Although planters displayed their wealth in the big house – using enough excess material in the drapes, for example, to form a luxurious puddle on the floor – their families didn't live a life of leisure, and children as young as five were expected to contribute to the running of the estate.

Beyond the main house, the grounds are dotted with buildings including a blacksmith, a chapel, and, unusually, an **African-American Museum** (Wed–Sat 10am–5pm, Sun 1–5pm; suggested donation $3), a one-room hotchpotch of local memorabilia, old photographs and good intentions. Much of the museum is given over to the local experience of slavery – an 1858 inventory of slaves working on the Houmas House plantation (see below) represents just some of the 750 people, aged from two months to 68 years, owned by sugar magnate John Burnside – but there are also potted histories of local black achievers (the nation's first African-American mayor, Pierre Caliste Landry, was formerly a slave at Houmas House). You can also see items of folk art, African masks and a jumble of artifacts from River Road churches, farms and homes.

Tezcuco's **restaurant** (daily 11am–2.30pm) serves reasonably priced, if unremarkable, salads, po-boys and hot lunches. The **accommodation** is more distinctive, and very good value, with a range of options from cute one-bedroom cottages – most with porches, rocking chairs and fireplaces – to a suite in the main house. Rates include a bottle of wine, a full Creole breakfast served in your room and a free house tour (☎225/562-3929; ❸–❽).

HOUMAS HOUSE

Map 5, B5. Daily: Feb–Oct 10am–5pm; Nov–Jan 10am–4pm; $8.
Flanked by colossal chemical plants, **Houmas House**, a couple of miles beyond Tezcuco on Hwy-942, is, in fact, two houses: the first, an early **Spanish colonial** structure, stands in the shadow of a far grander **antebellum** pile. In 1774 business partners Alexandre Latil and Maurice Conway snapped up 12,000 acres of land for 4¢ an acre from the local Houmas Indians, and proceeded to make their fortunes chopping down the forest of cypress around them. The simple, four-room house that they built was neither large nor ostentatious enough for the planters who lived here in the 1840s, who stuck a white, columned Greek Revival edifice in front of it.

In 1858 the plantation was bought for $1 million by Irishman **John Burnside**, the so-called "Prince of Sugar". Under his ownership it grew to become Louisiana's biggest sugar estate, its four mills and thousand slaves producing

20,000,000lb of the stuff per year – the largest volume in the nation. Though Burnside left no heirs, the plantation, which now covered twenty thousand acres, was eventually handed down to the son-in-law of one of his friends and continued to thrive until the Depression, when it fell into disuse. A decade later the house was bought by a doctor, who began a process of elegant restoration.

Tours start in the colonial building, where the kitchen, centering on a giant cypress table, displays racks of rustic domestic implements including a herb-filled spoon, which flavored as it stirred, and a rudimentary fat-skimmer. A holy water cabinet on the wall attests to the Creoles' Catholic piety. The dining room is similarly plain, and very Spanish-looking, with its low, beamed ceilings and whitewashed walls. In contrast, the antebellum home, filled with a wealth of paintings and sculpture, reflects the golden era of the plantation. Unlike in the earlier house, where cypress predominates, here you'll see an abundance of marble, especially on the fireplaces and mantels. Even the richest families couldn't outwit the climate, however: the oppressive parlor, with its Victorian furniture overstuffed with Spanish moss, features a press to squeeze buckled and dampened books into shape.

Two unusual hexagonal *garconnières* (see p.34) stand in the pretty **grounds**, which are planted with rose bushes and azaleas. The gnarled live oaks that form a shaded alley from the river to the main house are at least 150 years old – there used to be sixteen more of them until the construction of the levee in the 1930s swallowed up six acres of land.

If you're staying at one of the plantations, make sure to get out on the River Road after dark – it's an extraordinary spectacle, with the refineries twinkling like alien cities in a post-apocalyptic gloom.

MADEWOOD

Map 5, B7. Daily 10am–4pm; $6.

Taking a detour off the River Road south onto Hwy-308, which hugs Bayou La Fourche, brings you to the glorious Greek Revival **Madewood**, designed by eminent architect Henry Howard. It took four years to gather enough cypress and brick to build the 21-room house, and another four years till construction was completed in 1850. The owner died two years later, leaving his wife to raise fourteen children and manage the estate until her death in 1896. In the 1960s, the New Orleans-based Marshall family bought and restored the big house; they keep an apartment in the *garconnière* (see p.34), while a local family owns the land and maintains the sugar cane.

Everything about Madewood is imposing, without being oppressive: the walls, 18- to 24-inches thick, are made of solid brick covered with stucco and plaster, and the ceilings soar to 25ft. **Tours** are good on architectural detail and the history of the restoration, but it's the **B&B** at Madewood that's the real treat (☎504/369-7151 or 1-800/375-7151; ❾ including dinner). There are five huge rooms in the main building – most of them with balconies and giant four-posters – and three suites in a cottage on the grounds. Sleeping in these peaceful surroundings, with the freedom to pad around pretty much at will, is a great way to get the feel of the place. Evenings start with a wine and cheese reception; a candlelit dinner is served in the dining room, followed by brandy and coffee in the parlor. In the morning, you get coffee in bed and a superb full breakfast.

NOTTOWAY

Map 5, A5. Daily 9am–5pm; $10.

Back on the River Road, **Nottoway**, the largest surviving antebellum plantation home in the South, lies eighteen miles south of Baton Rouge on the west bank. Built in 1859 as the main house on a seven-thousand-acre sugar estate, the 64-room white Italianate and Greek Revival edifice was designed by Henry Howard about a decade after his work on Madewood plantation. When it was built, its indoor plumbing, gas lighting and coal fireplaces were innovations, but today it's the sheer opulence of the place that is most striking – in particular in the columned ballroom, all white and gilt, with sparkling crystal chandeliers.

Nottoway has a classy **restaurant** (daily 11am–3pm & 6–9pm) and luxurious **B&B** rooms (☎225/545-2730; **❼**), where rates include a welcome drink, wake-up call of coffee, muffins and juice, full breakfast and a house tour.

The Barataria Preserve and Lafitte

The name **Barataria** (roughly translating as "dishonesty at sea") was first seen on eighteenth-century French maps of the swamp-choked delta of the Mississippi River. Through these labyrinths of barrier islands, shallow bays and secluded bayous the Lafittes and their band of privateers smuggled slaves and luxury goods from the Gulf to New Orleans; Native American shell middens dotted along the levees made ideal storehouses for their misbegotten booty. Today the area is protected by the **Barataria Preserve**, where you can walk a number of easy trails or paddle a canoe through the ghostly swamp, watching out for alligators and snakes, and listening for the calls of wild birds.

Beyond the preserve, the road peters out altogether at the peaceful fishing community of **Lafitte**, where you can eat fresh seafood while gazing over the bayous. You're less than an hour away from New Orleans, but you could be in another world. To **get here** from downtown, take Hwy-90 and cross the bridge over the mesh of oil refineries and scrappy suburbs to the west bank of the Mississippi. From there, Hwy-45 – also known as Barataria Boulevard – sweeps you south. As the woods on either side of the road get thicker, and the flooded forest of the swamp creeps nearer, you know you're approaching the preserve.

If you don't have a car, see p.18 for a list of swamp tour operators that can provide transport from the city.

THE BARATARIA PRESERVE

The **Barataria Preserve** (Map 5, G7), part of the scattered **Jean Lafitte National Historical Park and Preserve** – which has another site in the French Quarter (see p.36) and at the Chalmette Battlefield (p.112) – encompasses not only swamp, forest, marsh and bayous, but also many remnants of human settlement, from Native American villages to nineteenth-century hunting and fishing camps. Most of the **animals** here are shy and nocturnal, though you may see reptiles, armadillos and nutria; if you visit during summer you might even spot an **alligator** or two sunbathing on a log. **Birdlife** includes herons, egrets and ibis, and you will hear woodpeckers and red-shouldered hawks.

THE BARATARIA PRESERVE

First stop should be the **Jean Lafitte National Historical Park and Preserve Visitor Center** (daily 9am–5pm; ℡504/589-2330), 7400 Barataria Blvd. Exhibits cover the ecology, wildlife and history of the preserve, and there's also a series of **talks**, guided **hikes, birdwatching** programs and **canoe treks** (some of which are moonlit). Ane they sell **mosquito repellent** wipes, which are absolutely essential, whatever time of year you visit.

Exploring the preserve

There are eight miles of **trails** (daily 7am–5pm) in the preserve, varying from dirt paths to paved roads and boardwalks. Each takes you through a variety of habitats and landscapes, and each offers a slightly different experience. Try to time your trip to coincide with one of the **ranger-led walks** (daily: Sept–May 2pm; June–Aug 10am), when guides will point out flora and fauna lurking in secret hiding places: **snakes** slither in and out of grasses by the path, **alligators** bob in the murky water, and above your head **spiders** weave enormous silky webs in the air – watch out for the Crab-Like Spiny Orb Weaver, which floats in its invisible web like a starfish, and the Golden Silk Weaver, whose silk is the strongest natural fiber on earth, traditionally used by local Native American tribes to make nets and fishing lines.

The **Palmetto** trail (0.9 miles one way) takes you from the visitor center to the Bayou Coquille trailhead, winding between the bayou's natural levee and the lower swamp, a virulent green from its carpet of plants. The **Bayou Coquille** trail (0.5 miles one way) starts at a Native American midden made of clam shells before weaving through forests of live oaks and red maple, past slopes of dense palmetto and into a liquid landscape of sodden bald-cypress and pumpkin ash. The trail eventually emerges into a vast, treeless freshwater marsh, which stretches to the horizon. You can continue from here on the **Marsh Overlook** trail (0.4 miles one way), where in summer you're almost guaranteed to spot an alligator, or return to the visitor center and set off on the **Ring Levee** trail (1.2-mile loop), which descends through dense forest and swamp. Keep your eyes open on this one for armadillos, turtles and otters.

Nine miles of **canoe routes** channel through the maze of narrow, silent canals into the heart of the swamp. You can almost picture the explorers and pirates of old, hacking their way through these impenetrable passages in search of adventure, or a new life. Check at the visitor center if you want to go with a **guide**; otherwise, the *Jean Lafitte Inn* rents canoes (see below).

The Jean Lafitte Inn

A mile south of the visitor center, at the junction of Hwy-3134, the *Jean Lafitte Inn* (☎504/689-3271; ❹) **rents three-person canoes** for $25 per day. They also have a few wood **cabins** that make a great base for forays into the swamp – but bear in mind that you're on the highway here and not hidden away somewhere picturesque. In the evenings – or, if you're not staying, at **lunch** – you can hang out with locals in the **bar**, which serves fried chicken, burgers, po-boys and cold beer, and hosts the occasional Cajun dance.

LAFITTE

South from the preserve, Hwy-45 takes you past a string of mobile homes, mansions and marinas to the fishing village of **Lafitte** (Map 5, G7). Dotted with fresh oyster and crab shacks, the road becomes less significant the further you go: most journeys around here are taken on the water.

If you're moved to **stay** in this land's-end community, the *Victorian Inn*, south of Goose Bayou Bridge, offers small rooms and a private lake (℡504/689-4757; ❹). A mile or so south, *Bouttes* (Tues–Sun 11am–10pm; ℡504/689-7978) is a great spot for a fishy **lunch**, with a wooden deck overlooking the bayou. The seafood is fresh from the water, and very good value; lunch specials go for $5. For something a bit more upmarket, try the seafood and German specialties at *Voleos* (℡504/689-2482), a little further south. It's here that land simply stops and water takes over: this is the **end of the road**, and – unless you have a boat, of course – there's nothing to do now but turn back.

Jazzland

Despite skepticism from critics who felt that its location – stuck out in the northeastern suburbs – would do nothing to drag tourists away from the French Quarter, the **Jazzland theme park** (Map 5, H5; summer daily 10am–10pm; winter Fri–Sun 10am–10pm; $31, children $26, parking $5), which opened in 2000, was a surprise success. True, most of the visitors are locals, who are able to make use of various money-saving passes, but for anyone with kids in tow and a car to hand – or simply a yen to be flung into the air at insane speeds – it's not at all bad. The theme, loosely, is Louisianan – thus rides with names like Bayou Blaster and Zydeco Twister fill areas such as Cajun Country and Mardi Gras – and the overall feel is of good, clean, and faintly nostalgic, fun.

The live performances in the park's Jazz Plaza are top-notch, featuring musicians you'd find in the city's best clubs.

Of the **rides**, star turns are the **Megazeph** wooden roller coaster, which at 4000ft long and 110ft high is one of the largest in the world, and the **skycoaster**, a gut-lurching bungee swing from 170ft. You can also go on all manner of swooping water rides, high-tech loop-the-loops and stimulated thrill rides.

Jazzland lies at the intersection of I-10 and I-510. To **get there**, take exit 246-A on I-10 to Lake Forest Boulevard, and follow the road about half a mile east. It's a drive of around thirty to forty minutes from downtown.

JAZZLAND

LISTINGS

Accommodation

New Orleans has some fantastic **places to stay**, from rambling old guesthouses, through hip boutique hotels in restored historic buildings, to the genteel *Windsor Court*, voted best hotel in the world by readers of *Condé Nast Traveler*. **Room rates**, never low (you'll be pushed to find anything half decent for less than $50), increase considerably for Mardi Gras, Jazz Fest and the Sugar Bowl, when prices can go up by as much as 200 percent. At other times, and especially during summer, when things slow down, it's worth asking about **special deals**. Guesthouse owners, especially, are often more willing to negotiate prices than to let rooms go empty.

New Orleans is not a city where you want to be stranded without a room, and though it's possible to take a chance on last-minute deals, you should ideally make **reservations** well ahead of time. This is especially true during the big festivals and special events – when hotels get booked solid months in advance – and weekends throughout the year. (Note also that many places, especially in the Quarter, have **minimum stays** of two nights on weekends – longer during special events.)

However, if you do turn up on spec, head immediately for the **information center** on Jackson Square (see p.9), which has racks of **discount leaflets** offering savings on same-day bookings (weekdays only).

ACCOMMODATION PRICE CODES

Accommodation prices throughout this book have been coded using the following symbols. Prices are for the least expensive double rooms available between October and May – the city's high season – though during Mardi Gras and Jazz Fest, rates can be double those quoted here. Where places have rooms with shared or private bath, we have quoted the cheapest room with bath, and where there is a large disparity between the cheapest and the most expensive rooms, we have quoted codes for both. Rates do not include the room tax of 12 percent.

- ❶ $40 and under
- ❷ $40–60
- ❸ $60–75
- ❹ $75–90
- ❺ $90–100
- ❻ $100–120
- ❼ $120–150
- ❽ $150–200
- ❾ above $200

Most people choose to pay a bit more to stay in the **French Quarter**, in the heart of things. Many accommodations here are in **guesthouses**, most of them in old Creole cottages or townhouses, furnished with antiques. These are some of the most beautiful, and atmospheric, lodgings in the city, ranging from shabbily decadent places with iffy plumbing to romantic honeymooners' hideaways. The odd few can be dark and a little musty inside – in the Creole tradition, they're shaded from the heat, sun and rain by lush patios and cranky wooden shutters – but many also have courtyards, balconies, verandas and pools. Most serve continental breakfast, and in the more expensive places you may also get complimentary evening drinks and hors d'oeuvres.

If you prefer to stay outside the Quarter – if you're on a very tight budget, say, or want to base yourself somewhere less intense – there are a number of possibilities throughout town. The **Lower Garden District** offers a handful of budget options near the streetcar line, while the funky

ROUGH GUIDES FAVORITES: HOTELS

The following are listed in ascending order of price.

Faubourg Marigny specializes in atmospheric bed and breakfasts – many of them gay-owned and -run – and the **Garden District** proper has a couple of gorgeous old places in historic buildings. The **CBD** is the domain of the city's boutique and chain hotels, catering mostly to conventioneers. We've reviewed the best of them in this chapter.

If you want to get **out of the city** altogether, many of the grand old plantation homes strung along the River Road offer B&B accommodation; they're reviewed in the "Out of the city" chapter (see p.133), along with a couple of options near the swamps that lie just thirty minutes' drive from New Orleans.

THE FRENCH QUARTER

Biscuit Palace
Map 4, H4. 730 Dumaine St at Bourbon ☏ 525-9949.
Well-run, friendly and spotless hotel, named for the old biscuit ad painted on its outside wall. It's housed in an 1820 mansion, complete with a pretty flagstoned courtyard, fish pond and tropical plants. The rooms, many of them suites, with balconies and antique baths, are creatively decorated – if you hanker after an opium-den ambience, ask for room no. 3. The attic apartment sleeps six. Rates drop considerably in summer, but there's a three-day minimum stay over weekends. ❺–❻.

Bon Maison Guesthouse

Map 4, G3. 835 Bourbon St at
St Ann ⓣ 561-8498,
Ⓦ *www.bonmaison.com*
Set back from the road
behind a brick courtyard, this
Creole townhouse has been
converted into a laid-back,
no-fuss guesthouse. The
atmosphere is wonderfully
peaceful, considering its
location, partly because there
are just five rooms, all with
bath and some with tiny
kitchenettes. It's particularly
popular with gay guests, but
everyone is welcome. ❹–❽.

Chateau Hotel

Map 4, I5. 1001 Chartres St at
St Philip ⓣ 524-9636,
Ⓦ *www.chateauhotel.com*
One of the best things about
this friendly hotel is its
location, in a quiet part of the
Quarter. Some of the rooms are
better than others, so if
you feel yours is too small or
a bit dark, check to see what
else is available. There's an
outdoor café-bar by the pool,

and rates include continental
breakfast. ❻.

Cornstalk Hotel

Map 4, H4. 915 Royal St at
Dumaine ⓣ 523-1515,
Ⓦ *www.travelguides.com/
bb/cornstalk*
Casually elegant hotel in a
turreted Queen Anne house
surrounded by a landmark
cast-iron fence (see p.52). The
appealing, high-ceilinged
rooms are each individually
furnished with antiques and
feature plenty of period detail;
all have showers, and four have
baths. Continental breakfast
can be taken in your room, on
the balcony or on the large
front veranda. Two-night
minimum at weekends. ❺–❽.

A Creole House

Map 4, G2. 1013 St Ann St at
Burgundy ⓣ 524-8076 or
1-888/251-0090,
Ⓦ *www.acreolehouse.com*
Though it borders on shabby
in places, this unfussy B&B
offers a variety of rooms

Drivers should note that few of the French
Quarter hotels offer free on-site parking.

THE FRENCH QUARTER

ranging from cozy hideaways with shared bath to antique-filled suites. Be specific about what you want when making reservations and feel free to negotiate. Rates include continental breakfast. ❹–❼.

Dauphine Orleans

Map 4, D2. 415 Dauphine St at Conti ⓣ 586-1800 or 1-800/508-5554, ⓦ*www.dauphineorleans.com*
Good-looking hotel in a historic complex of buildings with more than one hundred rooms. The best are set in brick cottages around tranquil, palm-filled patios and have their own jacuzzis. There's a pretty outdoor pool, a gym, bar (once the site of a brothel) and library, and they serve superb complimentary breakfast, afternoon tea, hors d'oeuvres and welcome cocktails. ❽.

Lafitte Guest House

Map 4, I3. 1003 Bourbon St at St Philip ⓣ 581-2678 or 1-800/331-7971, ⓦ*www.lafitteguesthouse.com*
This galleried antebellum house, on the quieter end of

Bourbon Street, across from the historic *Lafitte's Blacksmith Shop* (see p.57), is a romantic, welcoming, gay-friendly hotel. The fourteen antique-furnished rooms vary in size and style, though all feature original details, and many have balconies. Small touches, like the Egyptian cotton sheets, tranquil sound machines and silk sleep masks make this place extra special, as do the convivial wine and cheese socials held each evening in the red-and-gold parlor. Rates include in-room continental breakfast. ❼–❾.

Hotel Maison de Ville and Audubon Cottages

Map 4, E4. 727 Toulouse St at Royal ⓣ 561-5858 or 1-800/634-1600, ⓦ*www.maisondeville.com*
Very classy small hotel, favored by Elizabeth Taylor and Tennessee Williams (who worked on *Streetcar* in room 9) among others. Service is luxurious, with free evening sherry, overnight shoeshine, and continental breakfast brought to your room. The on-site *Bistro* (see p.178) is one

THE FRENCH QUARTER

of the best restaurants in the Quarter. Rooms in the main building, and around its courtyard and three-story fountain, are attractive, though small; the secluded Audubon Cottages, a block away on Dauphine Street, offer larger rooms, patios and a pool. Two-night minimum stay over weekends, and no children under 12 allowed. ❾.

Hotel Monteleone

Map 4, B4. 214 Royal St at Iberville ⓣ 523-3341 or 1-800/321-6710, ⓦ www.hotelmonteleone.com
Opened in 1886, New Orleans' oldest functioning hotel is also the tallest building in the Quarter, its sixteen stories making it something of a giant towering above Royal Street's antique stores. Another of Tennessee Williams' favorites, it has been restored and modernized somewhat – it now has more than 600 rooms – but manages to keep its distinctive character with a handsome baroque facade, elegant lobby and revolving *Carousel* bar (see p.208).

There's a gym, heated rooftop pool, beauty salon and three restaurants, and they offer a baby-sitting service. ❽.

Hotel Provincial

Map 4, I5. 1024 Chartres St at Ursulines ⓣ 581-4995 or 1-800/535-7922, ⓦ www.hotelprovincial.com
Though it has more than one hundred rooms, this is an intimate and relaxed place in a quiet part of the Quarter, with very nice, antique-filled rooms – each one of them different – opening onto peaceful, gaslit patios. Plus two outdoor pools and a bar. ❼.

Hotel Villa Convento

Map 4, J4. 616 Ursulines St at Chartres ⓣ 522-1793, ⓦ www.villlaconvento.com
It's *not* the original *House of the Rising Sun*, whatever the buggy-drivers might tell you, but rather a friendly, family-run place with the feel of an old European boarding house. The 25 no-frills rooms all have their own bath; some have balconies overlooking the street, while others lead onto the patio.

Complimentary continental breakfast is served in the covered courtyard, which is usually bustling with repeat visitors. ⑤–⑧.

Le Richelieu

Map 4, K5. 1234 Chartres St at Barracks ⓣ 529-2492 or 1-800/535-9653, ⓦ www.lerichelieuhotel.com
Handsome hotel in a restored factory and neighboring townhouse. Though the old-world ambience of the lovely lobby is not continued in the rooms, they are nonetheless comfortable and attractive, equipped with all mod cons. There's a small outdoor pool, overlooked by a café serving light meals and coffee, and free on-site parking – a rarity in the French Quarter. They also offer a baby-sitting service. ⑥–⑨.

Olivier House

Map 4, E3. 828 Toulouse St at Bourbon ⓣ 525-8456, ⓦ www .olivierhouse1.bizonthe.net
Family-run place in a large Creole townhouse with a warren of corridors, balconies and stairwells. Like many of the Quarter's old buildings, it can feel a bit dark, but it's immensely atmospheric and good value. The 42 rooms (all with bath) vary considerably in size and quality, but most of them are appealingly old-fashioned, with funky antique furniture, chandeliers, plush sofas and tall, shuttered windows. It's worth negotiating about rates; if money's no object, go for room no. 112, which has its own garden and fountain. There's a gorgeous tropical courtyard and a pool. ⑥–⑨.

Rue Royal Inn

Map 4, I4. 1006 Royal St at St Philip ⓣ 524-3900 or 1-800/776-3901, ⓦ www.rueroyalinn.com
The owners and their big fluffy cats make everyone feel welcome at this exceptionally good-value, gay-friendly hotel. Enormous, brick-walled, high-ceilinged rooms, which easily sleep four, all have bath, fridge and minibar; the priciest have balconies and jacuzzis. Rates include all-day coffee and continental breakfast, which

THE FRENCH QUARTER

you can take in the pretty courtyard. ④–⑧.

St Peter House Hotel

Map 4, F2. 1005 St Peter St at Burgundy ☏ 524-9232 or 1-888/604 6226, Ⓦ *www.frenchquarterneworleans .com/stpeter.html*
Darkish, comfortable rooms – some set around a courtyard, others with balconies – popular with a mixed gay and straight clientele. Though it's basic, and has less character than some of the Creole guesthouses – and can be noisy if you're staying at the front – it's clean and efficiently run. Rates include continental breakfast. ⑤–⑨.

Ursuline Guest House

Map 4, J4. 708 Ursulines St at Royal ☏ 525-8509 or 1-800/654-2351
No children allowed at this peaceful, modest place, which caters to a mixed gay and straight clientele. Rooms open onto a broad gallery or the courtyard (which has a jacuzzi); those with window air-conditioners can be noisy. Rates include continental

breakfast and evening drinks. ⑤–⑦.

W Hotel French Quarter

Map 4, C5. 310 Chartres St at Bienville ☏ 581-1200, Ⓦ *www.whotels.com*
Smaller and slightly less pretentious than its CBD counterpart (see p.165), this branch of the W chain offers the same concept, with stylish rooms, a trendy bar – the "Living Room" – in-room CD- and video-players, and even a dash of local flavor in the New Orleans courtyard. Despite the image, however, this is really a business hotel, affordable for expense-account travellers only. The superb nouvelle Italian restaurant, *Bacco*, is on site (see p.177). ⑨.

FAUBOURG MARIGNY, ESPLANADE RIDGE AND MID-CITY

The Frenchmen

Map 4, M6. 417 Frenchmen St at Decatur ☏ 948-2166 or 1-888/365-2775, Ⓦ *www.acreolehouse.com*

Popular, gay-friendly B&B in a great Faubourg location across from the Old US Mint. Spread across two quiet 1860 townhouses overlooking a tropical patio, the 25 rooms, which range from tiny to spacious, are all different, decorated with good-looking antiques and ceiling fans. There's a small pool on site and a jacuzzi. Rates include continental breakfast and (limited) covered parking. **⑤–⑦**.

India House Hostel

Map 1, D6. 124 S Lopez St at Canal ⓣ 821-1904, ⓦ *www.indiahousehostel.com* The Mid-City location of this funky backpackers' hostel, well away from the heart of things, doesn't seem to bother its young, enthusiastic crowd. Owned and run by keen travelers, it's probably the friendliest, and booziest, of the hostels, with pool parties, crab boils and the like. Dorm beds cost $14, and there are a few utilitarian rooms with shared bath, a pool, sun deck and even two pet alligators. The area isn't great at night. **❶**.

Maison Esplanade

Map 1, F6. 1244 Esplanade Ave at Tremé ⓣ 523-8080 or 1-800/892-5529, ⓦ *www.maisonesplanade.com* Good-value, no-smoking B&B in a lovely family home, with ten individually decorated rooms – some with balconies – named after local musicians. It's friendly and lived-in, with good-looking antiques and stripped hardwood floors, but you're on the fringes of the Faubourg here, near Tremé; don't wander around the neighborhood at night. Rates include continental breakfast, and there's free off-street parking. **❹**.

Rathbone Inn

Map 4, M1. 1227 Esplanade Ave at St Claude ⓣ 947-2100 or 1-800/947-2101, ⓦ *www.rathboneinn.com* Good-value guesthouse in an elegant 1850 mansion, with a porch, tropical patio and small jacuzzi. All twelve high-ceilinged rooms have private bath and kitchenettes; the sizeable suites sleep four. Rates

FAUBOURG MARIGNY, ESPLANADE RIDGE AND MID-CITY

include in-room continental breakfast. Reservations and deposit required; two-day minimum stay over weekends. See *Maison Esplanade*, above, for a caution about the neighborhood. **⑤**.

Royal Street Inn
Map 4, M4. 1431 Royal St at Kerlerec ⓣ 948-7499 or 1-800/449-5535, ⓦ *www.royalstreetinn.com*
Characterful Faubourg accommodation above the funky *R-Bar* (see p.213), and run by the same people. The five, good-looking rooms (all with private bath) are each decorated on a theme, ranging from Art Deco to bordello; those for two people are smallish, but the four-person suites with kitchenettes – including "Ghost in the Attic", under the eaves – are excellent value. Favored by a young crowd who spend evenings hanging out in the bar; rates include two free drinks per night. **⑤**.

CBD AND WAREHOUSE DISTRICT

International House
Map 3, M4. 221 Camp St at Common ⓣ 553-9550 or 1-800/633-5770, ⓦ *www.ihhotel.com*
Contemporary boutique hotel in a beautifully restored Beaux Arts bank building that changes its decor to fit in with the season or the latest festival. Beyond the swish design, however, this is yet another business hotel, though the very beige guest rooms are comfortable enough, filled with books about the city and photos of jazz musicians. Rates include continental breakfast. **⑧**.

La Salle Hotel
Map 4, A1. 1113 Canal St at Basin ⓣ 523-5831 or 1-800/521-9450, ⓦ *www.lasallehotelneworleans.com*
Few frills in this budget option, which skirts the Quarter and Tremé: just plain rooms – those without bath are a snip at $40 – free coffee,

and daily newspapers. Though the hotel is safe, the area can feel dodgy at night, so think about calling a cab. **3**.

Pelham Hotel

Map 3, M4. 444 Common St at Magazine ⓣ 569-0639 or 1-800/272-4583, ⓦ www .nolacollection.com/pelham
One of the city's more established boutique hotels, in a nineteenth-century building a couple of blocks from Canal Street. It's a laid-back, no-attitude kind of place, with comfortable, attractive rooms. Ask about special weekend deals or check the visitor center (see p.9) for brochures – and make sure to eat in the superb *Metro* restaurant downstairs (see p.192). **8**.

W Hotel

Map 3, M5. 333 Poydras St at S Peters ⓣ 525-9444, ⓦ www.whotels.com
From the outside this is just another CBD tower: inside, the slick, over-designed public spaces, including the over-hyped *Whiskey Blue Bar* and *Zöe Bistrot* – are scuttling

with fashion slaves and harassed business folk. If you prefer New York style and attitude – snooty service, hip furnishings and super-cool fellow guests – to rough-hewn New Orleans charm, you'll love the W, and may even be willing to pay the premium rates. **9**.

Windsor Court

Map 3, M5. 300 Gravier St at Tchoupitoulas ⓣ 523-6000 or 1-800/262-2662, ⓦ www .windsorcourthotel.com
This extremely luxurious hotel – a favorite of Bill Gates – was voted the best in the world by *Condé Nast Traveler* in 1998. The public spaces are palatial, dripping with Italian marble, Old Master paintings, colossal flower arrangements and priceless antiques, and the rooms themselves are as huge and special as you'd expect. Aristocratic pretensions abound in the swanky *Polo Lounge* bar and in the genteel afternoon teas, complete with live harp accompaniment. **9**.

CBD AND WAREHOUSE DISTRICT

LOWER GARDEN DISTRICT AND GARDEN DISTRICT

Henry Howard Inn

Map 3, I5. 2041 Prytania St at Josephine; also *Maginnis Mansion* at 2127 Prytania St ⓣ566-1515 (main office), ⓦ*www.HenryHowardInn.com*
Budget accommodation in two historic Lower Garden District houses with a total of 49 rooms (nine with shared bath). Rooms vary wildly in size, style and quality: the best, most of which are in *Maginnis Mansion*, feature lovely antique furnishings, but if you're fussy about cleanliness and atmosphere then avoid the cheaper options. Always make sure to ask what you're getting. There's a communal TV room in *Henry Howard Inn*, where they also serve a good breakfast (not included in room rate). ❷–❸.

HI-New Orleans Marquette House

Map 3, F4. 2253 Carondelet St at Jackson ⓣ523-3014, http://hometown.aol.com/hinewo rlns/marquettehouse.html
New Orleans' only official HI hostel is in a large antebellum house a block from the streetcar just outside the Garden District. Dorm beds cost $17 for members, $21 for nonmembers, and there are a few functional rooms (sleeping one to four), some with kitchens, in a separate building. The crowd is slightly older than at the city's other hostels – there's a ban on alcohol – and it's a favorite with families. Day use is allowed, and there's no curfew; reservations recommended. ❷–❹.

Josephine Guest House

Map 3, F6. 1450 Josephine St at Prytania ⓣ524-6361 or 1-800/779-6361.
Exquisite guesthouse in the gorgeous 1870s Italianate home of M. and Mme. Fuselier, set on the fringes of the Garden District. Rooms are decorated with unusual antiques and baroque flourishes; each has private bath and a balcony. Continental breakfast comes

with fresh orange juice, warm bread and café au lait, and drinks are served in the parlor. ❻.

Longpré House

Map 3, H5. 1726 Prytania St at Euterpe ☎ 581-4540, ⓦ *www .angelfire.com/la/longprezoo* The third of the city's budget hostels, in a run-down Italianate house in the Lower Garden District. Threadbare dorms ($12; $25 during festivals and special events) are somewhat cramped, but there are also a few private rooms, some of which sleep four or five. The cheapest rooms aren't bad value at $35 ($40 with bath), and there's a small pool, but the place as a whole is probably for die-hard hostelers only. No curfew, and no smoking in rooms. ❶.

McKendrick-Breaux House

Map 3, H6. 1474 Magazine St at Race ☎ 586-1700 or 1-888/570-1700, ⓦ *www.mckendrick-breaux.com* Laid-back B&B in two

nineteenth-century Lower Garden District homes. The large, antique-filled rooms are prettily decorated with fresh flowers and original paintings; all have bath and some feature balconies overlooking the patio (which has a jacuzzi). Rates include continental breakfast, served by the knowledgeable, personable hosts. ❻.

Prytania Park Hotel

Map 3, H5. 1525 Prytania St at Terpsichore ☎ 524-0427 or 1-888/498-7591, ⓦ *www.prytaniaparkhotel.com* One of the Lower Garden District's more upscale hotels, a spruce, peaceful place with a varied selection of historic and modern rooms, including good-value lofts that sleep four or five. All rooms have fridges and microwaves; rates include continental breakfast, which you can eat in the courtyard or in your room, and free use of the secure parking lot. ❻.

St Charles Guest House

Map 3, H5. 1748 Prytania St at Polymina ☎ 523-6556, ⓦ *www .stcharlesguesthouse.com*

Bohemian Lower Garden District guesthouse with rooms (all nonsmoking) ranging from basic cabins with no air-conditioning to en-suite doubles. None has phone or TV. It's a favorite with European backpackers who go for the 6ft by 8ft cabins ($35 – first-come, first-served), but for the pricier rooms you can get better value elsewhere. It's a friendly place, though, with a pool and café serving complimentary continental breakfast. Deposits required with reservations. ❶–❹.

St Vincent's Guest House

Map 3, H6. 1507 Magazine St at Race ☎ 566-1515, ⓦ *www .StVincentsGuestHouse.com* Run by the same people as the *Henry Howard Inn* and *Maginnis Mansion* (see p.166), this economical Lower Garden District lodging has more than seventy simple, bright rooms with private bath, in a huge 1861 orphanage. The atmosphere is peaceful, if a little institutional; rates include

breakfast, served in the pretty tearoom. There's a pool, too. They offer a year-round discount of five percent to *Rough Guide* readers. ❸.

Whitney Inn

Map 3, H5. 1509 St Charles Ave at Terpsichore ☎ 521-8000 or 1-800/379-5322, ⓦ *www.whitneyinn.com* No-nonsense hotel in renovated nineteenth-century townhouses on the streetcar line in the Lower Garden District. The modest rooms range from motel-type singles to a penthouse suite; all have private bath. There's a small communal kitchen, a little courtyard and a reading room. No smoking. ❺–❾.

UPTOWN

Columns Hotel

Map 2, J6. 3811 St Charles Ave at General Taylor ☎ 899-9308, ⓦ *www.thecolumns.com* Atmospheric hotel in an 1883 Italianate mansion. Standing in for a Storyville bordello in the 1977 movie *Pretty Baby*, the whole place seeps louche glamour, especially the superb bar (see p.216) and the columned veranda. The twenty rooms have hardwood floors and are decorated with antiques; some come with private bath and balcony, but there are no TVs. Complimentary continental breakfast is taken in a little tearoom. Rates increase by more than 200 percent at Mardi Gras, due to its excellent parade-viewing location on the streetcar line. **6**–**9**.

Park View Guest House

Map 2, C4. 7004 St Charles Ave at Walnut ⓣ 861-7564, ⓦ www.parkviewguesthouse.com Built for the 1884 Cotton Exposition, this large hotel on the edge of Audubon Park has an appealing, lived-in feel, with mismatched antique furniture, hardwood floors and a roomy veranda. Rooms, some with shared bath, are comfortable and good value, with many offering views of the park. Rates include continental breakfast and champagne reception. **5**.

Pontchartrain Hotel

Map 3, G5. 2031 St Charles Ave at Josephine ⓣ 524-0581 or 1-800/777-6193, ⓦ www.pontchartrainhotel.com Though time is taking its toll on the once-grand decor of this landmark building, it's still popular with visiting dignitaries and privacy-seeking celebs (Tom Cruise and Nicole Kidman canoodled here in happier days). The guest rooms are shabbier than the public spaces, but the location – on the fringes of the Garden District – is great, and the atmospheric *Bayou Bar* (see p.216), with its dark wood and romantic corners, remains a local favorite for a sophisticated night out. **7**.

St Charles Inn

Map 3, B4. 3636 St Charles Ave at Foucher ⓣ 899-8888. Sizeable and good-value, if unexciting, motel rooms in a prime location just beyond the Garden District, right by the streetcar stop. There's a communal lounge, and rates include continental breakfast taken in your room. Free covered parking. **4**.

UPTOWN

Eating

New Orleans is a gourmand's dream. Many visitors come here for the restaurants alone, while locals will spend hours arguing about where to find the fattest po-boy, the briniest raw oysters or the tastiest gumbo. The comings, goings and latest creations of local celebrity chefs are daily gossip, food festivals litter the calendar and restaurant openings make regular headlines.

The **food** itself, commonly defined as **Creole**, is a spicy, substantial – and usually very fattening – blend of French, Spanish, African, Caribbean and Cajun cuisine, mixed up with a host of other influences including Native American, Italian and German. It tends to be rich and fragrant, using heaps of herbs, peppers, garlic and onion. Some of the simpler dishes, like red beans and rice (traditionally served for Monday lunch), reveal a strong Caribbean influence, while others are more French, cooked with long-simmered sauces based on a **roux** (fat and flour heated together) and herby stocks. You'll often get surprising twinnings – oysters and tasso, say, or crabmeat and veal – and many dishes are served **étouffé**, literally "smothered" in a tasty Creole sauce (a roux with tomato, onion and spices), on a bed of rice.

Seafood is abundant and usually inexpensive – hardly surprising when you consider the city is almost entirely surrounded by water. Along with shrimp and softshell crabs, you'll get famously good **oysters**, shucked and slurped in their hundreds along marble-topped counters all around the city; they're in season from September to April. Once looked down on as "trash" food, **crawfish**, or mudbugs – which in the nineteenth century proliferated in standing puddles all over the city – are nowadays a real favorite. Closely resembling langoustines, they're served in everything from omelettes to bisques, or simply boiled in a spicy stock. Though you can get them any time from December through July, they're most plentiful between March and May, when locals throw huge crawfish boil parties to celebrate the season. To eat them, tug off the overlarge head, pinch the tail and suck out the juicy, very delicious flesh.

When deciding **where to eat** it can be difficult to choose between the city's fabulous special-occasion restaurants and its many neighborhood joints. Indeed, some of the best food in the city is served in scruffy little dives that you'd barely give a second glance elsewhere. That said, the atmosphere alone at New Orleans' swankiest, **old-guard restaurants** – including *Brennan's*, *Commander's Palace* and *Galatoire's* – all of which serve haute-Creole cuisine in elegant, jacket-and-tie surroundings, makes it worth splashing out for a special occasion. Many of them are owned by members of the extended Brennan family, a dynasty that has ruled the city's dining roost since the 1950s. There's no shortage of vibrant, **cutting-edge restaurants**, either, where stellar chefs throw even more influences – Southwestern, New American, Asian – into the pot. Currently, the most famous is *Emeril's*, brainchild of TV darling Emeril Lagasse, who stormed the restaurant scene in the 1990s after cutting his teeth at *Commander's*. Other top restaurants to try include *Bayona*, *Peristyle*, *Bistro at Maison de Ville* and *Upperline* – and keep an eye on the papers for news on the latest wunderkind chefs.

EATING

SOME NEW ORLEANS FOOD TERMS

Andouille (on-*doo*-we) Spicy pork sausage, often in gumbo.

Bananas Foster Flamboyant dessert invented at *Brennan's* restaurant. Sliced bananas, doused in rum and banana liqueur, are added to a mountain of brown sugar and set alight at your table to create the ultimate in boozy comfort food.

Barbecue shrimp Not BBQ as we know it; the shrimp are baked in their shells and served in a buttery, garlicky sauce.

Beignets (*ben*-yay) Deep-fried, square doughnuts without a hole, served hot and smothered in powdered sugar. Commonly thought to be French, in fact they derive from Spanish *sopapillas*, or fritters. Try them at the Café du Monde (p.200).

Biscuits Sourmilk scones, traditionally eaten at breakfast.

Boudin Spicy Cajun sausage of pork, crawfish or dirty rice.

Bread pudding Gooey dessert, made with French bread and raisins and usually drenched in sweet, liquor-filled custard.

Café brûlot Dark, spicy coffee flavored with brandy, orange liqueur, orange peel and spices, set alight before serving.

Chicken-fried Breaded and deep-fried.

Chicory Related to endive; a roasted, ground root used to flavor New Orleans coffee.

Chitlins Smoked, savory pig intestines – delicious soul food.

Debris Juicy meat leftovers, usually from slow-cooked roast beef or pork, often served in a sloppy po-boy.

Dirty rice Rice cooked with chicken livers, giblets, onions, peppers and spices.

Grillades (*gree*-yards) Sliced veal or beef served in a rich gravy, usually with grits, often for breakfast.

Grits Southern breakfast staple of mushy ground corn boiled and served with a dollop of butter, maple syrup or gravy.

Gumbo Thick soup-cum-stew made with seafood, chicken, vegetables or sausage. The name may come from *kombo*, a Native American word for filé (dried sassafras, ground by the local Choctaw to thicken soups, and often added to gumbos today) or *gombo*, the Bantu word for okra, which is another thickening agent. Gumbo z'herbes is a vegetarian option, created by African slaves for Lent.

Hush puppies Fried cornmeal balls.

Jambalaya Rice jumbled together with seafood, sausage, chicken, bell peppers, celery and onion. The name is thought to come from the Spanish or French words for ham (*jamon* and *jambon*), tacked onto the Spanish *paella*.

King Cake A ring of sweet brioche, iced in the carnival colors of gold, green and purple, eaten throughout Mardi Gras.

Macque choux Creamy stew of corn, tomatoes, onion and peppers.

Mirliton Squash.

Muffuletta Italian sandwich; a sesame-seed bun stuffed with aromatic meats and cheeses, dripping with olive and garlic dressing.

Oysters Rockefeller Concocted at *Antoine's* around 1900, and named for the oil magnate. These days most versions come baked in a creamy spinach sauce, but Antoine's secret recipe uses greens.

Pain perdu French toast ("lost bread").

Panéed Lightly breaded and fried in butter.

Po-boy French-bread sandwich crammed with oysters, shrimp, roast beef or almost anything else. They were created by two local bakers in 1929, who handed them out free to striking streetcar drivers ("poor" boys).

Praline (praw-leen) Tooth-rottingly sweet candy made from caramelized brown sugar, melted butter and pecans (pi-*cons*).

Ravigote Piquant mix of mayonnaise and capers, usually served with cold shellfish.

Rémoulade Chilled spicy sauce made with peppers, spring onion, horseradish and lemon, and slathered over cold shrimp.

Tasso Lean, spicy smoked ham.

SOME NEW ORLEANS FOOD TERMS

Although New Orleans does have a couple of good restaurants calling themselves **Cajun**, little of what they serve has much in common with the one-pot country food, cooked in a very dark roux, that is dished up along the bayous. After all, despite the nonstop accordion music that jangles from the tackiest tourist shops, New Orleans is not actually in Cajun country, which lies well to the west and southwest. What passes for Cajun food in the city is often a modern hybrid, tasty but not authentic: the "blackened" fish and chicken, for example, slathered in butter and hot spices, made famous by Cajun chef Paul Prudhomme in the 1980s.

New Orleans also has some good **ethnic** restaurants for Japanese, Chinese, Indian, Thai and North African food. Along with the handful of **vegetarian** places, these are the best bets for nonmeat-eaters, who otherwise need to be careful; even dishes that sound innocent – red beans and rice, collard greens – will probably yield fat chunks of smoked sausage or ham hocks, or will at the very least have been stewed with some juicy lump of flesh.

Gratifyingly, **prices** are not that high compared to other US cities – even at the best restaurants you can get away with $50 per head for a three-course feast with wine. Lunch, in particular, can be a bargain, even at the more upmarket places. And if you're on a really tight budget, don't despair: one of the great pleasures of New Orleans' dining scene is the scores of excellent neighborhood joints serving colossal portions at low prices.

New Orleans' best coffeehouses, most of which serve light lunches and snacks, are reviewed on pp.200–203; for picnic food, turn to the reviews of delis and food stores, which start on p.203.

EATING

DON'T MISS . . .

Garlicky Tuscan soup at Bacco see p.177
Sweetbreads and duck gumbo at Bayona see p.177
Raw oysters on the half-shell at Casamento's see p.196
Breakfast po-boy at Elizabeth's see p.190
Lunch and a café brûlot at Galatoire's see p.180
Louisiana shellfish in Girod's courtyard see p.181
Alligator sausage cheesecake at Jacques Imo's see p.197
Garlic chicken at Mr B's Bistro see p.184
Early drinks and antipasto at the Napoleon House see p.185
Barbecue oyster and shrimp combo – and pretty
  much anything at all – at Uglesich's see p.195

. . . AND DON'T BOTHER

In a city where restaurant openings make front-page news, it's all too easy to be taken in by the hype surrounding so many of them. But no one should have to waste precious vacation time and money eating at overrated places that for whatever reason – inflated prices, ordinary food, bad service, poor value – are just not worth the bother. For our money, in a city bursting with fantastic places to eat, you can safely disregard The Court of Two Sisters, Lemon Grass, NOLA, Pelican Club and Zöe Bistrot . . .

RESTAURANTS

No neighborhood can rival the **French Quarter** for sheer volume and variety of eating options, its narrow old streets jam-packed with everything from downhome holes in the wall to old-guard dining rooms serving glorious haute cuisine. If you can drag yourself away from the Quarter, your best bet for a special occasion is one of the

RESTAURANTS

RESTAURANT PRICES

The restaurant listings below are price-coded into three broad categories: inexpensive (under $15), moderate ($15–25) and expensive (over $25). This estimates how much you might pay, on average, for a two-course meal (appetizer and entrée, or entrée and dessert) for one person, not including tax or tip. All of this depends, of course, on what you order. Eating lobster at a restaurant we've classed as inexpensive will obviously push costs up, while many of even the swankiest restaurants offer very reasonable lunchtime deals.

swanky restaurants in the **CBD**, **Garden District** or **uptown**, while at the other end of the scale you'll find a clutch of good places in the **Faubourg** and **Bywater**, along Esplanade Avenue in **Mid-City**, in the **Lower Garden District** and throughout the studenty **Riverbend** area uptown.

THE FRENCH QUARTER

Acme Oyster House
Map 4, B3. 724 Iberville St at Bourbon ☎522-5973.
Sun–Thurs 11am–10pm, Fri & Sat 11am–11pm. Inexpensive.
With its checked tablecloths, tangle of neon signs, marble-topped oyster bar and fast, smart-talking staff, this noisy, characterful place has been

the French Quarter hangout for raw oysters and ice-cold beer for nearly one hundred years. A dozen briny bivalves on the half-shell costs just $6.50, or you can get them fried for around $11. In season, don't miss the fresh, buttery mudbugs, boiled in a delicious, pepper-hot stock. Or try the gut-busting medley of gumbo, jambalaya, and red beans and rice with sausage – not the finest in the city, but at a mere $8 the price can't be beat.

Bacco

Map 4, C5. 310 Chartres St at Bienville, in the *W Hotel* ⓣ522-2426.

Daily 11.30am–2.30pm & 6–10pm. Moderate–Expensive. Owned by Ralph and Cindy Brennan of the city's top restaurant clan, this gorgeous nouvelle Italian – all Venetian chandeliers, iron gates and ivory-colored booths scrawled with Italian love proclamations – is less expensive than you might expect, especially at lunch, when you can get two courses for around $17. Dinner can set you back, however, especially if you order foie gras pizza, and the homemade pasta, though tasty, is pricey. Good appetizers include the roasted garlic soup, rich with Romano cheese,

while for an entrée you could try wood-oven-roasted Gulf shrimp with greens, penne and feta dressing.

Bayona

Map 4, D3. 430 Dauphine St at Conti ⓣ525-4455.

Mon–Thurs 11.30am–2pm & 6–10pm, Fri 11.30am–2pm & 6–11pm, Sat 6–11pm. Moderate–Expensive. Splendid, romantic and relaxed restaurant in a seventeenth-century Creole cottage with a courtyard. Chef Susan Spicer creates dazzling "Global Cuisine", using organic ingredients and giving local dishes an Asian, Southwestern or European twist – grilled shrimp with black-bean cake and cilantro sauce, say, or salmon and choucroute with Gewürztraminer wine sauce. It's creative without being

Look out for the absurd Lucky Dogs giant hot-dog-shaped carts, set up on corners throughout the French Quarter. Featured in John Kennedy Toole's farcical novel A Confederacy of Dunces (see p.316), they've become something of an institution – though in truth the "dogs" themselves are nothing to write home about.

RESTAURANTS: THE FRENCH QUARTER

fussy; the simple garlic soup and sweetbreads with lemon caper butter are outstanding. The wine list is excellent, too, with more than 250 wines from around the world. To cut costs, go for lunch, when you can get three courses for less than $25.

Bistro at Maison de Ville
Map 4, E4. 727 Toulouse St at Royal ⓣ528-9206.
Mon–Sat 11.30am–2pm & 6–10pm, Sun 11am–2pm & 6–10pm. **Expensive.**
Nouvelle Creole cuisine and brasserie standards served in a romantic little restaurant linked to the historic hotel (see p.159). The place feels like an old French bistro with its red leather banquettes, bevelled glass mirrors and wooden floors, and the seasonal menu concentrates on the classics – sweetbreads, rack of lamb, moules-frites, snapper with sorrel beurre blanc, pan-seared scallops and crème brûlée. Prix-fixe options include a four-course feast for $40, and a three-course pre-theater menu for an incredible $18. Superb wine list.

Reservations advised.

Brennan's
Map 4, D4. 417 Royal St at Conti ⓣ525-9711.
Daily 8am–2.30pm & 6–10pm. **Expensive.**
Historic Creole restaurant, the first in the Brennan empire, with a dozen dining rooms and a tropical courtyard. It's famed for its long, luxurious breakfasts – choose from more than twenty poached egg dishes, hair-of-the-dog cocktails, grillades and grits and the like; though locals balk at spending $50 on eggs, tourists can't get enough of the place. Dinner proves better value, with four-course meals for $38.50: the long menu includes turtle and oyster soups, crawfish *sardou* (spicy crawfish tails in an artichoke, spinach and hollandaise sauce), and the definitive Bananas Foster (see p.172). The wine list is outstanding. Dress up and reserve.

Café Angeli

Map 4, J5. 1141 Decatur St at Gov Nicholls ☎ 566-0077.

Sun–Thurs 10am–4am, Fri & Sat 24hr. **Inexpensive.**

A favorite with night owls, hipsters and barflies, this big, dimly lit room is virtually an extension of the Lower Decatur scene outside. Picture windows allow diners to see and be seen, while cult movies flicker across the wall above the bar. Its late hours are a welcome rarity in the Quarter, and the Mediterranean salads, sandwiches and pastas are just the thing after a wild night out.

Clover Grill

Map 4, H3. 900 Bourbon St at Dumaine ☎ 598-1010.

Daily 24hr. **Inexpensive.**

All-night diner with counter seating and a few booths, usually crowded with a gay Bourbon Street clientele filling up on fries, burgers, omelettes and shakes. It's always lively and can get rowdy: come for a post bar-crawl breakfast of waffles, pancakes or Froot Loops,

then sit back and enjoy the scene.

Croissant d'Or

Map 4, J4. 617 Ursulines St at Royal ☎ 524-4663.

Daily 7am–5pm. **Inexpensive.**

Peaceful, absurdly cheap little place in a converted ice-cream parlor. Here you'll get the best French pastries and stuffed croissants this side of Paris, plus quiches, salads and steaming café au lait. There's a courtyard, but inside, with its marble floor, tiled walls, stained-glass and iron chairs, is even more atmospheric, usually filled with locals reading, writing and chatting. No smoking indoors and no credit cards.

Felix's Oyster House

Map 4, A3. 739 Iberville St at Bourbon ☎ 522-4440.

Mon–Thurs 10am–midnight, Fri & Sat 10am–1.30am, Sun 10am–10pm. **Inexpensive.**

Just across the road from the *Acme*, but less crowded, *Felix's* offers raw oysters on the half-shell just as fresh as its rival's and slightly cheaper, plus a broader range of tasty seafood dishes (oysters Rockefeller, oysters Bienville, seafood gumbo, oyster stew and the like) in sedate – some might say subdued – surroundings.

Fiorella's

Map 4, J6. 1136 Decatur St at Gov Nicholls ⓣ 528-9566.
Mon–Sat 7am–5pm.
Inexpensive.

Locals and traders have been coming to this shabby French Market diner for years, hooked on its soul food, fry-ups and French fry po-boys. Breakfast is good, while blue-plate specials are an amazing bargain. Go for the huge slabs of freshly fried chicken, which come with beans, bread and salad. The decor – old photos, rusting crawfish cages and sagging nets strewn across the walls – has seen better days, but that only adds to its charm.

Galatoire's

Map 4, B3. 209 Bourbon St at Iberville ⓣ 525-2021.
Tues–Sat 11am–9pm, Sun noon–9pm. **Expensive.**

Grand Creole restaurant, run by the same family since 1905. With its dark wood, black-and-white tiled floor, ceiling fans and old mirrors, it's quintessentially New Orleans: elegant, relaxed and not at all stuffy. It's best at lunchtime, on Friday or Sunday especially, when long, convivial hours can be spent gorging on rich food like turtle soup, oysters en brochette, crabmeat Maison (with capers, homemade mayonnaise, green onions and parsley in a secret French dressing) and filet mignon. Reservations are taken only for eight or more: smaller groups should go early and be prepared to wait. Jackets required after 5pm and all day Sunday.

Gamay

Map 4, C6. 32 N Peters St at Conti, in the *Bienville House Hotel* ⓣ 299-8800.
Tues–Thurs & Sat 6–10.30pm, Fri 11.30am–2pm & 6–10.30pm.
Moderate–Expensive.

The hotel dining room isn't the most atmospheric place to eat, but the contemporary Creole-Cajun food, brought to you by the same people behind *Gabrielle* (see p.199), is exceptional. The gumbos – roast duck and rabbit with smoked andouille, say – are great, as are entrées like truffle- and crabmeat-crusted Gulf fish with baked green onions and spinach crème fraîche. Dinner can be pricey, but for lunch you get three courses for less than $20; grilled eggplant soup, maybe, followed by fried softshell-crab salad with roasted tomatoes, and apple upside-down bread pudding.

Girod's Bistro

Map 4, D5. 500 Chartres St at St Louis ☏ 524-9752.

Tues–Sat 6–10.30pm.

Moderate.

Wonderful, romantic restaurant in the *Napoleon House* bar (see p.210). All cracked plaster, candlelight and age-old paintings, it's the perfect setting to linger over robust, creative Creole food with Mediterranean and Caribbean accents. Appetizers ($5–8) are a meal in themselves: try the garlicky barbecue shrimp, or savory cheesecake with mushrooms. Of the entrées ($12–18), most of which come with unusual, flavorful sauces, sure-fire winners include the chicken fricassée with garlic mash, and Louisiana shellfish with angel hair pasta and wild mushrooms.

Gumbo Shop

Map 4, F4. 630 St Peter St at Chartres ☏ 525-1486.

Mon–Thurs & Sun 11am–11pm, Fri & Sat 11am–midnight.

Inexpensive.

A relaxed, convivial spot for a quick lunch or to fill up before a night out, this touristy Creole restaurant is housed in an eighteenth-century building lined with murals of old New Orleans. Naturally the gumbo – seafood, chicken and andouille, or z'herbes – is the highlight; dark, subtly flavored and excellent value ($4–7). Entrées are good, too – try the crawfish étouffé, or the succulent grilled redfish smothered with shrimp Creole. The combination dinners, three courses for around $18, are a bargain.

RESTAURANTS: THE FRENCH QUARTER

Irene's Cuisine

Map 4, I5. 539 St Philip St at Chartres ☏ 529-8811.
Mon–Thurs & Sun 5.30–10.30pm, Fri & Sat 5.30–11pm.
Moderate–Expensive.

You can't reserve at this intimate, lively Italian place, so lines – and waits – are often very long. No one minds: settling down in the comfy piano bar with a good Italian wine is part of the experience. The dining room itself, lined with bookshelves and paintings, is just as cozy, packed with diners feasting on fantastic roast garlic chicken or rich pasta dishes packed with seafood.

Johnny's Po-Boys

Map 4, D5. 511 St Louis St at Decatur ☏ 524-8129.
Mon–Fri 8am–4.30pm, Sat & Sun 9am–4pm. Inexpensive.

A New Orleans institution, this no-frills, checked-tablecloth joint is heaving at lunchtime with local workers and in-the-know tourists. It's famed for its po-boys, of course, made to order – the mind-boggling choice of fillings includes pork chop, French fries, chicken Parmesan, and catfish – but they also serve good breakfasts and plate lunches for under $5. Prepare to wait at lunchtime, or call for deliveries. No credit cards.

K-Paul's Louisiana Kitchen

Map 4, D5. 416 Chartres St at Conti ☏ 524-7394.
Mon–Thurs 11.30am–2.30pm & 5.30–10pm, Fri & Sat 11.30am–2.30pm &.5.30–11pm.
Moderate–Expensive.

Renowned, rustic-smart restaurant serving the "blackened" cuisine, slathered in butter and spices, introduced to the nation by Cajun chef Paul Prudhomme in the 1980s. If you like your food hot and heavy you'll love it here; highlights among the dinner entrées ($20–30) include blackened beef tenderloin with a rich debris sauce, and bronzed swordfish crusted with roasted pecans, jalapeños and garlic. Gumbos are rich: try the seven-steak variety, or wild turkey and andouille. Most diners are tourists, who wait for ages for a table (reservations are accepted only for the more formal upstairs room); come for lunch, when lines are shorter, prices far lower, and there's time to walk it all off.

La Madeleine

Map 4, G5. 547 St Ann St at Chartres ⊤ 568-0073.

Daily 7am–9pm. **Inexpensive.** With a prime location on Jackson Square, this convenient refueling stop, part of the national chain, fits well in this most French of US cities. The ambience is nothing special, but it's the buttery smells and low prices that pull in the hungry artists and footsore tourists. Specialties include croques monsieurs, quiches and pies, as well as omelettes, pasta and fish; the *boulangerie* sells fresh bread, pastries and hot flaky croissants to go. No smoking.

Mama Rosa's

Map 4, E1. 616 N Rampart St at Toulouse ⊤ 523-5546.

Sun–Thurs 11am–10pm, Fri & Sat 11am–11pm. **Inexpensive.** Local favorite just a stone's throw away from the Quarter. The surroundings, service and decor are nothing to shout about, but the pizzas are fabulous: fresh, hot and topped with a mess of good ingredients. The menu also has muffulettas, salads and old Italian favorites – lasagne and eggplant Parmesan – but the pizzas are the real draw. Free delivery in the Quarter and Faubourg.

Maximo's

Map 4, J5. 1117 Decatur St at Gov Nicholls ⊤ 586-8883.

Daily 6–11pm. **Expensive.** Northern Italian food in a slick urban bistro, with counter seating, booths and moody jazz photos. It's especially buzzy at weekends, when people pile in to eat late. You can't go wrong with the pasta, especially penne crawfish diablo in a zippy cream sauce, and veal is great, be it cooked with garlic, lemon and wine, or pan-roasted with herbs. There's zabaglione to finish and around fifty good Italian wines, many of them served by the glass.

Mona Lisa

Map 4, K4. 1212 Royal St at Barracks ⊤ 522-6746.

Daily 11am–11pm. Inexpensive. Candlelit at night, with brick walls, cobblestone floors and wine coolers made from battered olive-oil cans, the funky – on the point of shabby – decor at this pizza place is a bit bohemian for many tourists, which keeps it a favorite with Quarterites. You can get pasta, sandwiches and salads, but the pizzas are the best thing here; try the Mediterranean, with spinach, feta, garlic, olives and sundried tomatoes. A 12in ($9–13) is more than enough for two. Choose from the wine list, or BYOB. Free delivery in the Quarter and Faubourg.

Moon Wok

Map 4, G3. 800 Dauphine St at St Ann ⊤ 523-6910.

Sun–Tues & Thurs 11am–10pm, Fri & Sat 11am–midnight. Inexpensive. Chinese food – unusual in the Quarter – dished up in modest, Deco-ish surroundings. At lunch it's busy with penny-pinching locals and a few stray tourists, while evening diners are usually young and hip, filling up before a big night out. The long menu includes all the Asian-American standards – chow mein, sweet and sour pork, egg foo yong – as well as more unusual choices like crawfish in black bean sauce. Lunch combos (11am–3pm) are good value at $6.95 (rising to $8.95 after 3pm). BYOB.

Mr B's Bistro

Map 4, B4. 201 Royal St at Iberville ⊤ 523-2078.

Mon–Sat 11.30am–3pm & 5.30–10pm, Sun jazz brunch 10.30am–3pm & 5.30–10pm. Moderate–Expensive. Another Brennans' winner: a casually chic European-style bistro with dark-wood booths, lots of etched glass, a relaxed, chatty buzz and spectacular food. It's difficult to choose from the star-studded contemporary Creole menu: the garlic chicken is the city's finest, served with wild rice drowned in a satiny reduction; the same accolade could go to the barbecue shrimp in sloppy sauce – you'll need the bib they tie around your neck. Other signature dishes include coconut- and beer-battered shrimp, pasta jambalaya and gumbo ya-ya with chicken and andouille.

Napoleon House

Map 4, D5. 500 Chartres St at St Louis Ⓣ 524-9752.
Food served Mon–Sat 11am–11pm, Sun 11am–6pm.
Inexpensive.

This fabulous old bar (see p.210) is one of the city's best lunch stops. Everyone comes here for the muffulettas, which they heat up to melt the cheese and mellow the flavors, but it's worth branching out to try their other Mediterranean sandwiches (the Franco, say, packed with herby mushroom salad, spinach and melted cheese), gumbos and salads (the Greek comes with baby spinach, roasted red peppers and warm grilled flatbread). There's also a terrific full-service bistro on site; see *Girod's* (p.181).

Old Dog, New Trick Café

Map 4, C4. 307 Exchange Alley at Bienville Ⓣ 522-4569.
Daily 11.30am–9pm.
Inexpensive.

Tiny vegetarian restaurant, with some outdoor tables. The food could be tastier, but for strict veggies it's the best choice in town, offering imaginative polenta and tempeh concoctions, lots of organic produce and even a few vegan options. Avoid the bland udon noodles and the crumbly burgers, and plump instead for pizzas, marinated tofu dishes or sandwiches. Wash it all down with iced hibiscus tea or choose from the good-value wine list.

Olivier's

Map 4, B6. 204 Decatur St at Iberville Ⓣ 525-7734.
Daily 11am–3pm & 5–10pm.
Moderate.

Great Black Creole food, served in smart surroundings in a charming old building. Family-owned, it's very welcoming, and the menu describes how each dish is cooked according to the recipe of a different family

RESTAURANTS: THE FRENCH QUARTER

member. To start, they offer four gumbos – the Creole variety is fantastic, packed with sausage and shrimp – while entrées include poulet au fromage, baked with five cheeses and served with shrimp, and Creole rabbit with oyster stuffing doused in a dark, herby sauce. They also do an expert crawfish étouffé, finely flavored and not as gloopy as it sometimes can be, and a killer butter-and-rum bread pudding.

Peristyle

Map 4, H1. 1041 Dumaine St at N Rampart ⓣ 593-9535. Tues–Thurs & Sat 6–10pm, Fri 11.30am–1.30pm & 6–10pm. **Expensive.**

Incongruously set on Rampart Street, this elegant restaurant – very New Orleans, all dark wood, checkerboard-tiled floors and mismatched mirrors – is one of the hottest places in town to eat contemporary French-Creole-New American cuisine. It's very congenial, for all its cachet – young chef Anne Kearney, superstar ascendant, regularly does the rounds to see how diners are enjoying her creations. The menu varies, but might include foie gras with grilled pear and ginger reduction, or pheasant and artichoke ravioli, with entrées ($22–25) such as poussin marinated in red wine with herbed basmati rice. Reservations essential; come early and have a drink in the lovely old bar.

Port of Call

Map 4, L3. 838 Esplanade Ave at Dauphine ⓣ 523-0120. Daily 11am–11pm. **Inexpensive.** Strung with tatty nets, lifebuoys and ship's lights, this lively neighborhood bar (see p.212) is the place for delicious, freshly made, half-pound burgers. The menu is short and to the point, with prices ranging from $6.50 for a plain burger to $7.75 with mushrooms and melted cheese. Eat them at the bar, in the cozy pub-like room or in the more formal dining area next door.

Quarter Scene

Map 4, H2. 900 Dumaine St at Dauphine ☎ 522-7533.
Mon & Wed–Sun 8am–midnight, Tues 5pm–midnight.
Inexpensive–Moderate.
During the day this casual, gay-owned restaurant lures you in with its plants and statuary, mismatched tables and splashy paintings lining the red-brick walls. It's great for breakfast and brunch, with lots of eggs benedict, fruit and pancake combinations; at night, flickering in the candlelight, it becomes sweetly romantic. The dinner menu, however, isn't terribly exciting, based on Creole standards, but specials do venture into Asian and Caribbean territory. BYOB; there's no corkage.

Redfish Grill

Map 4, A3. 115 Bourbon St at Iberville ☎ 598-1200.
Grill daily 11am–3pm & 5–11pm; oyster bar daily 11am–11pm. **Moderate.**
Relaxed, Ralph Brennan-owned fish restaurant, slightly twee with its ragwashed walls, fishy motifs and metallic palm

trees. It's not a place to linger, but the food is good value, especially the raw oysters ($4 for six) and the Bourbon Street sampler – coconut shrimp, barbecue oysters, alligator sausage and fish *beignets* – which, at just $11, is ample for two. Three-course lunch specials ($16 or so) might feature crawfish étouffé or a creamy oyster stew.

Rita's

Map 4, I5. 945 Chartres St at St Philip ☎ 525-7543.
Daily 11am–10pm.
Inexpensive–Expensive.
The French Quarter's coziest Black Creole restaurant, in an unpretentious dining room lined with news clippings and photos. The New Orleans soul food is substantial, tasty and good value: for dinner, try the blow-out "Taste of New Orleans" ($16) – gumbo, red beans and rice, jambalaya, barbecue ribs, crawfish pie, shrimp Creole, Louisiana yams, vegetable and bread pudding (which, covered with a hot praline sauce, you should order for dessert anyway). The cheaper lunch menu

RESTAURANTS: THE FRENCH QUARTER

(11am–4pm) includes po-boys and big plates of red beans and rice with fried chicken.

Royal Café

Map 4, F4. 700 Royal St at St Peter ☏ 528-9086.

Mon–Fri 11am–3pm & 5.30–10pm, Sat & Sun 10am–3pm & 5.30–10pm.

Moderate.

Located in the La Branche House (see p.51), with prime seating on its ornate, wraparound cast-iron balcony, the *Royal Café* is always full with tourists feasting on reliable Creole food. Though it looks rather elegant, it's actually a casual place, specializing in barbecue ribs in a good spicy sauce. Fish fans should go for the trout à la Branche, sautéed with crawfish and pecans; the salmon with mango is lighter, while the shrimp, another winner, comes with a delicious garlicky sauce.

Samurai Sushi

Map 4, B5. 249 Decatur St at Bienville ☏ 525-9595.

Mon–Thurs 11.30am–10pm, Fri 11.30am–10.30pm, Sat 5–10.30pm, Sun 5–10pm.

Moderate.

The only sushi bar in the Quarter, this sleek, minimal place offers good rolls and nigiri from $3, along with à la carte dishes including sushi and sashimi plates ($16–26), baked wasabi mussels, udon noodle soups, teriyaki, and a plate of tasty monkfish livers served with ponzu sauce. Lunch specials (Mon–Fri 11.30am–3pm) are a good deal, especially the sushi combo ($8.75). Free delivery in the Quarter, CBD and parts of the Faubourg.

Tally Ho

Map 4, D5. 400 Chartres St at Conti ☏ 566-7071.

Daily 6am–2pm. **Inexpensive.**

Tiny diner where hungover tourists wait in line on weekend mornings for no-frills fry-ups with New Orleans flair. If you're not up to wrestling with an alligator sausage, you might try the shrimp and pork boudin with grits – and they do all the usual breakfast items, too, served at a counter or small tables.

Tujague's

Map 4, G5. 823 Decatur St at Madison ⓣ 525-8676.

Daily 11am–3pm & 5–10.30pm. Bar 10.30am–11pm. Moderate. Things are kept simple at *Tujague's* ("Two-Jacks"), which at 150 years old is the second oldest restaurant in the city. The fixed-price menu – shrimp rémoulade or soup, followed by their famed boiled brisket with Creole sauce – has changed little since the 1850s, when butchers, dockers and traders feasted on *Tujague's* seven-course meals. Today it's an unpretentious, atmospheric place, with a classic New Orleans dining room and a nice old stand-up bar that's particularly good fun on Sunday when regulars gather to catch up and gossip. If you don't like beef, ask nicely and they just might cook you a fine chicken bonne femme, sautéed with mountains of garlic and parsley.

FAUBOURG MARIGNY AND BYWATER

Adolfo's

Map 4, N5. 611 Frenchmen St at Royal ⓣ 948-3800.

Mon–Sat 6–11pm. Moderate. Great Italian-Creole food in an intimate room tucked above the *Apple Barrel* bar (see p.212). Decorated with Christmas-tree lights, candles and Cubist art on the wood-paneled walls, it's the perfect setting for enjoying robust, rich, pasta and seafood. Every meal starts with a spaghetti Napoli appetizer; to follow, choose from entrées such as cannelloni stuffed with crabmeat, sweetcorn and ricotta or pan-sautéed softshell crab stuffed with shrimp.

Café Marigny

Map 4, M4. 1913 Royal St at Touro ⓣ 945-4472.

Sun–Thurs 11am–10pm, Fri & Sat 11am–11pm. Moderate. Creative Creole cuisine with Southwestern, Mediterranean and Asian accents, served in a casually chic neighborhood joint with a vaguely Tuscan decor. To start, try black-bean cakes served with crawfish and salsa, or mussels steamed with garlic and capers; good entrées include the cheese ravioli, smothered in a savory sauce of crawfish, roasted corn, tomatoes and basil. Daily specials, including veggie options, are good, and there's espresso and sumptuous pies to finish. BYOB; corkage $6.

Elizabeth's

Map 1, G6. 601 Gallier St at Chartres, in the Bywater ☎ 944-9272.

Tues–Sat 7am–2.30pm.
Inexpensive.

Even *Elizabeth's* logo, a cheery pig, can't prepare you for the size of the portions at this fabulous diner. Out in the Bywater, it pulls in a loyal crowd of local artists and blue-collar workers with its good food and low prices; for visitors, it's a perfect place to take a break from the Quarter. Breakfast (till 10.30am) will set you up for the day; try a po-boy overstuffed with scrambled egg, sausage and cheese. They do po-boys for lunch (from 10.30am), too, as well as unbelievably good specials ($6–7.50) such as chicken pie with biscuit crust or oyster meunière with grits. No credit cards.

Siam Café

Map 4, L6. 435 Esplanade Ave at Frenchmen ☎ 949-1750.

Mon–Fri 11.30am–2.30pm, Sat & Sun 11.30am–2.30pm & 6–11pm. **Inexpensive.**

Thai restaurant serving mountains of padh thai, zippy green and red curries and one-pot seafood dishes in funky gamblers' den-cum-opium pit surroundings. The hot sake is a hit with the hip, very young crowd who usually head upstairs to the *Dragon's Den* club (see p.230) after dining – you can order food up there, too, and eat it while sitting on floor cushions.

THE CBD AND WAREHOUSE DISTRICT

Emeril's

Map 3, L6. 800 Tchoupitoulas St at Julia ⓣ 528-9393.
Mon–Thurs 11.30am–2pm & 6–10pm, Fri 11.30am–2pm & 6–10.30pm, Sat 6–10.30pm.
Expensive.

Celebrity chef Emeril Lagasse's flagship restaurant is a noisy, flashy place, filled with delighted tourists and special-occasion locals enthusing over the decorative, cutting-edge Creole cuisine. Entrées ($20–35) include double-cut pork chop with green chile mole sauce, or duck confit with kiln-dried berries, Stilton, arugula and vanilla vinaigrette. For dessert most people go for the bus-sized banana cream pie or the "dessert storm", a sampler of the pastry chef's best. It's pricey, and service can be a pain, but Lagasse fans will love it. Reservations essential.

Herbsaint

Map 3, L4. 701 St Charles Ave at Girod ⓣ 524-4114.
Mon–Fri 11.30am–3pm & 5.30–10.30pm.
Moderate–Expensive.

Effortlessly elegant, and a little less formal than *Bayona* (see p.177), Susan Spicer's second restaurant offers French-influenced food in relaxed surroundings. It's especially good at lunchtime, when people come to enjoy themselves rather than to grab a hurried business lunch, and the streetcar rumbles past the huge windows. The food is deceptively simple, using good fresh ingredients in classics such as antipasto and roast chicken with lemon and olives. Leave room for the saffron semolina cake, a feather-light soufflé infused with lavender.

Liborio

Map 3, M5. 321 Magazine St at Gravier ⓣ 581-9680.
Mon 11.30am–2.30pm, Tues–Fri 11.30am–2.30pm & 6–9pm, Sat 6–9pm. Inexpensive.

The CBD lunchtime favorite is also good for inexpensive

RESTAURANTS: THE CBD AND WAREHOUSE DISTRICT

dinners: traditional Cuban dishes include *ropa viejo* ("old clothes") – shredded beef in tomato sauce with brown rice, black beans and plantain – and homemade tamales, while the *medianoche* – sweet bread stuffed with ham, cheese, pork and pickles – is an interesting variation on the classic Cuban sandwich. Don't miss the side dish of yucca with garlic.

Metro Bistro

Map 3, M4. 200 Magazine St at Common in the *Pelham Hotel* ☎ 529-1900.

Mon–Thurs & Sun 11am–2pm & 5.30–10pm, Fri & Sat 11am–2pm & 5.30–11pm.

Moderate–Expensive.

Splendid place that manages to be at once contemporary, comfortable, bustling and welcoming. The menu is excellent, mostly French-influenced, with lots of duck; try one of more than forty wines served by the glass and graze on white-bean dip and warm flatbread while you choose. Appetizers feature a cassoulet of duck confit, duck sausage and smoked pork; entrées to try include steak au poivre with rosemary frites or pan-seared scallops with andouille-potato hash. For something lighter, there's grilled fish on macque choux and a tangy bouillabaisse. The lunch menu features many of the dinner dishes, at half the price.

Mother's

Map 3, M5. 401 Poydras St at Tchoupitoulas ☎ 523-9656.

Mon–Sat 5am–10pm, Sun 7am–10pm.

Inexpensive–Moderate.

Though tourists go into a tizzy about *Mother's*, thrilled to be eating N'Awlins home cooking in a downhome ambience (brick walls, concrete floors, counter service, etc), locals complain that it's too pricey. That said, the portions are big, and the food is good – black ham (the sweet, crunchy skin of a baked ham) is a favorite, dished up with buttery biscuits and grits; the cholesterol-packed blue plates – fried chicken, beans and rice with sausage and so on – are not for the faint-hearted. No credit cards.

Palace Café

Map 3, N4. 605 Canal St at
Chartres ⓣ 523-1661.
Mon–Fri 11.30am–2.30pm &
5.30–10pm, Sat & Sun
10.30am–2.30pm & 5.30–10pm.
Moderate.

Lovely, casually elegant
restaurant on the edge of the
Quarter in a grand old music
store building. Always
buzzing, with the ambience
of a nineteenth-century
European café, it's big and
airy, with marble tables,
check-tiled floors, a spiral
staircase sweeping up to a
mezzanine and sunny walls
lined with French posters.
The food, Creole with a
contemporary spin, is first-
rate, from the creamy
crabmeat cheesecake with
mushroom sautée, or the
fragrant oyster pan roast, to
the potato pie mashed with
pork debris, spinach, melted
cheese and gravy. At lunch
they usually offer a "light"
option (fish, usually); after
that why not go on to ruin all
the good work with a slab of
white chocolate bread
pudding?

Rio Mar

Map 3, L6. 800 S Peters St at
Julia ⓣ 525-3474.
Mon–Thurs 11am–3pm &
6–10pm, Fri 11am–3pm &
6–11pm, Sat 6–11pm.
Moderate.

New Orleans seafood meets
Latin cuisine in this terrific
Warehouse District
restaurant. Appetizers are full
of flavor, with Spanish staples
like bacalao, escabeche,
grilled squid with gazpacho,
bouillabaisse, and tuna
empanadas, while for a main
course you can't go wrong
with a zingy ceviche. The
lunch menu adds a few tasty
seafood sandwiches –
crawfish cake, garlicky
shrimp, or fried oysters with
grilled corn and Serrano
ham.

LOWER GARDEN
DISTRICT AND
GARDEN DISTRICT

- -

Bluebird Café

Map 3, B4. 3625 Prytania St at
Foucher ⓣ 895-7166.
Mon–Fri 7am–3pm, Sat & Sun
8am–3pm. **Inexpensive.**

RESTAURANTS: LOWER GARDEN AND GARDEN DISTRICT

Though it looks like a run-of-the-mill diner, the *Bluebird*, on the fringes of the Garden District, is in fact a vaguely hippyish hangout serving good, healthy home cooking. Lines form outside, especially at the weekend, for the big all-day breakfasts, which include huevos rancheros, corned-beef hash, buckwheat pancakes and "power" eggs (with tamari and yeast). They also do daily plate lunch specials, which you can wash down with virtuous herbal teas and fresh OJ. No reservations; no credit cards.

Commander's Palace

Map 3, D5. 1403 Washington Ave at Coliseum ☎ 899-8221. Mon–Fri 11.30am–2pm & 6–10pm, Sat 11.30am–1pm & 6–10pm, Sun 10.30am–1.30pm & 6–10pm. **Expensive.**
Haute Creole restaurant in a Garden District mansion, with a maze of rooms and a tropical courtyard always full with the city's finest. The best dishes, most of which come garnished with lots of adjectives (check the double-cut veal chop with goat's cheese thyme stoneground grits and wild mushroom woodland sauce) are heart-thumpingly rich; specialties include turtle soup, truffle and wild mushroom stew and roast quail stuffed with andouille and sweet potato. And don't miss the bread pudding soufflé. À la carte is pricey (dinner entrées $25–30), but the prix-fixe menus (lunch from $15) are good value. Jacket required for dinner and Sunday lunch; no shorts, T-shirts, running shoes or jeans at any time. Reservations essential.

Juan's Flying Burrito

Map 3, F7. 2018 Magazine St at St Andrew ☎ 569-0000. Mon–Sat 11am–11pm, Sun noon–10pm. **Inexpensive.**
A funky Tex-Mex joint in the Lower Garden District, with groovy music, local art on the walls and low, low prices. Star dishes include tacos, house special quesadilla and overstuffed burritos – go for jerk chicken or vegetables – loaded with sour cream and guacamole. They also offer

daily specials and happy-hour deals on bottled beers and margaritas (Mon–Fri 4–7pm).

Uglesich's

Map 3, I4. 1238 Baronne St at Erato ☎ 523-8571.

Mon–Fri 10.30am–4pm, plus one Sat per month (call to check). Moderate.

Shabby seafood joint, two blocks from the streetcar in the Lower Garden District. Yugoslavians Gail and Anthony Uglesich ("Yewgle-sitch") draw on Eastern European cuisine to create arguably the best food in the city. Everything is spectacular, from the softshell crabs and crawfish macque choux, or the barbecue oyster stew, to the phenomenal sizzling shrimp Gail. Ask the Uglesichs, or any of their overworked, charming staff, for recommendations, and feast on freshly shucked oysters at the bar while you wait for a seat (which can be a while). No credit cards.

UPTOWN

Brigtsens

Map 2, A2. 723 Dante St at River ☎ 861-7610.

Tues–Sat 5.30–10pm.

Moderate–Expensive.

Elegant restaurant spread across a handful of cozy rooms in an old Riverbend house. The long, handwritten menu of Creole-Cajun dishes changes daily; of the entrées ($15–30) the fish is especially good, be it served in a gumbo or fragrant bisque, blackened, or smothered in creamy sauces; you can't go wrong with roast duck, either, especially with cornbread dressing and honey pecan gravy. Prices are reasonable, especially for the early-evening specials, but can mount up. Reservations advised.

Camellia Grill

Map 2, B2. 626 S Carrollton Ave at St Charles ☎ 866-9573.

Mon–Thurs 9am–1am, Fri & Sat 8am–3am, Sun 8am–1am.

Inexpensive.

Housed in a genteel, columned Riverbend building, where the streetcar line turns inland, this tiny diner has become an institution for burgers, omelettes, fries and grilled sandwiches – lines can be long, especially at weekends, but it's worth the wait. A maître d' seats you on benches until a stool becomes free at the double-horseshoe counter; there, brisk wait staff, in jackets and bow ties, bark your orders to the cooks frying right behind them. The chilli cheese omelette, with potato and onion, packs a punch; round it off with a sticky pecan waffle. No credit cards.

Casamento's

Map 2, I7. 4330 Magazine St at Napoleon ☎ 895-9761.
Mid-Sept to May Tues–Sun 11.30am–1.30pm & 5.30–9pm.
Inexpensive.

Spotless, wonderfully old-fashioned oyster bar – all dazzling white and floral tiles – that's been here since 1919. Other than the unmissable oysters, shucked at the marble bar (for a truly heavenly experience, order a grilled cheese sandwich on the side), good choices include the oyster or trout "loaf", a buttery, overstuffed sandwich made from hunks of white bread. No credit cards.

Dante's Kitchen

Map 2, A2. 736 Dante St at River ☎ 861-3121.
Tues–Sat 11.30am–2.30pm & 6–10pm, Sun 10.30am–2.30pm.
Moderate–Expensive.

Classy New American cuisine in a Riverbend shotgun. Star appetizers include lavender- and herb-rubbed seared Gulf fish with lentils, or duck confit and root vegetable hashcake with baked apple butter. Entrées ($13–22) are just as good, especially the jasmine tea-steamed free-range chicken with brown rice, bok choi and ginger plum dipping sauce. Vegetarians will love the wondergrain hash, made from quinoa, amaranth and a slew of oddly named goodies. Lunch salads and sandwiches are far more ordinary. Reservations advised for dinner.

Dunbar's

Map 2, G4. 4927 Freret St at Upperline Ⓣ 899-0734.
Mon–Sat 7am–9pm.
Inexpensive.
Family-run, absurdly cheap place dishing up spectacular Creole soul food. Gut-busting breakfasts – pork chops, French toast, smoked sausage, grits and biscuits – will keep you going all day; at lunch or dinner, go for red beans and rice (the house specialty) or smothered turkey necks with mustard greens, candied yams and cornbread. Take a cab.

Frankie & Johnny's

Map 2, E8. 321 Arabella St at Tchoupitoulas Ⓣ 899-9146.
Mon–Thurs 11am–10pm, Fri & Sat 11am–midnight, Sun 11am–10.30pm. Inexpensive.
This homey, noisy neighborhood restaurant gets packed at weekends with families and large parties. Food is downhome Cajun-Creole – turtle soup, crawfish pie, gumbo, softshell crabs, fried seafood platters and the like – and their po-boys are consistently voted best in the city.

Jacques Imo's

Map 2, B1. 8324 Oak St at Cambronne Ⓣ 861-0886.
Mon–Thurs 5.30–10pm, Fri & Sat 5.30–10.30pm. Moderate.
Funky, very friendly Riverbend restaurant with a colorful covered patio. The cooking, an inventive Creole-Caribbean take on soul food, is fantastic value, and everything – garlicky fried oysters, chicken livers, buttery blackened redfish, ambrosial alligator cheesecake, smothered rabbit with cornbread dressing, to name but a few – is quite delicious. Sides include macque choux, sweet potatoes, butterbeans with rice and the like – you'll leave feeling stuffed. It's *the* place to eat before a gig at the *Maple Leaf* club (see p.233), but highly recommended at any time.

Nirvana

Map 2, I7. 4308 Magazine St at Napoleon Ⓣ 894-9797.
Tues–Sun 11.30am–2.30pm & 5.30–10.30pm.
Inexpensive–Moderate.
Uptown's prettiest Indian

restaurant serves beautifully prepared, authentic food ranging from Goan dishes, through biryani and tandoori, to creative fusions. Vegetarian choices are good: go for the potato patties topped with curried garbanzo beans, the naurattan curry with vegetables and creamy paneer, or a thali. Entrées start at $11; the lunch buffet is great value at $6.95.

Upperline

Map 2, G6. 1413 Upperline St at Prytania ⊤ 891-9822.
Wed, Thurs & Sun 5.30–9.30pm, Fri & Sat 5.30–10pm.
Expensive.

Lovely, bright restaurant filled with a jumble of local paintings, prints and ceramics. The food, contemporary Creole, is just as attractive, with creative menus often based on a theme. Try the fried green tomatoes rémoulade or gazpacho to start, followed by roast duck with garlic port and sweet potato chips, or grilled Gulf fish with warm salade niçoise and tapenade. If

you've got room, order the twice-baked spinach soufflé on the side – it's fabulous. One of the charms of this place is the friendly atmosphere – even owner JoAnn Clevenger finds time every night to stop and chat with diners.

MID-CITY AND ESPLANADE RIDGE

Christian's

Map 1, D5. 3835 Iberville St at S Scott ⊤ 482-4924.
Tues–Fri 11.30am–2pm & 5.30–9.30pm, Sat 5.30–9.30pm.
Expensive.

In an elegantly restored Lutheran church near City Park – the stained-glass and vaulted ceilings are still intact – this local favorite serves superlative, innovative French-Creole food. Highlights include smoked softshell crab, flash-fried oysters en brochette, saffron bouillabaisse, seafood-stuffed filet steak and trout amandine meunière. It's not cheap – dinner will set you back about $40 – but during their early-evening specials (Tues–Thurs 5.30–6.30pm) you can get four courses for less than $25.

Dooky Chase

Map 1, E5. 2301 Orleans Ave at Miro ☏ 821-0600. Sun–Thurs 11.30am–10pm, Fri & Sat 11.30am–11pm. Moderate–Expensive.

Classy Creole soul food dished up in a cozy dining room favored by movers and shakers in the city's black community. Of the entrées ($10–18), the fried chicken, oyster-stuffed chicken breast, and filé gumbo with seafood and okra are all amazing. Side dishes, in soul-food tradition, are huge; the sweet potatoes are meltingly good. For the best value, go for the four-course special ($28) or the Creole feast ($40). Take a cab.

Gabrielle

Map 1, E5. 3201 Esplanade Ave at Mystery ☏ 948-6233. Oct–May Tues–Thurs & Sat 5.30–10pm, Fri 11.30am–2pm & 5.30–10pm; June–Sept Tues–Sat 5.30–10pm. Expensive.

Chefs Greg and Mary Sonnier serve spectacular contemporary Cajun-Creole cuisine in this tiny triangle of a restaurant near City Park. Traditional-sounding dishes all come with a creative spin: go for lobster and corn bisque, barbecue shrimp pie, cracker-crusted rabbit with black-eyed peas, greens and corn bread, or whole salt-baked flounder with roasted garlic and lemon basil butter, and make sure to leave room for the stunning homemade desserts.

Lola's

Map 1, E5. 3312 Esplanade Ave at Mystery ☏ 488-6946. Mon–Thurs 6–10pm, Fri & Sat 11.30am–2.30pm & 6–10.30pm, Sun 11.30am–2.30pm & 6–10pm. Inexpensive.

Funky little Spanish place that has become a firm local favorite for mouthwatering, cheap and authentic food. To start, choose from lentil or garlic soup, gazpacho, or lip-licking grilled shrimp, perhaps following with grilled rack of lamb or pork loin. Star attractions, however, are the paellas, cooked to order in the open kitchen, served in a cast-iron skillet and packed with seafood, meat or vegetables, or a combination of the three. Be sure to order the fresh bread, which comes warm, with garlic-packed butter. No reservations, so you may have to wait, and no credit cards. BYOB.

COFFEEHOUSES

European-influenced New Orleans has always been *the* American city for **coffee**. Fresh, strong and aromatic, it's been a big part of life here since long before upstart Seattle laid claim to the notion, and today locals drink twice the national average.

Most of the coffeehouses listed below serve inexpensive snacks and pastries, too, and many will rustle up breakfasts and light lunches.

The city's fondness for smoky **chicory** coffee – which for many visitors takes some getting used to – dates back to the early European colonists, who had learned to stretch out their precious coffee supplies back home by adding the ground root of the endive plant. This money-saving ruse became particularly popular in New Orleans during the impoverished days of the Civil War – when the entire city developed a taste for the stuff – and has endured ever since.

Café du Monde
Map 4, G6. 800 Decatur St at St Ann ☎ 581-2914.
Daily 24hr.
Despite the hype, the crowds and the sugar-sticky tabletops, this is an undeniably atmospheric place to drink steaming café au lait, imbued with chicory, and snack on piping hot, sugary *beignets* for a couple of dollars – apart from orange juice and hot chocolate, they serve little else. Come early, when it's quiet, or late at night when

you can gaze at the starry sky from the covered patio.

CCs Community Coffeehouse

Map 4, I4. 941 Royal St at St Philip ⓣ 581-6996.
Mon–Thurs 6.30am–11pm, Fri & Sat 6.30am–midnight, Sun 7.30am–10pm. Other branches all around town.
Locals linger for hours at the counter or in the plump leather armchairs, chatting, reading or people-watching out of the open French windows. The brews are good and strong – try the Mochassippi, a creamy iced espresso with a choice of flavors. Also quiches, pastries and muffins, and teas. The other French Quarter branch, at 528 St Peter St on Jackson Square, is cramped and rather subdued in comparison (Mon–Thurs 8am–7pm, Fri–Sun 8am–8pm). No smoking.

Cuccia Chocolate Café

Map 4, E4. 622 Royal St at Toulouse ⓣ 1-800/25-CUCCIA.
Mon–Thurs & Sun 9am–8.30pm, Fri & Sat 9am–11pm.

The espresso and specialty drinks are as good as you'll find anywhere, but it's the delicious handmade chocolates that really set this French Quarter coffee shop apart from the crowd. The open on-site kitchen produces a range of delicacies from tiny, exquisite truffles to chocolate-dipped strawberries – just the thing to go with a strong espresso.

Flora Café

Map 1, G6. 2600 Royal St at Franklin ⓣ 947-3866.
Daily 6.30am–10pm.
Grungy-cool coffee bar/gallery in deepest Faubourg Marigny. The decor is funky, the crowd is bohemian and the coffee is good. Regular poetry slams and an open-mic night on Monday (9–11pm).

La Marquise

Map 4, E5. 625 Chartres St at Wilkinson Row ⓣ 524-0420.
Mon–Thurs 7am–7pm, Fri–Sun 7am–8pm.
Though the coffee isn't the best in town, this

COFFEEHOUSES

neighborhood patisserie, sister shop to the *Croissant d'Or* (see p.179), is worth a stop for its delectable French pastries, croissants and quiches. The friendly staff and local clientele make it a pleasant place to linger, either in the cozy interior or in the shady courtyard.

New Orleans Net Café
Map 3, K5. 900 Camp St at St Joseph ⊤ 523-0990.
Mon & Tues 9am–5pm, Wed–Sat 9am–10pm, Sun 11am–5pm.
The best thing about this café, linked to the city's premier contemporary art gallery (see p.87), is that internet access is free – and they serve espresso, tea, wine, sandwiches and pastries to boot.

PJs Coffee and Tea
Map 4, N4. 634 Frenchmen St at Royal ⊤ 949-2292.
Mon–Fri 7am–midnight, Sat & Sun 8am–midnight. Other branches all around town.
There's nothing special about the decor at this much loved

local chain, but it's a favorite for its expertly made coffee, muffins, bagels and gourmet sandwiches. The iced coffee is the best in town. Other locations include a Garden District branch at 2727 Prytania (in the Rink mall) and another at 3000 Magazine St.

Royal Blend
Map 4, E4. 621 Royal St at St Peter ⊤ 523-2716.
Mon–Fri 6.30am–10.30pm, Sat & Sun 6.30am–midnight.
Convenient French Quarter coffeehouse hidden behind a pretty courtyard dotted with fountains and statuary. In addition to coffees, espressos and herbal teas, they offer a limited menu – at $6, the gumbo with half a sandwich makes a good, cheap lunch.

Rue de la Course
Map 2, L6. 3128 Magazine St at Ninth ⊤ 899-0242.
Mon–Fri 7am–midnight, Sat & Sun 7.30am–midnight
With their pressed-tin walls, café-au-lait decor, ceiling fans and reading lamps, the *Rue*

coffee shops have an old-Europe ambience. Liveliest of the lot, this Garden District branch is usually teeming with students poring over fat textbooks or playing Scrabble. The coffee, brewed with beans from around the world, is great – for a real indulgence, try the caffe crema and there are plenty of biscotti, cakes and bagels. Other locations include 219 N Peters St in the Quarter (☎523-0206; Mon–Thurs & Sun 7am–11pm, Fri & Sat 7am–midnight) and 1500 Magazine St in the Lower Garden District (☎529-1455).

True Brew
Map 3, L6. 200 Julia St at Fulton ☎524-8441.
Mon–Fri 6.30am–9pm, Sat & Sun 8am–9pm (later during performances).
Comfortable Warehouse District coffeehouse-cum-theater (see p.239) that serves good espresso, plus healthy sandwiches, soups, salads and quiches in a relaxed atmosphere.

DELIS, FOOD STORES AND MARKETS

A&P
Map 4, F4. 701 Royal St at St Peter ☎523-1353.
Daily 24hr.
The smallest A&P in the world is the largest supermarket in the Quarter. Its central location keeps it bustling: you'll rub shoulders with horn players and living statues, tourists and bus boys all "making groceries", as food shopping is known in these parts.

All Natural Foods and Deli
Map 2, F7. 5517 Magazine St at Octavia ☎891-2651.
Mon–Thurs 10am–7pm, Fri & Sat 10am–6pm, Sun 10am–5pm.
Uptown health-food grocery, with a deli counter serving chunky black-bean samosas, vegetarian tamales, overstuffed sandwiches, falafel, miso broth and smoothies, all at low prices.

DELIS, FOOD STORES AND MARKETS

In good weather eat at benches on the sidewalk or in a small patio.

Central Grocery

Map 4, H5. 923 Decatur St at Dumaine ⊤ 523-1620.
Mon–Sat 8am–5.30pm, Sun 9am–5.30pm.
Famed for its muffulettas (half for $5, whole for $9), this fragrant old Italian deli, open since 1906, offers a range of good picnic staples, with giant cheeses and salamis hanging from the ceiling and big tubs of olives marinating in herby oils. Most people take out, but there is some counter seating. No credit cards.

Crescent City Farmers Market

Map 3, L5. 700 Magazine St ⊤ 861-5898.
Sat 8am–noon.
Neighborhood market in the Warehouse District, with stalls selling fresh herbs, flowers, breads, cheese and organic wines. They also have live music and celebrity chef demonstrations.

Martin Wine Cellar

Map 2, I5. 3827 Baronne St at Napoleon ⊤ 896-7380.
Mon–Sat 9am–7pm, Sun 10am–2pm.
Gourmet uptown wine shop/deli offering wine tastings, cooking demonstrations, free samples and superior po-boys and hot plates.

Progress Grocery

Map 4, H5. 915 Decatur St at Dumaine ⊤ 525-6627.
Daily 9am–5.30pm.
Old Italian deli, much like the nearby Central Grocery, but cheaper (half a muffuletta $4, whole $7) and less crowded. They also serve a small menu of plate lunches – red beans and rice, barbecue ham, and the like – and gumbos.

Verti Marte

Map 4, J4. 1201 Royal St at Gov Nicholls ⊤ 525-4767.
Daily 24hr.
French Quarter corner grocery with an astonishingly good 24-hour hot-food take-out counter: pick up mountains of baked chicken,

fried oysters, barbecue ribs, stuffed eggplant, macaroni, dirty rice and gumbo for ridiculously low prices. Perfect after a night out on the town. Free delivery in the Quarter and Faubourg.

Vieux Carré Wine Shop
Map 4, D5. 422 Chartres St at St Louis ☏ 568-9463.
Mon–Sat 10am–10pm, Sun 10am–7pm.
Huge range of wines, bottled beers and spirits – a few of them somewhat obscure – from around the world. With its TV and chairs, it's

something of a meeting place for local *bons vivants*.

Whole Foods Market
Map 1, E5. 3135 Esplanade Ave at Ponce de Leon ☏ 943-1626.
Daily 8.30am–9.30pm.
Mid-City health-food grocery, with a good, though not all that cheap, deli counter serving smoothies, salads and sandwiches. Hot food includes chunky vegetable soups, lasagne, baked eggplant, and grilled chicken, which you can eat on benches outside.

DELIS, FOOD STORES AND MARKETS

Drinking

As befits its image as a hard-drinking, hard-partying town, New Orleans has dozens of truly great **bars**. Locals love to drink, and tourists, it seems, even more so, and there are more than enough places to cater for all of them. Gratifyingly, too, in this city of neighborhoods, many establishments are within walking distance of each other, making bar-hopping all the easier. It can be difficult to separate the drinking scene from the **live-music scene** – most bars feature music, at least one night of the week, and many places now known best as live-music venues started their days as humble taverns. Many establishments listed in this chapter feature live music, but are not best known for it – see the "Live Music" chapter, p.218, for music venues that double as great places to drink.

If you've run out of cash and there's no ATM in sight, there's a very good chance of finding one in the nearest bar – designed, of course, to get you to spend as much money as possible on drink.

Despite the popular misconception, there's more to drinking in New Orleans than the French Quarter, and there's far more to drinking in the French Quarter than

Bourbon Street. A boozy enclave of beer stalls, karaoke clubs, strip joints and daiquiri bars – and even the odd jazz venue – Bourbon is usually heaving by nightfall, along with many of its guests, leaving plenty of room in a host of great bars elsewhere in the Quarter. That said, it's a pretty unusual first-time visitor who doesn't spend at least an hour or so on Bourbon Street, stumbling through the hollering crowds with a lurid cocktail to go – perhaps in a pink plastic goblet molded into the form of a nubile woman, or a neon-green alien-shaped beaker – before dipping out again to find more atmospheric haunts nearby. The bedlam of dance music and shrieking revelers at the gay clubs *Oz* (see p.267) and *Parade* (see p.266), on the 800 block, where Bourbon meets St Ann, heralds the **gay** stretch of Bourbon Street. Beyond here, the further you head toward Esplanade Avenue, the quieter and more residential the street becomes. Once you've crossed Esplanade you're in the **Faubourg Marigny**, where Frenchmen Street features a handful of bars and music venues that attract a stylish, arty and youthful crowd.

Bars in the **CBD** and **Warehouse District** tend to be after-work drinking holes – not bad for a quick beer, but little competition for the atmospheric places **uptown**, many of which are accessible from the streetcar line along St Charles Avenue.

While many tourists come to New Orleans intending to drink the place dry of **cocktails**, the city also offers some interesting **beers**. Abita is the local brew, with varieties including the caramelly Amber, raspberry-flavored Purple Haze, and the seasonal Christmas Ale. *The Acadian Beer Garden*, based in Mid-City at 201 N Carrollton Ave, also brews its own pilsner, which is served all over town.

DRINKING

- -

For gay and lesbian bars, most of
which welcome straights, see p.266.

- -

ROUGH GUIDES FAVORITES: BARS

Though **24-hour drinking licenses** are common, don't expect every bar to be open all night – even on Bourbon Street many places close whenever they empty, which can be surprisingly early during slow periods. Uniquely in the United States, it's legal to drink on the streets, though not from a glass or bottle – simply ask for a plastic "**to go**" cup in any bar and carry it with you. You'll be expected to finish your drink before entering another bar, however. The **legal drinking age** is 21; it's best to carry photo ID, though few bartenders bother asking for it.

THE FRENCH QUARTER

Bombay Club

Map 4, C3. 830 Conti St at Dauphine ☎ 586-0972.

La-di-da martini bar, a favorite with power brokers and peachy-skinned belles. The atmosphere evokes an English gentlemen's club, with paintings of Winston Churchill and sleek thoroughbreds on the wall, plump leather chairs, and lots of dark wood. A pianist plays Wed–Sat, when food is served till 1.30am.

Carousel Bar

Map 4, B4. *Hotel Monteleone*, 214 Royal St at Iberville ☎ 523-3341.

Gimmicky hotel bar, favored by a high-spirited conventioneer and tourist crowd. The central bar is kitted out like a fairground carousel, with the stools set on a revolving floor; it takes fifteen minutes to do one full rotation. Drinks are a little pricey, but you get free snacks, and it's a fun stop on a bar crawl. If you're feeling dizzy you can settle at stationary booths illuminated by a trompe l'oeil starlit sky, but that's missing the point somewhat.

The Dungeon

Map 4, E4. 738 Toulouse St at Bourbon ⊕ 523-5530.

Hidden away down a spooky side-alley, this Stygian hideout is said to appeal to visiting rock stars, who enjoy anonymity in the web of nooks and crannies lit only by the dimmest red lightbulbs. It features good specials, such as 3-for-1 mixed drinks on Fridays from 1am to 4am, and occasional Goth and fetish nights. Open Tues–Sun from midnight; $3 cover on weekends.

Fahy's

Map 4, E2. 540 Burgundy St at Toulouse ⊕ 586-9806.

The friendliest of the French Quarter's handful of Irish bars, with a loyal local clientele – many of them service industry workers unwinding after a long hard night – and not a tourist to be seen.

Keuffer's Bar

Map 4, E5. 540 Chartres St at Toulouse ⊕ 523-8705.

Though it's smack bang in the heart of the Quarter, this unpretentious neighborhood bar, another favorite of local service industry workers, lacks any New Orleans atmosphere, which, perversely, is part of its charm. A good place to stop off for a couple of quiet beers and a game of pool or table tennis.

Lafitte's Blacksmith Shop

Map 4, I3. 941 Bourbon St at St Philip ⊕ 523-0066.

Dim, ancient bar frequented by artists, writers (how they see by the candlelight remains a mystery) and a few stray tourists. One of the oldest buildings in the Quarter, bought by notorious pirate Jean Lafitte in 1809 (see p.57), it's a tumbledown shack with beamed ceilings

THE FRENCH QUARTER

and a blackened brick fireplace (where Lafitte's treasure is said to be stashed). At night, a gloriously cheesy piano player pounds out cocktail-lounge standards to a gaggle of drunken reprobates – there's a patio for those who want a quieter time.

Molly's at the Market

Map 4, J5. 1107 Decatur St at Ursulines ⓣ 525-5169.

Once famed for being a genuine local Irish bar, haunt of politicos and media stars, *Molly's* now pulls in a happy mix of locals, rowdy tourists, service industry workers and grungy street punks. It's a very New Orleans kind of place, stubbornly remaining open during hurricane alerts, and organizing street parades for Mardi Gras, St Patrick's Day and Halloween. There's good Guinness on tap, filling burgers from Dana's patio kitchen around the back (daily 3pm–1am) and a photo booth in the corner.

Napoleon House

Map 4, D5. 500 Chartres St at St Louis ⓣ 524-9752.

Exuding a classic, relaxed New Orleans elegance, the *Napoleon House* is quite simply one of the best bars in the United States. The venerable building was once the home of Mayor Girod, who schemed with Jean Lafitte to rescue Napoleon from exile (see p.43); the shadowy interior is romantic in the extreme, its crumbling walls lined with ancient-looking oil paintings and the old, well-stocked wooden bar dominated by a marble bust of the frowning emperor. The customers, an interesting mix of tourists and regulars, dally for hours, either indoors, where chatter mingles with classical music on the CD player, or in the gorgeous courtyard, fringed with lush plants. The bar food (see p.185) and restaurant (see p.181) are superb, too. Closes 7pm on Sunday.

Pat O'Brien's

Map 4, F4. 718 St Peter St at Bourbon ⓣ 525-4823.

One of the most famous bars in New Orleans, spilling over

COCKTAILS

It is said that the cocktail was invented in New Orleans in the 1790s. Operating from 437 Royal St, Haitian pharmacist Antoine Peychaud served medicinal tonics of brandy and bitters in little china egg-cups called coquetiers, which Anglo-Americans translated as "cocktails". Since then, several potent concoctions have been dreamed up in New Orleans, many of them the signature drinks of the city's classier establishments.

Hurricane The number one choice for gonna-drink-till-we're-sick out-of-towners; a headache-inducing concoction – made with sugar, fruit juice and rums – which many bars refuse to serve. It's traditionally drunk, in reckless quantities, by the tourists at *Pat O'Brien's* (see opposite), but in fact *Lafitte's* (see p.209) shakes up a better one. Anyone with a death-wish can buy chemical-laced Hurricane mixes in plastic packs from the tourist stores.

Pimm's Cup The specialty of the *Napoleon House* (see opposite), served simply in a long cool glass with a slice of cucumber.

Ramos Gin Fizz A frothy swirl of gin, lemon juice, milk, egg-white, powdered sugar and orange-flower water, invented by barman Harry Ramos around 1900. It was later perfected at the *Sazerac Bar* in the swanky *Roosevelt Hotel*, now the *Fairmont* (see p.214) – still the best place to order one.

Sazerac Another drink associated with the *Roosevelt* and its *Sazerac Bar*: a caramel-colored mix of rye whiskey, bitters, lemon, and ice, stirred together in a glass rinsed out with aniseed liqueur.

COCKTAILS

with drunken tourists and bellowing frat packs, most of them guzzling the requisite Hurricane cocktail (see p.211), served in 29oz hurricane-lamp glasses ($2 deposit). As well as the main bar, there's a large patio and a raucous "dueling" piano bar, where players compete to play loudest. If you love Bourbon Street you'll want to make a beeline for *Pat's*; if you don't, keep well away.

Port of Call

Map 4, L3. 838 Esplanade Ave at Dauphine ☎ 523-0120.
Though best known for its fantastic fresh burgers (see p.186), *Port of Call* is also an unpretentious drinking hole haunted by a noisy mix of Quarterites, Faubourg denizens and in-the-know tourists who put the world to rights around the large wooden bar or at small tables. A scattering of grubby nautical accoutrements is the only concession to style – this place is the archetype of a guileless, classic American bar, and all the more loved for it.

FAUBOURG MARIGNY AND BYWATER

Apple Barrel

Map 4, M5. 609 Frenchmen St at Chartres ☎ 949-9399.
Tiny place beneath *Adolfo's* restaurant (see p.189). Its cozy, pub-like atmosphere (there's even a darts board, though the darts went astray years ago) seems a little out of place on this supercool stretch, but it holds its own with a core group of laid-back regulars and drop-ins from the Frenchmen Street bar-hop circuit.

Checkpoint Charlie's

Map 4, L5. 501 Esplanade Ave at Decatur ☎ 947-0979.
Boozy, dingy laundromat/bar, which hosts unknown grunge rock bands and serves sandwiches and burgers until late. The young, grumpy-looking crowd makes more use of the pool tables, slot and pinball machines than the incongruous lending library or coin-operated washing machines.

dba

Map 4, M5. 618 Frenchmen St at Chartres ⊤ 942-3731.
Housed in an old theater, with picture windows and high ceilings, this dimly lit bar sashayed into town in 2000 flashing its big-city credentials (the original *dba* opened in New York in 1994) and a choice of beers that leaves most local bars reeling. It's a bit slick – not very New Orleans – but the drinks are good, if pricey, with more than twenty draught premium beers, classy cocktails and a range of spirits. Happy hour daily 5–8.30pm.

R-Bar

Map 4, M4. 1431 Royal St at Kerlerec ⊤ 948-7499.
The quirky, thrift-store decor at this attitude-free bar – Buddhist prayer flags, peeling bordello mirrors on the red walls, 1970s armchairs and the like – gives it an edge, making it popular with a convivial twentysomething set that includes visitors staying at the guesthouse upstairs (see p.164). The pool table is played by some of the coolest sharks in town.

Saturn Bar

Map 1, G6. 3067 St Claude Ave at Clouet, in the Bywater ⊤ 949-7532.
Atmospheric, junk-filled neighborhood dive (it's an electrical repair shop by day), with a funky New Orleans cachet. The easy-going regulars – artists, intellectuals and off-duty service industry workers – are often joined by hip out-of-town celebrities (Nicolas Cage, Sam Shepard and the like). Go late, and take a cab there and back.

TREMÉ

Ernie K-Doe's Mother-in-Law Lounge

Map 1, F6. 1500 N Claiborne Ave at Columbus ⊤ 947-1078.
Despite the untimely death of eccentric R&B veteran Ernie – who, along with his wife Antoinette, simply fixed up his home with a bar and a few chairs, opened it to the public and called it a lounge – the Mother-in-Law Lounge

TREMÉ

has, for now at least, remained open. Sporadic music performances are not quite the same without the strutting, self-styled "Emperor of the World" himself, but as a memorial to a great man this remains an experience not to be missed. Take a cab there and back.

THE CBD AND WAREHOUSE DISTRICT

Ernst Café

Map 3, M5. 600 S Peters St at Lafayette ⓣ 525-8544.
No-frills blue-collar joint – said to be a favorite of honorary New Orleanian John Goodman – with pressed-tin walls and a fine old wooden bar. Quiet during the day, it fills in the evening with an older, mellower set of regulars than you'll find in the other CBD after-work haunts. You can soak up the beer with blue-plate specials, gumbo and po-boys, served in the bar or in a small dining room.

Happy hour with free snacks every Friday 4–7pm.

Lucy's Retired Surfers' Bar

Map 3, L5. 701 Tchoupitoulas St at Girod ⓣ 523-8995.
Something of a twenty- and early thirtysomethings pick-up joint, this gimmicky Warehouse District bar is packed after office hours with a white-collar clientele. In an attempt to evoke a West Coast scene, the walls are lined with surfboards, beach movies flicker on the TVs and chirpy bar staff dole out garish, frosted cocktails. They also serve decent Tex-Mex food.

Sazerac Bar

Map 3, N3. *Fairmont Hotel*, 123 Baronne St at Canal ⓣ 529-4733.
Swanky, historic Art Deco bar in the grand old hotel that was, until 1965, the *Roosevelt*. Serving champagne, fine wines, tip-top cocktails and desirable desserts, it attracts a well-dressed uptown and business traveler clientele – a very different scene from

the shabby French Quarter bars, but just as much part of the New Orleans landscape. It's the best place in town to sip their signature cocktails (see p.211). Closed Sunday & Monday.

Top of the Mart

Map 3, N6. World Trade Center, Canal St at the river ℡ 522-9795.

Deliciously tacky cocktail bar, high in the sky on the 33rd story of the World Trade Center. Though you pay through the nose for a drink, the ambience is appealingly kitsch, stuck somewhere in the 1960s with its tired red and gilt decor, chandeliers and bored waitresses. Mostly, however, you come here for the unbeatable views: one ninety-minute revolution spans the startling bend in the river across to the west bank, the tiny, congested grid of the French Quarter, the drab roofs of the CBD towers, and the poker-straight channel of Canal Street.

LOWER GARDEN DISTRICT AND GARDEN DISTRICT

Audubon Hotel

Map 3, I5. 1225 St Charles Ave at Erato ℡ 568-1319.

Not for the faint-hearted, this Lower Garden District flophouse-cum-techno-rave venue attracts a wild, half-crazed band of lost souls – from tortured teens to down-and-outs – knocking back cocktails as if their lives depended upon it.

The Bulldog

Map 3, B5. 3236 Magazine St at Toledano ℡ 891-1516.

Laid-back bar with a thirtysomething after-work crowd and lively, local scene at night. The main appeal is the wide range of beers – some fifty on tap and more than 200 in bottles – from around the world. Video trivia games are hugely popular, as are the occasional acoustic music sets, and in warm weather the benches out on the street are filled until the wee hours.

Parasol's

Map 3, D6. 2533 Constance St at Third ⓣ 897-5413.

Anyone in town on or around St Patrick's Day should make a beeline for this Irish Channel bar – their street parade is a blast, awash with green beer, green beads and green-haired revelers (see p.281). The rest of the year, it's a welcoming neighborhood bar, with good roast beef po-boys, boudin sandwiches and sport on the TV. Take a cab there and back.

UPTOWN

Bayou Bar

Map 3, G5. *Pontchartrain Hotel*, 2031 St Charles Ave at Josephine ⓣ 524-0581.

Though the bar, like the hotel, has seen better days, the ambience is very uptown, all exposed brick, glossy dark wood, and canvas murals of Louisiana wildlife. Popular with a cocktail-sipping set, it's one of the city's landmark bars, and probably more interesting for who has drunk there than anything else. Past denizens include Tennessee Williams and the Rat Pack; more recently it's said to have been a favorite of local author Anne Rice, who has used it as a location in a number of her novels.

Carrollton Station

Map 2, C1. 8140 Willow St at Dublin ⓣ 865-9190.

Welcoming, laid-back neighborhood bar opposite the streetcar barn, near *Jimmy's* and the *Maple Leaf* (see pp.233 & 234). Lots of good beers on draft, plus darts, and live rock, folk and funk Thurs–Sun, when there may be a small cover charge.

Columns Hotel

Map 2, J6. 3811 St Charles Ave at General Taylor ⓣ 899-9308.

Gorgeous, atmospheric hotel (see p.168) on the edge of the Garden District, with a louche old bar, richly decorated in dark wood and faded velvet. You can drink in a number of rooms, all of which exhude faded grandeur with their chandeliers, baroque mirrors and vases of plump pink roses; on warm evenings, customers make for the columned veranda, which overlooks the St Charles streetcar line. Occasional live Latin, jazz and piano.

F&M Patio Bar
Map 2, H8. 4841 Tchoupitoulas St at Lyons ☏895-6784.

A favorite on the post-*Tipitina's* (see p.233) circuit since the 1960s, this friendly, drunken, local hangout has it all – pool tables, a patio, great jukebox and cholesterol-packed snacks served until late. Traditionally it's *de rigueur* to guzzle Bloody Marys and dance on the pool table, but no one will mind if you don't.

Ms Mae's
Map 2, I7. 4336 Magazine St at Napoleon ☏895-9401.

Another post-*Tipitina's* haunt, open 24hr, which attracts a mixed crowd of serious-drinking locals and students. The atmosphere is less frenetic than at *F&M*, and the pool table sees more cue balls than pratfalls, but it's still very lively, especially at weekends.

Snake and Jake's Christmas Club Lounge
Map 2, C2. 7612 Oak St at Hillary ☏861-2802.

Distinctive drinking hole in a tumbledown shack with perennial Yuletide decorations fading in the gloom. Nothing much happens before 2am, when it fills up with a jubilant local crowd of musicians, journalists and students. The jukebox is superb, with a playlist of New Orleans music, classic soul and R&B.

UPTOWN

Live music

New Orleans is quite simply one of the best places in the world to hear **live music**. From lonesome street musicians, through the shambling, joyous brass bands, to international names like Dr John and the Neville Brothers, music remains integral to the Crescent City, the thread that stitches the whole place together. At any time of year – especially during the festivals – the sheer quantity, variety and quality of what's on offer is staggering.

For a history of New Orleans' music, with a discography of essential CDs, see p.322.

While the French Quarter has its share of atmospheric clubs and bars, there are plenty of good venues elsewhere. To decide **where to go**, check the listings papers *Offbeat* or *Gambit* (see p.10), and keep an ear cocked to local radio station WWOZ (90.7FM; see p.11), which announces local events and offers ticket competitions. You could also take potluck: most clubs have an eclectic booking policy, but as a general rule you can be pretty sure of seeing **brass bands** at *Donna's*, sophisticated **modern jazz** at *Snug Harbor* and *Sweet Lorraine's*, **trad jazz** at the *Palm Court* and *Preservation Hall*, **blues** and **R&B** at the *Maple Leaf* and a **mixed bag** at *Funky Butt*, *Kermit's*, *Rock'n'Bowl* and *Tipitina's*.

ROUGH GUIDES FAVORITES: MUSIC VENUES

Visitors making a beeline for **Bourbon Street**, hoping to find it crammed with cool, smoky jazz clubs, will be disappointed by the string of 3-for-1 cocktail stands, drab strip joints and karaoke bars. That said, even this tawdriest of streets has a couple of good places to hear jazz and blues, and at any time of day you may well stumble upon superb musicians – Guitar Slim Jr, Eddie Bo, Rockin' Dopsie Jr – playing happy-hour sets in even the dingiest alcohol-soaked dives.

As for timing your night out: with **24-hour drinking licenses** common (see p.208), the music often doesn't get going until around midnight, even if the show is listed as starting at 10pm. A number of places put on **two sets** a night, often by different performers, so with a little creative club-hopping you could easily see three outstanding gigs in one evening. Bear in mind also that **club hours** are always open to change, especially during Mardi Gras and Jazz Fest, when many places get started early and stay open for all-night jams.

Many musicians, especially those in the brass bands, get the bulk of their income from playing for tips. When in a club, or when watching street bands, always have a dollar or so ready for when the bucket is passed around.

Another distinctive feature of New Orleans' nightlife is that many shows can be seen – and heard – from the street. Perhaps it's something to do with the climate – faced with a room of hot, dancing, drinking people on a warm evening there's little to do but fling doors and windows open wide. If you hear something you like, but don't want to pay the **cover charge** – low or nonexistent in bars, but as much as $15 in some clubs – it's perfectly acceptable to stand outside with a "to go" cup (see p.208), drifting on when the fancy takes you.

Oddly, for a city so defined by its music, it can be difficult to predict how big a **crowd** will turn up to a gig. New Orleans is a small place, with a lot of clubs, and occasionally, especially during slow times, you may find yourself in the extraordinary position of sitting with just two or three others, listening to a local legend who sold the place out the night before.

JAZZ

Jazz in New Orleans remains an evolving art form, and you're spoiled for choice for places to hear it. Local, world-class musicians, including the multitalented **Marsalis** family, **trumpeters** Terence Blanchard, Irvin Mayfield and Nicholas Payton, and **scat** singer Charmaine Neville (of *the* Nevilles) all play regularly. Of the **pianists**, don't miss Henry Butler – whose superb, superfast modern jazz is matched by his mean R&B and blues repertoire – or Davell Crawford, who infuses traditional New Orleans piano with heartfelt gospel. On a Monday night, you may be lucky enough to catch one or more of the above at *Donna's*, when Bob French and his Original Tuxedo Jazz Band showcase the cream of the city's talent.

Although **brass bands** have been integral to New Orleans' street music and parade culture since the nineteenth century, their resurgence in the 1980s and 1990s led to an explosion of energy on the local jazz scene. Ragtag groups of musicians, many of them from Tremé, the brass bands blast out a joyful, improvised and eminently danceable sound, a kind of homegrown party music that goes down as well in the student bars as in the Second Line parades. Favorites include the **ReBirth**, whose ear-splitting spin on old and original tunes has won them a massive following, the more traditional **Tremé** and **Olympia** bands, and the **Soul Rebels** and **Coolbone**, who mix a cacophony of horns with hard funk, hip-hop and reggae. Traditionally, many of the younger band-members go on to become beloved performers in their own right – one of the city's favorite trumpeters, **Kermit Ruffins**, cut his teeth with the ReBirth.

On any given week you'll find a handful of brass bands in the music listings, but it's even more fun to catch them at neighborhood bars, parades and festivals in **Tremé**, when they really let rip. These are some of the hardest-working musicians in town: don't be surprised to find that the bunch of horn-blasting buskers attracting crowds in Jackson Square is made up of the phenomenal musicians you paid $10 to see at a club the night before.

For details of Dixieland jazz cruises along the Mississippi, see p.106.

Incidentally, when looking for a jazz gig, don't overlook the **"other" live music venues** reviewed in the section of this chapter that starts on p.226. It's always worth checking the line-up at *Le Bon Temps Roulé*, uptown (p.232), *Café Brasil*, in the Faubourg (p.232), *Red Room*, in the Garden District (p.232), and *Shim-Sham* (p.229) and *El Matador* (see p.228) in the Quarter.

THE FRENCH QUARTER

Donna's

Map 4, G1. 800 N Rampart St at St Ann ⊤ 596-6914.

Mon & Thurs–Sun from 6.30pm.

Run by the formidable Donna and husband Charlie, *Donna's* feels like a locals' place – there's no stage, and you have to fight your way

JAZZ RESOURCES

Jazz enthusiasts should make sure to visit the New Orleans Jazz National Historical Park Visitor Center and the Old US Mint/Jazz Museum (both on p.39). And for anyone seriously interested in the history of America's indigenous art form, there are two good libraries open to the public: the William Ransom Hogan Jazz Archive, Tulane University (☎ 865-5688, ⓦ www.tulane.edu/~lmiller/jazzhome.html), which is a superb repository for New Orleans jazz research, and the Williams Research Center, 410 Chartres St (Tues–Sat 10am–4.30pm; ☎ 598-7171, ⓦ www.hnoc.org), which includes the Bill Russell collection of jazz artifacts, documents and recordings.

through the blasting horns to get to the bathroom – but it attracts a big out-of-town crowd. With a roster of brass band and trad jazz acts it's a must-see, especially during Jazz Fest and Mardi Gras, and on Monday night it's the *only* place to be. That's when old-timer Bob French runs the show, drumming with a who's who of local stars who pop in after their own gigs to check out the scene. These are some of the finest jam sessions – jazz, spirituals, R&B, blues – you're likely to hear, in a wonderful old-style jazz house party atmosphere. Charlie cooks up tasty food, too –

ribs, chicken, red beans and rice – at low prices. Cover $5.

Funky Butt

Map 4, G1. 714 N Rampart St at Orleans ☎ 558-0872.
Daily 9pm–3am.

Stylish, intimate and atmospheric club named for an early haunt of jazz legend Buddy Bolden. The eclectic decor resembles an Art Deco bordello-cum-speakeasy-cum-Seventies pad, while the music – mostly contemporary jazz and R&B – is exceptional. On a good night many people drift back and forth between here and *Donna's* (see above). Poetry slams on some nights. Cover varies, rising to $15, but you can drink in the bar for free.

Palm Court Jazz Café

Map 4, J5. 1204 Decatur St at Gov Nicholls ☎ 525-0200.

Wed–Sun 7–11pm.

The jazz aficionado's favorite: top-notch trad jazz played in elegant supper-club surroundings. New Orleans jazz memorabilia adds atmosphere, and they also sell collector's items and records. Reservations are recommended for dinner; shows start at 8pm. Cover varies, but a seat at the bar costs nothing.

Preservation Hall

Map 4, F4. 726 St Peter St at Bourbon ☎ 523-8939.

Daily from 8.30pm.

Unbelievably shabby room – with no bar, air-conditioning or toilets, and just a handful of benches – long lauded as the best place to hear trad jazz in New Orleans. Though the building is as old as it looks, the hall itself opened in the 1960s, since when it has changed little. The dereliction is a bit hokey, but the music, played by old pros, is outstanding. The Hall is always bursting at the seams with tourists, and lines form well before doors open; sets, each about 45min with 15min gaps, run 8.30–11.45pm. The $5 cover allows you to stay as long as you like, and people move out steadily, so you're bound to get a seat in the end.

Storyville District

Map 4, A3. 125 Bourbon St at Iberville ☎ 410-1000.

Daily 5pm–1am; food served 5pm–11pm, plus Sun brunch 10am–2.30pm.

Swish entertainment complex, with bars, dining areas (it's part-owned by Ralph Brennan of the city's famous restaurant clan) and two stages featuring live music, from ragtime through big bands to modern jazz.

Call a cab (see p.13) to get to and from any of the music venues outside the French Quarter or Faubourg.

JAZZ: THE FRENCH QUARTER

Geared toward tourists, it's all a bit sanitized, with superb acts playing their hearts out to provide background music for the chattering crowd. Low or nonexistent cover charge.

Sweet Kathleen's

Map 4, C6. 311 N Peters St at Bienville ⓣ 568-0080.
Daily 5.30pm–1am.

Though the beers are pricey and the food no great shakes at this long, narrow, vaguely saloon-themed bar, the lively Dixieland music is faultless, played to an appreciative crowd of high-spirited tourists. The jukebox is a jazz enthusiast's dream.

FAUBOURG MARIGNY AND BYWATER

Snug Harbor

Map 4, N5. 626 Frenchmen St at Royal ⓣ 949-0696.
Daily 5pm–2am.

Sophisticated Faubourg jazz club in a small, two-story space packed tight with tables and chairs. Regulars include Astral Project, who play cool modern jazz, drum maestro Johnny Vidacovich, Charmaine Neville and pianist Ellis Marsalis. The restaurant, which serves Creole standards, closes at 11pm (midnight at weekends), but the bar, from where you can hear the gigs – and watch them, on the tiny closed-circuit TV– stays open late. Shows at 9pm and 11pm; cover $8–25.

Tin Roof Café

Map 4, M5. 532 Frenchmen St at Decatur ⓣ 948-3100.
Sun & Tues 9pm–1am, Wed & Thurs 9.30pm–1am, Fri & Sat 10pm–2am.

The Faubourg went into shock when the *Dream Palace* closed its doors in 2000; luckily, its successor has proved a roaring success. Virtuoso clarinetist Jack Maheu transformed the old building into an intimate trad jazz club, with small, candlelit tables, sepia photos around the walls and a vibe that practically purrs with pleasure. Though there's a small cover when guest musicians play, Maheu's own weekend shows are free – a real bargain.

Vaughan's

Map 1, G6. 4229 Dauphine St at Lesseps, in the Bywater ⓣ 947-5562.

Daily 11am–3am.

Tiny neighborhood bar that fills to bursting on Thursday, Kermit Ruffins' night. It's all very convivial, with the band crammed against the hard-dancing audience – a mixed bunch of high-spirited college students, the players' friends and family, and other musicians; between sets, help yourself to all-you-can-eat beans and rice from a massive pot. Cover $10 (Thurs only).

TREMÉ

Joe's Cozy Corner

Map 1, F6. 1532 Ursulines St at N Robertson ⓣ 561-9216.

Daily 24hr.

Few tourists head out to this friendly local bar, where on Sunday evenings Kermit Ruffins plays a lively end-of-the-week set to a crowd of friends and family. This part of Tremé, just blocks from the Quarter, can be dangerous after dark, and it may be difficult to get a cab to pick you up; book one in advance, and call the club to make sure there'll be live music. Cover varies.

Kermit Ruffins' Jazz and Blues Hall

Map 1, F6. 1533 St Philip St at N Robertson ⓣ 299-0790.

Fri–Tues 10pm–2am.

In 2001 Kermit realized a long-cherished dream and opened his own place just down the block from *Joe's*. It's an intimate venue, with a low stage, small tables and just enough space to dance, and it's packed on Saturday night, when the man himself plays; the rest of the week he books the best in brass, piano, R&B and jazz. The crowd is a happy mix of savvy tourists, local musicians and New Orleanians from all over town.

Sweet Lorraine's

Map 1, F5. 1931 St Claude Ave at Touro, Ninth Ward ⓣ 945-9654.
Thurs–Sun 5pm–2am.

This classy Ninth Ward venue – on the fringes of Tremé and the back end of the Faubourg – has established itself as a top spot for contemporary jazz. The room is small, but musicians love to play here, certain of an enthusiastic, attentive response. Cover varies.

LOWER GARDEN DISTRICT

St Mary's Bar

Map 3, G7. 961 St Mary's St at Magazine ⓣ 410-1421.
Dark, atmospheric bar, all candles, dim red lights and brick floors. The scene gets even cooler on music nights, when in-the-know locals come to enjoy jazz trad and modern.

OTHER LIVE MUSIC

There's far more to New Orleans than jazz. Though the "**New Orleans sound**", an exuberant, carnival-tinged hybrid of blues, parade music and R&B, had its heyday in the early 1960s, many of its greatest stars are still going strong. Check listings papers for gigs by the Neville Brothers, either all together, or, in Cyril's case, fronting his own barnstorming horn ensemble; Eddie Bo, who hots up traditional New Orleans piano with funk and soul; and "soul queen of New Orleans" Irma Thomas, whose classic hits *Breakaway*, *It's Raining* and *Ruler of My Heart* never fail to send shivers down the spine. Super-talented songwriter-producer Allen Toussaint, who gave many of them their big breaks, is still hard at work, too, showcasing new acts and even performing occasionally.

Since the 1960s New Orleans has also been known for its homegrown **funk** – Galactic and Papa Grows Funk are currently the hottest on the scene, and Art Neville's funky

Meters still play occasionally. If you want to see New Orleanians really let rip, however, try to catch a rare show from graying local heroes The Radiators, whose noisy blend of R&B, funk and rock has been bringing the house down for decades. **Blues** fans should look out for guitarists Snooks Eaglin and Walter "Wolfman" Washington, the younger, urban bluesman Kipori "Baby Wolf" Woods, Delta-blues guitarist John Mooney, and, for powerful gospel-blues, the formidable Marva Wright.

In the late 1990s, the **swing** revival took off in a big way in New Orleans: jumping and jiving Johnny Angel still dominates the scene, dragging behind him a diehard following of hip young things dressed to the nines and sipping fancy cocktails. **Latin** music is popular, too – with a strong fan-base for the smooth sounds of Irvin Mayfield and Los Hombres Calientes – and there's a growing fascination with **tango**, which appeals to the city's love of drama, passion and sheer camp.

Hip-hop has spun its way center stage in the last few years, primarily due to the phenomenal international success of local rappers Master P and Mystikal. You're most likely to witness New Orleans' dance-oriented version of rap, known as **bounce**, at big venues like House of Blues, where emerging stars such as transvestite Katey Red and bounce maestro DJ Jubilee attract huge local crowds. Meanwhile, fusion bands like Soul Remedy, who blend funk, hip-hop and R&B, pack smaller clubs all over the city.

For a list of venues staging the biggest, international touring acts, see p.236.

Though many people associate New Orleans with **Cajun** music, it's not indigenous to the city: that said, locals do love to *fais-do-do* (the Cajun two-step), and there are a couple of fantastic places to dance to **zydeco**, its bluesier black

OTHER LIVE MUSIC

relation. The city has also taken **klezmer** to its heart, and in particular the local Klezmer Allstars, who bang out a frenzied blend of Yiddish folk, jazz and funk. Finally, for something totally unique, scour the listings for **Mardi Gras Indians** (see p.310) such as the Wild Magnolias or Golden Eagles, whose rare gigs – you're most likely to catch them around Mardi Gras or Jazz Fest – are some of the funkiest, most extraordinary performances you're ever likely to see.

THE FRENCH QUARTER

El Matador

Map 4, L5. 504 Esplanade Ave at Decatur Ⓣ 569-8361.
Mon–Thurs 9pm–3am, Fri–Sun 5pm–3am.
The decor – all pressed-tin ceiling, red velvet booths, Spanish kitsch on the walls and, best of all, a huge circular bar to drape yourself over – is pure New Orleans, as is the oddball crowd of eccentrics, artists, loners and serious drinkers. The music, meanwhile, is eclectic and inspired: early evening flamenco (with cut-price sangria); Europop go-go parties; trad jazz jam sessions; hip-hop; and long-lost R&B legends. Every Wednesday the Soul Rebels play three sets to a hard-partying crowd. Cover varies.

House of Blues/The Parish

Map 4, B5. 225 Decatur St at Iberville Ⓣ 529-2583.
Daily 8pm–3am; food served 11am–midnight, plus Sun gospel brunch (see below).
Enormous, slick venue, part of the national chain, with

To glimpse Bourbon Street bawdiness at its old-fashioned best, check out Chris Owens' one-woman variety show. Glitzy, spangly and unashamedly camp, Chris has been high-kicking and grinding for donkeys' years; you'll find her at 500 Bourbon St.

Southern folk art-themed decor. While the high prices and un-New Orleans attitude (the bouncers and wrist tags led detractors to nickname it "House of Rules") can be off-putting, they book the best in everything from blues, funk, reggae and zydeco to rap, hip-hop and rock. Big names have included Bob Dylan, Ray Charles, Johnny Cash and Lee "Scratch" Perry, as well as local stars like the Nevilles and Dr John. There's a gospel brunch on Sunday (9.30am, 11.45am & 2pm; call to reserve) and regular DJ dance nights, while up-and-coming local bands play at the *Parish*, an intimate room above the box office.

Mama's Blues

Map 4, E1. 616 N Rampart St at Toulouse ⓣ **488-4463.**
Thurs–Sun 9pm–2am.
Brought to you by the same people as the *Funky Butt*, which is just up the road, this is the only club in town devoted exclusively to blues. It's above *Mama Rosa's* (see p.183), so you can order hot pizza to go with your beer. Marva Wright, John Mooney and Walter "Wolfman" Washington are regulars. Cover varies.

Shim-Sham Club

Map 4, E4. 615 Toulouse St at Chartres ⓣ **565-5400.**
Daily 2pm–6am
Witty, creative club that flings together an offbeat mix of music and styles and comes up trumps. Conceived loosely as a decadent cabaret lounge in old Bourbon Street-style, *Shim-Sham* is a little dark and slightly daring, but it's a friendly place for all that, and never takes itself too seriously. Among the punk 'n' porno nights, the Eighties nights and the "dark dance" nights, look out for the Shim-Shamettes burlesque review, various cabaret and swing titans, and the Port of New Orleans jazz band, a hot young trad combo with a crowd of wild fans. Cover varies.

Tipitina's French Quarter

Map 4, B6. 233 N Peters St at Iberville ⓣ **566-7095.**
Opening hours vary.

OTHER LIVE MUSIC: THE FRENCH QUARTER

Geared toward tourists who've heard of the famed uptown venue (see p.233) but don't want to leave the Quarter, this branch of *Tip's* lacks the atmosphere of its older sibling and can feel oddly empty, even when it's rocking with a "gonna-have-fun-if-it-kills-me" conventioneer crowd. They haven't quite got the formula right, and for now the performances – R&B, rock, funk and blues – are rare. Cover varies.

FAUBOURG MARIGNY

- - - - - - - - - - - - - - - -

Café Brasil

Map 4, M5. 2100 Chartres St at Frenchmen ⓣ 949-0851.
Mon–Thurs & Sun 6pm–2am, Fri & Sat 6pm–4am.
Minimalist, arty club at the center of the Faubourg scene. It's known for its eclectic live music (Latin, jazz, klezmer, reggae, world) and poetry readings, and there's a small adjoining bar (where they crank the CD-player up loud to drown out the bands). The windows are huge, so it all feels very open, and the young, gorgeous crowd tends to spill onto Frenchmen Street to create a lively block party. Cover varies.

Dragon's Den

Map 4, L6. 435 Esplanade Ave at Frenchmen ⓣ 949-1750.
Daily 6pm–3am.
Tucked above the *Siam Café* (see p.190) in a crumbling townhouse, this bohemian, opium-den style bar/club is a favorite of local bright young things. While there is some seating on the perilously decrepit balcony, most people loll on the velvet floor cushions, crowd the low tables or dance like demons next to the tiny stage. Music is a mixed bag of R&B, blues, jazz and brass bands, and there's a wild poetry slam, Madpoet Express, on Thursday at 8pm. Monday is 2-for-1 sake night.

TREMÉ

- - - - - - - - - - - - - - - -

Ernie K-Doe's Mother-in-Law Lounge

Map 1, F6. 1500 N Claiborne Ave at Columbus, in Tremé

Ⓣ 947-1078.
Daily 6pm till late.

Offbeat venue in the home of flamboyant R&B veteran Ernie K-Doe. Since his death in July 2001 the lounge has become a memorial to the great man, and remains a good place for a friendly drink (see p.213). It's still open for occasional music shows (call to check), when you may catch his old warm-up act, Rico Watts, an Elvis soundalike with a melodious organ – playing his heart out to a motley crew of die-hard K-Doe fans, family and thrill-seeking hipsters. Low or no cover.

THE CBD AND WAREHOUSE DISTRICT

Circle Bar
Map 3, J5. 1032 St Charles Ave at Lee Circle Ⓣ 588-2618.
Daily 4pm–4am.
Run by the same people who brought you *Snake and Jake's* (see p.217), the *Circle*, incongruously set in a crumbling house in the

shadow of the Expressway, crams live bands into its tiny space most nights, and pulls in an artsy set for its eclectic, hip booking policy. It gets very crowded, and half the party usually ends up mingling on the sidewalk. Happy hour 4–8pm; music starts around 11pm. No cover.

Howlin' Wolf
Map 3, L6. 828 S Peters St at Julia Ⓣ 522-WOLF.
Mon–Sat 3pm till late.
Big, bare-bones Warehouse District club that attracts a mixed bunch of grungy young locals and tourists for alternative rock, funk and R&B, and regular acoustic open-mic nights. Happy hour Mon–Fri 4–7pm. Cover varies.

Le Chat Noir
Map 3, L4. 715 St Charles Ave at Girod Ⓣ 581-5812.
Tues–Sat 4pm–2am.
Ritzy bar with a small stage and dance floor surrounded by cocktail tables. It's the perfect setting for cabaret, trad jazz, piano and torch singers, and pulls a laid-back thirtysomething crowd.

OTHER LIVE MUSIC: THE CBD AND WAREHOUSE DISTRICT

Mermaid Lounge

Map 3, J6. 1102 Constance St at John Churchill Chase ℡ 524-4747.

Tues–Sat 9pm–3am.

Hidden away down a dead-end alley in the Warehouse District, this tiny local bar features a mixed bag of garage, punk, klezmer, blues, funk and Cajun (don't miss the ancient Hackberry Ramblers). Cover varies.

Mulate's

Map 3, L6. 201 Julia St at Convention Center Blvd ℡ 522-1492.

Daily 11am–11pm.

Very touristy Cajun restaurant, filled with conventioneers cheerily two-stepping to first-rate live bands (from 7pm). Good fun, but not quite up to *Tipitina's* weekly *fais-do-do* (see p.233) or *Mid-City Lanes'* zydeco nights (see p.234).

LOWER GARDEN DISTRICT AND GARDEN DISTRICT

Le Bon Temps Roulé

Map 2, H7. 4801 Magazine St

at Bordeaux ℡ 895-8117.

Daily 11am–3am.

A spirited mix of locals and hard-drinking students fill this long-running, convivial neighborhood bar – the name is a variation on the Cajun phrase "let the good times roll". Kermit Ruffins plays every Wednesday, the Soul Rebels every Thursday, and on Friday and Saturday it's a mixed bag of blues, acoustic, funk, brass, zydeco, R&B or rock. They also offer food specials – free oysters, free red beans and rice and the like – a wide selection of beers, pool, a great jukebox and a patio. Low or no cover.

Red Room

Map 3, G5. 2040 St Charles Ave at Josephine ℡ 528-9759.

Daily 5pm–2am.

Swanky supper club, housed in a restaurant that was, amazingly enough, removed from Paris' Eiffel Tower and brought to New Orleans in 1986. It's a sumptuous, scarlet setting for smooth jazz, swing and Latin bands, and attracts a supercool uptown set. Also DJ nights, with hip-hop and funk, Latin disco and contemporary R&B. Cover varies; there's a dress code at weekends.

UPTOWN

Jimmy's

Map 2, C1. 8200 Willow St at Dublin ⓣ 861-8200.

Tues–Sat 8pm–3am.

Long-established rock club, with a big dance floor, usually commandeered by raucous college students; it also books Latin, hip-hop and reggae bands. Cover varies.

Maple Leaf Bar

Map 2, B1. 8316 Oak St at Dante ⓣ 866-9359.

Daily 3pm–4am.

Friendly old bar with pressed-tin walls, a dance floor and a patio. Established for more than 25 years, it's much beloved of locals, who fill the place – and the sidewalk outside – for a nightly menu of New Orleans piano, R&B, brass (ReBirth's Tuesday night gigs are legendary) and blues. There's chess and pool, too,

and poetry on Sunday afternoons. Cover varies.

Tipitina's

Map 2, I8. 501 Napoleon Ave at Tchoupitoulas ⓣ 891-8477.

Daily 4pm–4am.

Legendary venue, named for a Professor Longhair song and sporting a banner with his likeness above the stage. Though there's a smaller branch in the Quarter (see p.229), this is the original and still the best, with a consistently good funk, R&B, brass and reggae line-up, spanning the range from local favorites to national acts. The Cajun *fais-do-do* (Sun 5–9pm) is great fun, too, with free red beans and rice. Cover varies.

MID-CITY

Lion's Den

Map 1, D6. 2655 Gravier St at S Broad Ave ⓣ 822-4693.

Days and hours vary.

Tiny club part-owned by R&B legend Irma Thomas, who performs very occasionally, usually during festivals (check listings papers, or call), when she may even prepare beans and rice for her devoted fans. The neighborhood is desolate; take a taxi. Cover varies.

Mid-City Lanes Rock'n'Bowl

Map 1, D5. 4133 S Carrollton Ave at Tulane ☎ 482-3133. Daily noon–2am.

Eccentric ten-lane bowling alley-cum-live music venue in an unprepossessing mall. Thursday night is zydeco night, when greats such as Geno Delafose stir the crowd into such a frenzy that you can barely hear the crashing of the pins. For the rest of the week they book good local R&B, blues, Latin and swing. There are two stages; on P.O.P nights you pay one price to dash from one to the other, in between trying to get a strike. Fantastic fun, especially if you're in a group. Take a taxi. Cover varies.

Theater and the arts

Despite the city's long association with the **performing arts** – from the earliest years of the French colony, when short dramas were performed in private drawing rooms, through to the nineteenth-century golden era, when theaters, ballrooms and the glorious French Opera House were packed every night – few visitors come to New Orleans for opera or the ballet. However, while the high-arts scene poses little competition for bigger, wealthier cities – arts funding is pitifully low – New Orleans does have respected **operatic** and **orchestral** companies, a small **ballet** company, a couple of **rep theaters** and a handful of places showcasing **avant-garde** and experimental works.

There's little in the way of comedy, but **spoken word** performances have a loyal following in local bars. The Sunday afternoon poetry reading series at the *Maple Leaf* (see p.233) is the oldest in the South, and features top-quality literary work; the slams and open-mic nights hosted by the *Dragon's Den* (p.230), *True Brew* (p.203), *Funky Butt* (p.222) and *Flora Café* (p.201) are less sedate.

Though America's first purpose-built movie house opened on Canal Street in 1896, it's long since been torn down. Nonetheless, the city does have its fair share of mainstream cinemas and a few places to catch independent and art-house **films**, as well as a respected festival, held each fall (see p.284).

For a filmography of movies made in or about New Orleans, see p.332.

One of the best things about the high-art scene in New Orleans is the **Louisiana Philharmonic Orchestra** (⊤523-6530; ⓦ*www.lpomusic.com*), owned by its members, which puts on fine classical concerts at the grand old Orpheum Theater; tickets cost between $20 and $50. The highly regarded **New Orleans Opera** (⊤529-3000; ⓦ*www.neworleansopera.org*) and the **New Orleans Ballet Association** (⊤522-0996; ⓦ*www.nobadance.com*) both stage short, well-received seasons at the Mahalia Jackson Theater of the Performing Arts, and in smaller venues around town; tickets start at $15 for dance, $30 for opera.

To check what's happening on any particular night, check the **listings** pages of *Gambit*, or the *Lagniappe* supplement of the *Times-Picayune* (see p.10). Ticketmaster (⊤522-5555, ⓦ*www.ticketmaster.com*) sells **tickets** to most of the bigger productions; they have a booth (daily 10am–7.30pm) in Tower Records, 408 N Peters St.

THEATERS AND PERFORMANCE VENUES

Contemporary Arts Center
Map 3, K5. 900 Camp St at St Joseph ⊤528-3800,

ⓦ*www.cacno.org*
Modern gallery and performance space in the Warehouse District, features

hosting and one-off art exhibitions, dance, performance art, video installations, art-house movies and experimental theater. For more on the CAC, see p.87.

Le Chat Noir

Map 3, L4. 715 St Charles Ave at Girod Ⓣ 581-5812, Ⓦ *www.cabaretlechatnoir.com* Tues–Sat 4pm–2am.
Cabaret, musical revues, dance, stand-up comedy and alternative theater in a swish, supper club-style venue in the CBD.

Mahalia Jackson Theater of the Performing Arts

Map 4, G1. Louis Armstrong Park, Rampart St at St Ann Ⓣ 529-3000.
A large, lavish setting for touring musicals, classical concerts, opera and ballet, ice spectaculars, boxing and so on. The theater is named after the New Orleans-born gospel singer Mahalia Jackson, also known as "the Queen of Gospel Song".

Municipal Auditorium

Map 4, G1. Louis Armstrong Park, Rampart St at St Ann Ⓣ 565-7470.
Another large venue for touring companies and big concerts.

New Orleans Arena

Map 3, J2. Sugar Bowl Drive, adjacent to the Superdome Ⓣ 587-3800, Ⓦ *www.neworleansarena.com* In the shadow of its older sibling, the Superdome, the Arena seats about 20,000 for big-name rock concerts – Bruce, Tina, Britney and the like. It's also home to the city's unlikely ice hockey team, the New Orleans Brass.

NOCCA

Map 1, G6. 2800 Chartres St at St Ferdinand Ⓣ 861-8832, Ⓦ *www.nocca.com* The new campus of the highly respected New Orleans Center for Creative Arts is a handsome building, melding old cotton warehouses with cutting-edge design. It's occasionally open to the public for jazz,

THEATERS AND PERFORMANCE VENUES

237

poetry and drama performances.

Orpheum Theater

Map 3, M3. 129 University Place at Common ⓣ 524-3285, ⓦ *www.orpheumneworleans.com*
Historic venue, built in 1918 as a vaudeville theater and movie house. Today, seeping faded grandeur, it makes a characterful base for the Philharmonic Orchestra.

Petit Théâtre du Vieux Carré

Map 4, F5. 616 St Peter St at Chartres ⓣ 522-2081.
The nation's longest-running community theater, formed in 1919 by the Drawing Room Players, who first trod the boards in private homes. The building, on the corner of Jackson Square in the French Quarter, is a pretty setting for middle-of-the-road musicals, comedies and drama, and an atmospheric venue for the annual Tennessee Williams Literary Festival (see p.282).

Saenger Theater

Map 4, A1. 143 N Rampart St at Canal ⓣ 524-2490.
Beautifully restored 1920s movie theater, replete with classical statuary, glittering chandeliers and a star-spangled night-sky ceiling. It's a lovely, special-occasion venue for touring Broadway productions and big-name concerts.

Southern Rep Theater

Map 4, A7. Canal Place shopping mall, 333 Canal St ⓣ 861-8163, ⓦ *www.southernrep.com*
Conveniently situated, intimate venue in one of downtown's best malls (see p.242). For most of the year, it features the work of Southern playwrights – up-and-coming and established – performed by local actors; it also doubles as a movie theater during the annual film festival (see p.284).

State Palace Theater

Map 4, A1. 1108 Canal St at N Rampart ⓣ 522-4435, ⓦ *www.statepalace.com*
Gorgeous old theater, built as

a vaudeville house in the 1920s. A regular venue for big-name rock, rap, ska and R&B concerts, it's also notorious for its occasional raves.

Superdome

Map 3, K2. Sugar Bowl Drive ⓣ 587-3800, ⓦ *www.superdome.com*

The gargantuan stadium variously used for Saints' football games, teeming trade shows and overblown rock concerts. For more on the building and its history, see p.87.

True Brew Theater

Map 3, L6. 200 Julia St at Fulton ⓣ 524-8440.

Small theater in a Warehouse District coffeehouse (see p.203). Shows, usually on the weekend, tend to be short dramas or comedies of local interest, and there are some stand-up and open-mic events.

Zeitgeist Alternative Arts Center

Map 3, H4. 1724 Oretha Castle Haley Blvd at Polymnia ⓣ 525-2767, ⓦ *www.crosswinds.net/~zte*

This peripatetic avant-garde arts center (keep track of its current location through the Web site) currently shares space with the offbeat *Barrister's* gallery. One of the city's few truly alternative venues, it is a great place for movies (lots of gay, lesbian and world cinema), live music of all varieties, performance art, theater, lectures, workshops and readings.

CINEMAS

For details of the **New Orleans Film and Video Festival**, held each October, see p.284.

Joy

Map 3, N2. 1200 Canal St at Elk Place ⓣ 522-7575.

Downtown cinema, just outside the French Quarter, screening the latest mainstream releases.

Landmark Cinemas at Canal Place

Map 4, A7. Canal Place shopping mall, 333 Canal St ⓣ 581-5400.

Conveniently located in an expensive downtown mall (see p.242), this four-screen cinema features mainstream releases along with independents and world cinema. In October, it's the main venue for the city's film festival (see p.284).

Prytania

Map 2, F6. 5339 Prytania St at Leontine ⓣ 891-2787.

The only remaining single-screen cinema in the city, this atmospheric old uptown movie theater is a delight. It shows art-house, Hollywood and independent movies and acts as a venue for the city's annual film festival (see p.284).

CINEMAS

Shopping

Shopping in New Orleans, where mega-malls play second fiddle to small, stylish stores, can be a lot of fun. In a place where hanging out is a priority, most visitors spend a lot of time browsing and window-shopping, whether their budget extends to a framed WeeGee original or to one-of-a-kind crafts by local designers.

The **French Quarter** has its share of tacky tourist shops hawking T-shirts, ersatz voodoo gris-gris and cheap little ceramic masks – but beyond these are some superb antique shops (concentrated on Royal Street, the "Main Street" of the old Creole city), and individualistic places to buy art, clothes, books and music.

On Saturdays, when the Quarter can get choked with tourists, you're best off heading for the antique shops, thrift stores and workshops along six-mile **Magazine Street**, which starts at Canal in the CBD and runs through the Warehouse and Garden Districts to Audubon Park. You could also spend a day browsing in the **Riverbend** area and around **Maple Street**, the studenty uptown district at the end of the streetcar line. If you've got serious money to spend on contemporary art, head for the galleries of the **Arts District** (see p.81).

Sadly, the fine old department stores that once graced **Canal Street** are slowly disappearing; the elegant buildings are filled today with swanky hotels, questionable electrical stores, luggage stores, fast-food outlets and sportswear chains. If you're looking for a department store, head for the **malls**.

For details of Louisiana's Tax-Free shopping scheme, whereby the state's nine percent sales tax is reimbursed to foreign visitors, see p.289.

MALLS

Canal Place
Map 4, A7. 333 Canal St at N Peters ⓣ 522-9200.
Mon–Sat 10am–7pm, Sun noon–6pm.
A tranquil place to shop, with upmarket national chains like Williams-Sonoma, Pottery Barn, Laura Ashley, Saks Fifth Avenue, Jaeger, Gucci, Betsey Johnson and Banana Republic plus local stores RHINO (see p.260) and the shop of New Orleans jewelry designer Mignon Faget. It also has a four-screen **cinema** (see p.240), **rep theater** (see p.238) and **gym** (see p.288). The food court isn't bad, but you're near enough to the Quarter here to give it a miss.

Jackson Brewery (JAX)
Map 4, E6. Decatur St between Toulouse and St Peter ⓣ 566-7245.
Mon–Sat 10am–9pm, Sun 10am–7pm.
The least appealing of the downtown malls, filling a restored 1891 brewery with more than fifty brash stores. Among the ubiquitous pralines, hot sauces, T-shirts and crawfish-emblazoned neckties, you'll find branches of Gray Line, The Limited and Sunglass Hut, as well as a Planet Hollywood and Virgin Megastore (see p.262). The food court, despite its riverside terrace, is entirely missable.

Riverwalk

Map 3, M6–7. 1 Poydras St, on the Mississippi ☎ 522-1555. Mon–Sat 10am–9pm, Sun 11am–7pm.

Bustling, touristy mall running along the river from Julia Street to the Plaza d'España. Its three stories house 150 shops, including DeVille Books (see p.250), and chains such as the Disney Store, Banana Republic, Gap, Warner Bros, Victoria's Secret, Body Shop, Abercrombie and Kent and Footlocker. There's also a *Café du Monde* (see p.200) and a good food court where you can eat outside above the river. For more on the mall, see p.112.

ANTIQUES AND VINTAGE STORES

Partly due to its strong links with Europe, especially France, and its crucial nineteenth-century role as a port, New Orleans is a world-class **antiques center**. You'll need serious money if you want to buy from the places on elegant **Royal Street**, many of which have been trading since the late 1800s. If your budget doesn't stretch to Persian rugs or eighteenth-century armoires, check out the vintage stores along the 1100 and 1200 blocks of **Decatur Street**: great for bric-a-brac and funky retro furniture. Or go store-hopping along **Magazine Street**, where thrift and rummage stores sit alongside classy antiques warehouses.

For antique **maps** and **prints** see p.246; for rare and antique **books**, see p.249.

Animal Arts

Map 4, E5. 617 Chartres St at Wilkinson Row ☎ 529-4407. Mon–Sat 10am–5pm.

Animal-themed antiques – oil paintings, ceramics, upholstery, majolica and a huge selection of Palissy. Also large pieces of wooden furniture and primitive art.

ANTIQUES AND VINTAGE STORES

Barakat

Map 4, H4. 934 Royal St at St Philip ☏ 593-9944.

Mon & Thurs–Sun 11am–5pm.

A cross between an antique store and a rummage store, *Barakat* sells funky junk, retro furniture, coffee sets, hats and the like, along with primitive rural furniture, textiles and old postcards.

James H. Cohen

Map 4, D4. 437 Royal St at Conti ☏ 522-3305.

Daily 9.30am–5.15pm.

Musty specialist store dealing in rare coins and antique weapons; though the bulk of the stuff dates from the Civil War (flags, photos, swords, muskets), there are also presidential buttons, vintage magazine ads and pieces of eight from the 1700s.

Gerald D. Katz

Map 4, D4. 505 Royal St at St Louis ☏ 524-5050.

Daily 10am–5.30pm.

Gorgeous old store, with the nation's largest hoard of antique jewelry (mostly nineteenth-century), plus china and oil paintings.

Lucullus

Map 4, E5. 610 Chartres St at Wilkinson Row ☏ 528-9620.

Sept–May Mon–Sat 9.30am–5pm; June–Aug closed Mon.

Named for the Roman general who held notoriously lavish banquets, this is *the* place for dining-related antiques – coffee pots, table linens, earthenware jars, cut-glass decanters, oyster forks, candlesticks – dating from the 1600s onwards. There's another branch at 3932 Magazine St (☏ 894-0500; same hours).

Manheim Galleries

Map 4, D4. 409 Royal St at Conti ☏ 568-1901.

Mon–Sat 9am–5pm.

One of Royal Street's finest, in a handsome bank building designed by Benjamin Latrobe. Famed for their collections of jade and porcelain Boehm birds, they also have paintings, wooden furniture, tapestries and porcelain.

Nineteenth-Century Antiques

Map 2, H7. 4838 Magazine St at Lyons ☎ 891-4845.

Mon–Sat 10am–5pm.

A jumble of small, quality pieces, including a fantastic selection of unusual clocks and watches, china and cut glass, in one of Magazine Street's best-established stores.

Orient Expressed Imports

Map 2, I7. 3905 Magazine St at General Pershing ☎ 899-3060.

Mon–Sat 10am–5pm.

Eclectic, sprawling shop that sells unusual antiques and imports including Mexican wooden *santo* figures, masks and icons, Thai buddhas and antique Chinese ancestors. Also contemporary gifts, including ceramics, candles and children's clothes.

Quarter Past Time

Map 4, E5. 606 Chartres St at Toulouse ☎ 410-0000.

Mon, Tues & Thurs–Sun 10am–6pm.

Deco clocks, watches and lamps, cocktail sets and novelties; fun to browse, even if you're not buying.

M.S. Rau

Map 4, E4. 630 Royal St at Toulouse ☎ 523-5660.

Mon–Sat 9am–5.15pm.

Third-generation-owned store, specializing in nineteenth-century American antiques, with chandeliers, silver, ironwork, Cartier and Tiffany jewelry, early Edison phonographs and pieces by Prudent Mallard, New Orleans' foremost nineteenth-century cabinet maker.

Vintage 429

Map 4, D4. 429 Royal St at St Louis ☎ 529-2288.

Mon–Thurs 10am–6pm, Fri & Sat 10.30am–6.30pm, Sun 10.30am–5.30pm.

The place to come for autographs – from local boy Kermit Ruffins through Elvis to Greta Garbo (whose autographed and framed photo will set you back $4000) and the elusive J.D. Salinger. Cheaper stuff includes 1950s cocktail sets, lunchboxes, cigarette cases and concert posters, plus pens and postcards.

ANTIQUES AND VINTAGE STORES

ART, PRINTS, POSTERS AND MAPS

There are scores of places to buy **art** in New Orleans, from the cheapest poster to the classiest antique oil painting, and a whole lot of distinctive, interesting stuff in between. It seems that every second shop in the Quarter, especially along Decatur and Royal, sells **posters** and **prints** – the overload can become enervating, especially as the same, tired images pop up time and time again. Best buys include official and unofficial Jazz Fest and Mardi Gras posters, reproduction historical prints, and old maps.

Don't overlook the artists who display their work in **Jackson Square**, either – along with portraits and caricatures, usually at very low prices, you'll find abstracts, quirky local scenes, and folk art (look out for Big Al Taplet, whose humorous, boldly colored ads for his shoeshine service, painted on slates, have become collectibles). All works are originals.

If your budget for artworks runs to **fine oil paintings**, see the antiques stores detailed on pp.243–246. And if you're in the market for **cutting-edge works**, check the Arts District galleries listed on p.81.

Bergen Galleries

Map 4, F4. 730 Royal St at Orleans ⊤ 523-7882.
Sun–Thurs 9am–9pm, Fri & Sat 9am–10pm.
Huge print and poster store, featuring local artists Michalopoulos (vivid, dreamlike streetscapes) and Rodrigue (whose little blue dog pops up everywhere), along with Vargas and Erté, etchings, and the best Jazz Fest and Mardi Gras posters. They ship worldwide.

Berta's and Mina's Antiquities

Map 2, I7. 4138 Magazine St at Jena ⊤ 895-6201.
Daily 10am–6pm.
Misleadingly named store

crammed with the inventive folk art of Nicaraguan-born Nilo Lanzas, who started painting at the age of 63. His brash dioramas, many of them painted on old wooden window frames, portray quirky biblical and rural scenes, or depict life in the imaginary town of Niloville, all of them daubed with witty, touching captions.

The Centuries

Map 4, D5. 517 St Louis St at Decatur ☎ 568-9491.

Mon–Thurs & Sun 10.30am–6pm, Fri & Sat 10.30am–6.30pm.

Antique prints and maps, engravings and etchings. The print bins are well labeled, and the laid-back staff are happy to let you browse. Categories include architecture, towns, countries, fashion and literature.

Eugene's

Map 4, I4. 940 Royal St at St Philip ☎ 561-8851.

Mon & Thurs–Sat 11am–5.30pm, Sun noon–5pm.

One of the best places in town for top-quality black, Southern and folk art, with an emphasis on local artists. Prices aren't low, but the works are originals.

A Gallery for Fine Photography

Map 4, C4. 322 Royal St at Bienville ☎ 568-1313.

Daily 10am–6pm.

Superb place, more of a gallery than a store, with antique and classic photographs to look at or to buy. Many prices reach four figures, and rare platinum prints can go for as much as $12,500. Works date from 1839 and include pictures by Edward S. Curtis, Jacques-Henri Lartigue, WeeGee, Diane Arbus, Helmut Newton and David Bailey. Look out for Walker Evans' photos of the 1930s French Quarter, a host of jazz portraits, and Clarence White's ghostly double-exposed images. The books section includes rare nineteenth-century titles.

ART, PRINTS, POSTERS AND MAPS

THE FRENCH MARKET

New Orleans' French Market, a restored arcade taking up five blocks of Decatur Street downriver from Jackson Square, has been a marketplace since the Choctaw traded here in the 1700s. Today, along with the tourist shops selling T-shirts, Cajun and jazz music, cookbooks, Mardi Gras beads, masks, pralines and posters, there's a 24-hour Farmers Market, which starts at the 1100 block of N Peters St, selling fresh seasonal produce, sacks of beans and nuts, coffee, pyramids of spices and the like. The 1200 block is occupied by a flea market: a jumble of plants, jewelry, junk, and used and new clothes, with some interesting Latin American and African crafts among the tourist trinkets. It's open daily, but busiest at weekends; haggling is acceptable.

ART, PRINTS, POSTERS AND MAPS

Historic New Orleans Collection
Map 4, E4. 533 Royal St at St Louis ☎ 523-4662.
Tues–Sat 10am–4.45pm.
Terrific French Quarter museum (see p.49) shop with a great collection of old maps and prints on subjects including New Orleans, the Civil War, Napoleon, and Audubon's "botanicals". It's also worth checking their postcards (early city plans, paintings of the Quarter in the 1930s, old photos, etc), and the shelves of new and used books.

Peligro
Map 4, C5. 305 Decatur St at Bienville ☎ 581-1706.
Mon–Fri 10am–6pm, Sat 10am–8pm, Sun noon–6pm.
A hoard of contemporary Southern folk art and sculpture along with South American icons, tin boxes and bottle-top saints. Prices range from affordable to seriously expensive.

Shadyside
Map 2, K7. 3823 Magazine St at Peniston ☎ 897-1710.
Mon–Sat 10am–5pm.
Studio for the pottery of

Charles Bohn, who uses the "raku" process – whereby high-sand content earthenware is fast fired and cooled – to create gorgeous turquoise and copper, emerald green, or ethereal white "crackle" hues. Prices range from $25 to $450. Call for details of the occasional classes.

Vincent's

Map 4, E5. 631 Decatur St at Wilkinson Row ☎ 522-2773. Mon–Fri 10am–5.30pm, Sat & Sun 10am–6pm.
Good selection of mainstream prints, Mardi Gras and Jazz Fest posters, at reasonable prices. The staff are helpful and knowledgeable.

BOOKS

New Orleans is a dream for bibliophiles, with plenty of places that carry specialist and used **books**, a handful of much-loved neighborhood stores and a couple of national chains. For **nonfiction**, new and used, you could also try the record stores (p.261), Le Monde Creole (p.259), and the Historic New Orleans Collection (p.248).

Beaucoup Books

Map 2, F7. 5414 Magazine St at Jefferson ☎ 895-2663. Mon–Sat 10am–6pm, Sun noon–5pm.
New fiction, including many titles by local authors. Also cookbooks, art books, travel guides, Granta periodicals, foreign-language titles, cards and postcards. Frequent author readings.

Beckham's Books

Map 4, B6. 228 Decatur St at

Iberville ☎ 522-9875. Daily 10am–6pm.
Thousands of old editions, rare and out-of-print titles, and vintage magazines in a rambling, two-story bookstore. You could browse here all day. There's a sister branch, Librairie Books, at 823 Chartres St at St Ann (daily 10am–8pm; ☎ 525-4837).

Bookstar

Map 4, D6. 414 N Peters St at St Louis ☎ 523-6411.

Mon–Sat 9am–11pm, Sun
9am–10pm.

Conveniently located
megastore with a wide range
of local and regional titles,
plus books on travel, cookery,
literature and music, and lots
of magazines. Many
discounts, particularly on
hardbacks.

Dauphine Street Books
Map 4, D3. 410 Dauphine St at
Conti ☎ 529-2333.
Mon & Thurs–Sun 11am–7pm.
A gem of a store, with piles
of used books, especially
strong on local fiction,
history, photography and
Latin American translations.
The helpful owner is happy
to make recommendations.

DeVille Books
Map 3, M6. Riverwalk Mall
☎ 595-8916.
Mon–Sat 10am–9pm, Sun
11am–7pm.
Very good choice of local
titles, history, mysteries and
thrillers, travel guides, avant-
garde works and sections
dedicated to blacks and
women. The branch at 344
Carondelet St (Mon–Fri

9.30am–5.30pm; ☎ 525-
1846) also sells used paper-
backs.

Faubourg Marigny Bookstore
Map 4, M5. 600 Frenchmen St
at Chartres ☎ 943-9875.
Mon–Fri 10am–8pm, Sat & Sun
10am–6pm.
The city's oldest gay and lesbian bookstore, selling travel
guides, regional titles, postcards and calendars.

Faulkner House Books
Map 4, F5. 624 Pirate's Alley
at Chartres ☎ 524-2940.
Daily 10am–6pm.
Tucked into the building
where the novelist lived
while writing *Soldier's Pay*,
his first book. Along with
Faulkner, it stocks works by
other Southern writers and
many local-interest titles,
including first editions and
poetry. The owners, who are
a good source of
information on local literary
events, organize their own
annual literary festival (see
p.282).

Garden District Bookshop

Map 3, D5. The Rink, 2727 Prytania St at Washington ☎ 895-2266.

Mon–Sat 10am–6pm, Sun 11am–5pm.

Strong selection of local titles, new fiction and limited editions. One of the many authors who hold book signings here is Anne Rice – it's next door to her own store (see p.259), and they stock rare editions and autographed copies of her books.

George Herget Books

Map 2, L6. 3109 Magazine St at Eighth ☎ 891-5595.

Mon–Sat 10am–5.30pm, Sun 11am–5pm.

Cool, musty store, good for rare and out-of-print titles. They stock more than 20,000 used books, covering fiction, music, art, Louisiana, New Orleans, the Civil War, Americana, black studies, travel and cookery.

Kaboom Books

Map 4, K2. 915 Barracks St at Dauphine ☎ 529-5780.

Daily 11am–6pm.

Kaboom's floor plan helps you negotiate the narrow aisles, which are stuffed full of used volumes including fiction (lots of crime), drama, travel, movie books, biographies and photography. It's strong on history, especially of the South, and has a good African-American section.

Maple Street Book Shop

Map 2, C3. 7523 Maple St at Cherokee ☎ 866-4916.

Mon–Sat 9am–9pm, Sun 10am–6pm.

Lots of local titles, classic and contemporary, and a great art/photography selection in this beloved Riverbend store. They host frequent book signings and can do searches for hard-to-find titles. The same people own the children's bookshop next door.

BOOKS

CLOTHES AND ACCESSORIES

Though not famed as a fashion city, New Orleans is without doubt a stylish one. Locals adore dressing up, be it in haughty haute couture or flamboyant secondhand gladrags – **vintage clothes**, in particular, are a hit with a population that not only revels in nostalgia and drama, but also numbers many penniless musicians and artists. In addition to the vintage stores reviewed below, check the crop of warehouse-style rummage stores in the 1100 and 1200 blocks of Decatur, where you can pick up old Mardi Gras costumes and retro suits among the dusty old mirrors, records and family mementos.

Many of the clothes stores listed here also sell **jewelry** – look out especially for the work of local designer Mignon Faget, whose striking metal pieces are inspired by local wildlife and architecture – and other accessories. And if you crave a hep-cat hat to top that sharp suit there are also a couple of serious **hat stores**.

We've listed here mostly one-off, local stores; for **chain stores**, check the malls listed on pp.242–243 and for **sportswear**, head for Canal Street. See also **costume**, on p.256, and the **antique shops** listed on pp.243–245.

Frock Candy

Map 4, I5. 520 St Philip St at Decatur ☎ 566-1133.
Mon–Thurs & Sun 10am–6pm, Fri & Sat 10am–7pm.
Full of bright young things rifling through skinny T-shirts, retro shades, sex-kitten shoes and handbags. Glamorous and fresh, though not all that cheap.

Grace Note

Map 4, H4. 900 Royal St at Dumaine ☎ 522-1513.
Mon–Sat 10am–6pm, Sun 11am–5pm.
Offbeat store selling fabulous hats, vintage and designer women's clothes, jewelry and gloves – all very New Orleans, with lots of velvets, satins, embroidery and

fringing. Check out the 1930s chiffon dresses: perfect for debauchery on a wrought-iron balcony. They also do a good line in folk art and postcards.

Hemline
Map 4, E5. 609 Chartres St at Toulouse ☎ 529-3566.
Mon–Sat 10am–6.30pm, Sun 10am–6pm.
Funky women's clothes, hats, jewelry and shoes with a definite New Orleans panache. There are branches at 7916 Maple St (Mon–Sat 10am–6pm; ☎ 862-0420) and 3025 Magazine St (☎ 269-4005), while Simplicity by Hemline, 838 Royal St (Mon–Thurs & Sun 10am–6pm, Fri & Sat 10am–6.30pm; ☎ 522-8577), sells a less flamboyant range, including shoes, jackets and sweaters.

House of Lounge
Map 3, F7. 2044 Magazine St at Josephine ☎ 671-8300.
Mon–Sat 10am–6pm, Sun noon–5pm.
This glamorous salon, a throwback to 1930s Hollywood, is a drop-dead

gorgeous setting to splash out on vampish lingerie and boudoir attire – all feathers, satin and fishnet. They also do a nice line in froufrou accessories and jewelry.

Thomas Mann
Map 3, G7. 1804 Magazine St at Felicity ☎ 581-2113.
Mon–Sat 11am–6pm.
Local artist Mann's "Techno-Romantic" jewelry – soft, quirky forms melded from burnished metals and found objects – is modern, inventive and witty. New Orleanians love the cockroach pins, but you can also get beautifully crafted charm bracelets, broken-heart earrings and simple pendants; prices stretch from affordable to very expensive. The store also carries sculpture, clocks and mirrors, all worked from metal.

Meyer the Hatter
Map 3, N4. 120 St Charles Ave at Canal ☎ 525-1048.
Mon–Sat 10am–5.45pm.
Traditional, old store for characterful hats. Most of the space is taken up by Biltmores – the New Orleans

CLOTHES AND ACCESSORIES

jazzman's favorite – but you'll also find stetsons, baseball caps and Kangols.

Ragin' Daisy
Map 2, L6. 3125 Magazine St at Ninth ⓣ269-1960.
Mon–Sat noon–6pm.
Rock'n'roll spandex, Goth crushed velvet and punk PVC for men and women, plus a few vintage dresses and suits, costume jewelry, neat little hats, beatnik accessories, bags and shoes.

Rapp's Luggage
Map 3, N4. 604 Canal St at St Charles ⓣ568-1953.
Mon–Sat 10am–6pm.
The most reputable baggage store on Canal Street, with a good, reasonably priced selection including Samsonite, Tumi, Timberland and Jans backpacks, along with briefcases and purses, and a repair service.

Sole Starr
Map 4, J6. 1200 Decatur St at Gov Nicholls ⓣ566-0777.
Daily noon–6pm.
A riot of glitter, sequins and shiny fabrics: inexpensive women's clothing, shoes, wigs and accessories. Flashy, trashy and fun.

Winky's
Map 3, F6. 2038 Magazine St at Jackson ⓣ568-1020.
Mon–Sat 11am–6pm.
Fashionable store on the lower, slightly funkier end of Magazine Street. Selling hip clothes and accessories – mostly for women – it's bright and fun, youthful and pricey, with offbeat furnishings upstairs and a tiny gallery, Art Lab (Wed–Sat noon–6pm; ⓣ581-7009) tacked onto the back.

VINTAGE CLOTHING

Fiesta
Map 2, L7. 3322 Magazine St at Louisiana ⓣ895-7877.
Mon & Thurs–Sun noon–5pm, Tues & Wed 2–5pm.
Small store packed full with Hawaiian shirts, denim jackets, 1950s dresses and seersucker swimsuits, 1970s disco gear, smoking jackets and Mardi Gras costumes. Also shoes, shades, retro

VINTAGE CLOTHING

neckties and jewelry, with a nice line in vintage lamps.

Funky Monkey

Map 2, L7. 3127 Magazine St at Louisiana Ⓣ 899-5587.

Mon–Sat 11am–6pm, Sun noon–5pm.

Fabulous designer costumes, vintage rags, wigs, bags, shoes and make-up, with a good choice of men's suits. It's just the place to throw together a unique costume or disguise.

Le Garage

Map 4, K6. 1236 Decatur St at Barracks Ⓣ 523-4467.

Tues–Sat noon–5pm.

The biggest and the best of the rummage stores on this decadent stretch of Decatur: a warren of old uniforms, vintage Mardi Gras costumes, hats, suits and dresses, along with furniture and books.

Paisley Babylon

Map 4, J6. 1129 Decatur St at Ursulines Ⓣ 529-3696.

Wed–Mon noon–6pm.

Friendly store for secondhand jeans, party frocks and the like, with a good selection of Hawaiian shirts and sharp suits for men. Not always that cheap, but there's something for everyone.

Jim Smiley

Map 3, G7. 2001 Magazine St at Felicity Ⓣ 528-9449.

Mon–Sat 11am–5pm.

Fine antique clothing, hats, shoes and textiles on Lower Magazine Street. It's more of a place to admire the goods than to buy – which isn't to say that the prices aren't just. Some items, like the 1950s leather jackets (around $150), are good value.

Trashy Diva

Map 4, G5. 829 Chartres St at St Ann Ⓣ 581-4555.

Daily noon–6pm.

Pricey, top-of-the-range period clothes; beautiful 1940s suits, 1930s evening wear and a wide range of sexy antique corsets. Their own line of vintage-look chiffon dresses and satin dresses are as exquisite and expensive as the real thing.

VINTAGE CLOTHING

COSTUMES, MASKS AND DISGUISES

New Orleanians love to **dress up**, and, so it seems, do the tourists. Scores of shops sell cheap masks, feather boas and whacky hats to satisfy exhibitionist impulses, but for serious **costuming** – at Mardi Gras, say, or Halloween – you should head first for the specialist shops listed below. Even off season they're worth a browse: the older, deliciously shabby, Mardi Gras suppliers in particular are full of weird treasures.

See also Fifi Mahony's for **wigs** and supercool **accessories** (p.262) and all the stores listed under **Vintage Clothing** on pp.254–255.

Accent Annex
Map 4, E4. 633 Toulouse St at Royal ⓣ 592-9886.
Daily 10am–6pm.
Mardi Gras minimarket, with a king's ransom of glittery masks, hats, costumes, T-shirts and souvenirs. It's good year-round for wigs, fancy dress and stage make-up.

Little Shop of Fantasy
Map 4, H5. 523 Dumaine St at Decatur ⓣ 529-4243.
Mon–Sat 11am–6pm, Sun 1–6pm.
The French Quarter's first stop for fabulous designer masks. What with these, and the big velvet hats, cloaks, boas, tiaras, satin flowers and angel wings, you'll be playing dress-up here for hours. They also have a roomful of kitsch toys and accessories.

MGM
Map 3, H5. 1617 St Charles Ave at Euterpe ⓣ 581-3999.
Tues–Fri 9.30am–5.30pm, Sat 9.30am–5pm.
Hollywood's MGM studio was renowned for its big-budget extravaganzas – now you can kit yourself out in costumes worn by the stars. Rental only, from $25 to $500 per day.

Royal Rags
Map 4, H4. 627 Dumaine St at Chartres ⓣ 566-7247.
Wed–Mon 11am–6pm.

Handmade outfits stuffed into a closet-sized store: wings and outrageous headdresses, ball gowns and satin opera gloves, hoop skirts, spats, drag gear, feathery antennae and the like. The staff are happy to let you rifle before making that crucial decision between sequinned leggings or shocking-pink tutu. They'll custom-design, too, given enough notice.

Uptown Costume and Dancewear Company

Map 2, I7. 4326 Magazine St at Napoleon ⓣ 895-7969.
Mon–Fri 10am–5pm, Sat 10am–6pm.

Cavernous warehouse packed tight with inexpensive wigs, masks, costumes, hats, shoes, accessories and make-up. Staff are informative and helpful, even when rushed off their feet during Mardi Gras (when the place is milling with krewe members and marching bands) and Halloween (stage make-up and hideous latex heads are particularly popular). Opening hours are extended during these busy periods.

Vieux Carré Hair Store

Map 4, G4. 805 Royal St at St Ann ⓣ 522-3258.
Mon–Sat 10am–5pm.

They take their business seriously at this dusty old theatrical supplier, despite the shrieking novelty doormat and "yes! we have warts" sign. It's a surreal place, with shelves of decrepit polystyrene heads sporting off-center woollen wigs, rubber masks, sideburns and false noses. They also sell stage make-up, much of which is stored behind the old-fashioned glass-fronted counter.

FOOD AND DRINK

A glut of tourist stores in the Quarter do a rapid turn-around in easily transportable **foodie gifts**, from café au lait and *beignet* mixes to red beans and rice and jambalaya spices. Other buys include cans of Community blend coffee laced with chicory, filé (for gumbo), peppery crab-boil and sugary pralines, along with hundreds of brands of hot sauce – some of them emblazoned with flaming toilets, burning butts and such in an effort to seem hotter than the next – and the evil, inexplicably popular, make-your-own Hurricane mixes (see p.211), packed with sugar and artificial additives.

For **picnic food**, head for the neighborhood groceries and delis reviewed in the "Eating" chapter, on p.203, or the Farmers Market, covered on p.248.

Café du Monde Coffee Shop

Map 4, G6. 800 Decatur St at St Ann ☎581-2914.

Daily 24hr.

Beignet mix and cans of chicory coffee, along with *Café du Monde* souvenirs.

N'Awlins Cajun and Creole Spices

Map 4, J6. 1101 N Peters St, in the Farmers Market ☎566-0315.

Daily 24hr.

One of the better stops for hot sauces, coffee, spices and mixes – everything imaginable in a packet.

Orleans Coffee Exchange

Map 4, F4. 712 Orleans St at Royal ☎522-5710.

Daily 7am–5pm.

Hundreds of teas, specialty coffee blends and beans – including Kona and Jamaican Blue Mountain – in a quiet little coffee bar in the heart of the Quarter.

GIFTS

While you could buy souvenirs in many of the stores listed in this chapter, there's also a host of hard-to-categorize places selling well-made, good-looking objects that are perfect to give as **gifts**. The best finds, as ever, are in the Quarter and along Magazine Street.

The Anne Rice Collection

Map 3, D5. The Rink Mall, 2727 Prytania St at Washington Ⓣ899-5996.

Mon–Sat 10am–6pm, Sun 11am–4pm.

Gift shop in which everything is either designed or personally chosen by Rice. There's something for everyone, from lightswitch plates featuring Stefan, Arnaud or Claudia, to Lestat key-chains ("Lestat sucks"), wine, and cologne ("A Scent to Die For"). You'll also find Catholic icons, signed items of Rice's clothing, and artworks by husband Stan.

Big Life Toys

Map 2, L7. 3117 Magazine St at Louisiana Ⓣ895-8695.

Mon–Sat 11am–6pm, Sun noon–5pm.

This kitsch emporium is not just for kids, though the piles of tricks and games will keep the little ones happy. Meanwhile, young-at-heart hipsters will delight in the miniature go-go girls, Mexican wrestlers and debutantes, along with disguises, Tiki toys, cartoon clocks, retro furnishings and the like. There's a children's branch down the street at no. 5430 (Mon–Sat 10am–6pm; Ⓣ899-8697).

Casa del Corazon

Map 4, H5. 901 Chartres St at Dumaine Ⓣ569-9555.

Daily 10am–5pm.

French Quarter corner store crammed with colorful, kitsch Mexican stuff: icons, Jesus gear-stick knobs, glittery Frida Kahlo boxes, tin mirrors, Day of the Dead skeletons, plastic wrestlers and nightlights.

Le Monde Creole

Map 4, E4. 624 Royal St at Toulouse Ⓣ568-1801.

Daily 10am–5pm.

Eclectic little store set back from the street in a courtyard. Run by the people who lead the superb city and plantation tours (p.15), it specializes in ceramics, games, furniture, CDs, videos and antiques, all related to the Creoles. They also carry a great selection of books.

GIFTS

The Living Room

Map 4, H4. 927 Royal St at St Philip ⓣ 595-8860.

Daily 11am–5pm.

Quirky, individualistic crafts with a Southern folk-art feel: glittery jewelry boxes, pop shrines studded with plastic dolls and found objects, Elvis art, jewelry, retro-style glasses and ceramics. You'll also find some antiques, including religious icons.

RHINO

Map 4, A7. Canal Place Mall ⓣ 523-7945.

Mon–Sat 10am–7pm, Sun noon–6pm.

Interesting, varied work – jewelry, ceramics, collages, greeting cards, textiles, hats, glassware, sculpture, clothing – produced by a local co-op that also runs workshops and exhibitions.

Scriptura

Map 2, F7. 5423 Magazine St at Jefferson ⓣ 897-1555.

Mon–Sat 10am–6pm, Sun noon–5pm.

Exquisite store selling delicate handmade notebooks, art papers, rich inks, classy writing paper and designer cards. They also have a selection of butter-soft leather diaries and address books.

Three Dog Bakery

Map 4, H4. 827 Royal St at Dumaine ⓣ 525-2253.

Daily 10am–6pm.

High-camp concept for the pampered pooch – home-baked treats include truffles, petits fours and birthday cakes. Bestsellers include "bark'n'fetch" cookies – try fat-free apple, oatmeal or carob. They also sell doggy-sized tuxes and tutus, aromatherapy healing kits for Fido's down days, and even a "We Pity the Kitties" range of fishy snacks for cats.

HEALTH AND BEAUTY

For a list of **pharmacies**, see p.289. For **spas** (perfect for post-debauchery detox), see p.288.

Fifi Mahony's

Map 4, G5. 828 Chartres St at St Ann ⓣ 525-4343.

Daily noon–6pm.

Fabulous wig store, staffed by friendly, gorgeous boys and girls with neon hair and sparkling eyelids. You can try the hairpieces at a big, lightbulb-edged mirror, or rifle through all manner of nail polish, hair mascara and eye jewels. Wide range of brands, from Urban Decay and Cookiepuss to Fifi's own.

Hové Parfumeur

Map 4, G4. 824 Royal St at St Ann ⓣ 525-7827.

Mon–Sat 10am–5pm.

There's a distinctly old-world ambience at this elegant parfumier. Best seller is the Tea Olive, made from the sweet olive blossom, common in New Orleans gardens; sniff out too the Magnolia, Carnaval and musky Rue Royale. Packaging is beautiful; they also do mail order.

MUSIC

New Orleans has plenty of places to buy good **music**. Prices tend to be lower at the used record stores, but though these are excellent for rare and collectible stuff, they may not have as wide a choice of new releases as the well-stocked superstores.

For a history of New Orleans music, plus discography, see p.322.

Jim Russell Records

Map 3, G7. 1837 Magazine St at St Mary ⓣ 522-2602.

Mon–Sat 10am–7pm, Sun 1–6pm.

Large collection of rare vinyl, along with singles, cassettes and CDs, specializing in soul, R&B, rap and blues.

Louisiana Music Factory

Map 4, B6. 210 Decatur St at Iberville ⓣ 586-1094.

Daily 10am–10pm.

A great source of local music at low prices; one entire wall is lined with eight listening stations for jazz, R&B, Cajun and zydeco. They also deal in

MUSIC

vinyl, along with hard-to-find secondhand music books, posters and T-shirts. The expert staff organize frequent in-store performances.

Magic Bus

Map 4, D5. 527 Conti St at Chartres ⓣ522-0530.

Daily 11am–7pm.

This cavernous old record store may not have as varied a choice as some of the others, but it does offer bargains, especially on local jazz and blues cassettes. Also new, used and rare CDs and vinyl.

Rock and Roll Collectibles

Map 4, K6. 1214 Decatur St at Gov Nicholls ⓣ561-5683.

Daily 10am–8pm.

The place for rare vinyl, this shambolic old store sells the best in secondhand blues, jazz, soul and British imports. Prices can be steep ($80 for a rare Dr John LP, say, and as high as $600 in some cases) but are sometimes negotiable.

Tower Records

Map 4, D6. Riverfront Marketplace, 408 N Peters St

ⓣ529-4411.

Daily 9am–midnight.

Especially good for local sounds – the room dedicated to Louisiana music has a wider choice than many of the specialist record stores – as well as rock, pop and classical music. They also stock videos and books – with the emphasis on alternative titles – and have a Ticketmaster stand (see p.290). Prices tend to be slightly lower than at Virgin, and the choice is better.

Virgin Megastore

Map 4, E6. Jackson Brewery Mall ⓣ671-8100.

Mon 10am–12.30am, Tues–Sun 10am–midnight.

Three floors of CDs, tapes and videos. The local selection is small but well chosen, and there are some books – regional and local titles, mostly, plus music books and photography. The small café, with a terrace overlooking the river, is one of the few places you can sip espresso while watching the activity on the Mississippi, but it's a lackluster place that doesn't invite you to linger.

Gay New Orleans

New Orleans is one of the easiest and most enjoyable cities in the United States for **gay travelers**. The French Quarter, in particular, has a sizeable gay community and a host of gay-owned restaurants, hotels, bars and businesses to serve it. In the anything-goes atmosphere of the Quarter, however, it can be hard to distinguish between gay-only and straight establishments – most places accept most people.

If you're after a wild time, try to plan your visit to coincide with one of New Orleans' **festivals** – especially those that involve dressing up, like Halloween (see p.284) and, of course, Mardi Gras (see p.269) – when the French Quarter bars and clubs are even livelier than usual. One of the biggest gay festivals is the cross-dressing, heavy-drinking extravaganza known as **Southern Decadence** (see p.283), held in the Quarter the weekend before Labor Day. In the fall, there's a **Gay Pride** parade (see p.283), but perhaps because there are so many other opportunities for gay celebration and expression – political activism tends to take second place to partying – it's neither as outrageous nor as well attended as Pride festivals in bigger cities.

CHAPTER FIFTEEN

GAY ACCOMMODATION

Although gay travelers will feel comfortable staying in most places in the city, the following gay-run or -owned guesthouses, concentrated in the French Quarter and Faubourg, are particularly welcoming.

Bon Maison, 835 Bourbon St   ☏ 561-8498; see p.158

The Frenchmen, 417 Frenchmen St   ☏ 948-2166; see p.162

Lafitte Guest House, 1003 Bourbon St   ☏ 581-2678; see p.159

Maison Esplanade, 1244 Esplanade Ave   ☏ 523-8080; see p.163

Rue Royal Inn, 1006 Royal St   ☏ 524-3900; see p.161

St Peter House Hotel, 1005 St Peter St   ☏ 524-9232; see p.162

Ursuline Guest House, 708 Ursulines St   ☏ 525-8509; see p.162

PUBLICATIONS

Ambush, which hits the stands every other Friday, is New Orleans' major gay **listings paper**, available free from clubs, bars, cafés and record stores. Covering the Gulf South region, it's an entertainment paper first and foremost, heavy on juicy gossip and anecdote and low on political editorial. Its online arm, Ⓦ *www.ambushmag.com*, includes a searchable database of back issues. Other useful **Web sites** include Ⓦ *www.gaynewordeans.com* and Ⓦ *www.ambushonline.com*, both of which are worth checking for links to local gay publications, attractions, bars and clubs. Look out, too, for the *Gay and Lesbian Yellow Pages*, which although primarily aimed at residents, does include listings for accommodation, coffeehouses, restaurants and, usefully, dungeons.

PUBLICATIONS

SHOPS AND RESOURCES

Alternatives

Map 4, H3. 909 Bourbon St at Dumaine ☎ 524-5222. Sun, Mon, Wed & Thurs 11am–7pm, Fri & Sat 11am–9pm.

Gift shop selling cards, clothes, books and toys – including a fine selection of trailer-trash Barbies – as well as more practical accessories like condoms and lubricants.

Faubourg Marigny Bookstore

Map 4, M5. 600 Frenchmen St at Chartres ☎ 943-9875. Mon–Fri 10am–8pm, Sat & Sun 10am–6pm.

This friendly gay and lesbian bookstore has been around for some thirty years, selling travel guides, regional titles, fiction, postcards and calendars, and acting as a de facto information center.

GAY TOURS

Run by the exemplary Bienville Foundation, which leads a number of alternative walking tours (see p.15), the **Gay Heritage Tour** (2hr 30min; $20; ☎ 945-6789) is a lively, informative scoot around the French Quarter, concentrating on the gay characters – and homophobes – who have contributed so much to its rich cultural life. Tours leave from outside *Alternatives* (see above), on Wednesday and Saturday at 2pm; call to check and reserve a place.

GAY BARS AND CLUBS

Most of New Orleans' **gay bars and clubs** are in the Quarter or the Faubourg: though the majority of them are geared toward the boys, most of them welcome lesbians, and the ones along Bourbon Street at least are happy to serve straights. The so-called **Rampart Strip**, however, a string of bars and drag joints along North Rampart Street, attracts more locals than tourists, and is not the place for curious straights, however well-meaning. Every place listed below features a dizzying series of daily happy hours and special deals – check the publications listed on p.264.

735

Map 4, G3. 735 Bourbon St at St Ann ⊤ 581-6740.

Daily from 8pm.

Though it's not an exclusively gay venue, the astounding light shows, huge dance floor, pounding hot house and techno, theme nights and top-notch international DJs make this Bourbon Street club a favorite on the gay circuit. There's the usual range of drag parties and dancing boys, plus special girls-only nights.

Bourbon Pub/Parade

Map 4, G3. 801 Bourbon St at St Ann ⊤ 529-2107.

Pub daily 24hr; Parade Mon–Sat from 9pm, Sun from 5pm.

Noisy, sweaty video-bar and club at the heart of the Quarter's gay scene. *Parade*, upstairs, is the liveliest of the gay dance clubs, still hopping long after other places have emptied out. Other draws include frequent happy hours, tea dances, C&W nights and talent contests. Cover varies at *Parade*, but is usually no more than $8.

Café Lafitte in Exile and Balcony Bar

Map 4, H3. 901 Bourbon St at Dumaine ⊤ 522-8397.

Daily 24hr.

Reputedly the oldest gay bar in the nation (continually in operation since the 1950s), this rambunctious, welcoming gay men's bar is a much-loved favorite, with a balcony that becomes party central during Mardi Gras. Drinks specials Mon–Sat 4–9pm, Sun 4–10pm.

Golden Lantern

Map 4, K4. 1239 Royal St at Barracks ⊤ 529-2860.

Daily 24hr.

Established neighborhood gay/drag bar, headquarters for

the Southern Decadence festival (see p.283), usually full with a crowd of devoted regulars. Happy hour daily 5–9am & 5–9pm.

Good Friends and Queen's Head Pub
Map 4, G3. 740 Dauphine St at St Ann ⓣ 566-7191.
Daily 24hr.
In a quiet part of the French Quarter, this good-natured bar has a cozy, neighborhood feel, with a working fireplace and a pool table. The *Queen's Head*, upstairs, is more refined, with a mock-English ambience, a much-used dartboard and a piano player on Sunday afternoon. Daily drinks specials, and daily happy hour 4–9pm.

Le Roundup
Map 4, D3. 819 St Louis St at Dauphine ⓣ 561-8340.
Daily 24hr.
Relaxed neighborhood haunt, favored by drag queens and transsexuals. Allegedly, the C&W jukebox is a favorite of movie star Ashley Judd, who regulars claim

hung out here while taking breaks from filming *Double Jeopardy*.

Oz
Map 4, G3. 800 Bourbon St at St Ann ⓣ 593-9491.
Daily 24hr.
Noisy, high-tech disco with a wild balcony. It's directly opposite the *Bourbon Pub* (see opposite) and very similar, with drag nights, talent shows, fabulous go-go boys and game shows. Cover $4–6 at weekends.

Rawhide 2010
Map 4, G2. 740 Burgundy St at St Ann ⓣ 525-8106.
Daily 24hr.
Hard-core leather and denim bar, with brutalist garage decor, that keeps going around the clock. During Mardi Gras, the Bourbon Street costume awards – the biggest, most flamboyant gathering of revelers in the city – is staged on the sidewalk outside. Happy hour daily 4–9pm.

GAY BARS AND CLUBS

Tonix

Map 4, B3. 216 Bourbon St at Iberville ☎ 299-3900.
Fri & Sat 10pm–dawn.

Swish Bourbon Street club – not exclusively gay – which competes with *735* (see p.266) for the hardest techno, house, garage and hi-NRG.

Voodoo at Congo Square

Map 4, F1. 718 N Rampart St at Orleans ☎ 527-0273.
Daily 24hr.

Friendly neighborhood pub opposite Louis Armstrong Park, home to a loyal crowd hanging out and catching up on local gossip.

Festivals

As befits this party-loving, parade-crazy, multicultural city, New Orleans' calendar is packed with **festivals**. The big one, of course, is the pre-Lenten bacchanalia of **Mardi Gras** – closely followed by the superb **Jazz Fest** – but whenever you come you're bound to coincide with some celebration or other, be it a saint's day or a sinner's beanfeast. Whatever the festivity, music and food feature prominently, as do **street parades**, which occur at the drop of a hat throughout the year. Parades are particularly important in Tremé, where local Social Aid and Pleasure clubs organize lively processions featuring the city's best **brass bands**, followed by a dancing Second Line.

If you're planning to come to New Orleans for Mardi Gras or Jazz Fest, be sure to reserve a hotel room well in advance; see p.155.

MARDI GRAS

New Orleans' **carnival season** – which starts on Twelfth Night and runs for the six weeks or so until Ash Wednesday – is unlike any other in the world. Though the name is used to define the entire season, **Mardi Gras** itself, French for "Fat Tuesday", is simply the culmination of a whirl of parades, parties, bohemian street revels and secret masked balls, all inextricably tied up with the city's byzantine social, racial and political structures. It's hard to imagine another city in the developed world that could, for more than a month, devote all its energy, resources and infrastructure to the simple pursuit of pleasure – and while it's by far the busiest **tourist season**, when the city is invaded by millions

TOP TEN CARNIVAL TUNES

Carnival in New Orleans reels along to its own exuberant soundtrack, much of it penned during the 1950s and 1960s, when Crescent City R&B was in its heyday. Anyone who has danced to Mardi Gras music knows it to be an expresson of sheer life-affirming joy: a peculiarly New Orleans cocktail of R&B mixed with Mardi Gras Indian chants, Second Line beats, barroom boogie-woogie, and Caribbean and African rhythms. Every local recording artist includes a handful of Mardi Gras songs in his or her repertoire: the versions listed below – in chronological order – are agreed to be the definitive and the best.

Carnival Time, Al Johnson
Archetypal 1950s Mardi Gras anthem, all catchy lyrics, driving piano and ear-splitting horns.

Jock-a-Mo, Sugar Boy Crawford
Infectious calypso-tinged hit, recorded in 1953, that flings together Indian patois with hard-driving guitar from Snooks Eaglin.

Mardi Gras Mambo, The Hawkettes
1950s R&B-meets-mambo hit, featuring a 17-year-old Art Neville on vocals and keyboards.

MARDI GRAS

of people, Mardi Gras has always been, above all, a party that New Orleanians throw for themselves. Visitors are wooed, welcomed and shown the time of their lives, but without them carnival would reel on regardless, dressing wildly, drinking and dancing its bizarre way into Lent.

Much of official carnival revolves around the members-only **krewes** (see p.309), who as well as organizing the public **parades** also hold elite society **balls**, glittering,

---

Go to the Mardi Gras, Professor Longhair
The usual piano wizardry from the Prof, plus a young Mac Rebennack (who later reinvented himself as Dr John) on guitar.

Big Chief Part 2, Professor Longhair
Probably the finest carnival song ever; a fabulously danceable tribute to the Mardi Gras Indians, to New Orleans and to the sheer pleasure of being alive.

Indian Red, Wild Tchoupitoulas
Venerable Mardi Gras Indian incantation recorded in 1972 by the Neville Brothers and the Wild Tchoupitoulas.

Mardi Gras in New Orleans, Dirty Dozen Brass Band
Longhair's rollicking Second Line classic performed with customary verve by the elder statesmen of the contemporary brass bands.

New Suit, Wild Magnolias
Hard funk homage to the Indians and their "pretty" outfits, driven by the foghorn vocals of Big Chief Bo Dollis.

Gimme My Money Back, Tremé Brass Band
Contemporary Second Line parade classic.

Do the Fat Tuesday, Kermit Ruffins
High-spirited call to dance in tongue-in-cheek 1960s style.

arcane affairs that are strictly invitation-only. But visitors are more likely to be drawn into unofficial carnival: a whirlwind of satirical shindigs thrown by **alternative krewes** (see p.277), impromptu parades and spur-of-the-moment carousing in the French Quarter and the Faubourg, and always, everywhere, the city's phenomenal **live music**. Of course, there's also the heavy drinking, stripping off and throwing up on **Bourbon Street**, where carnival gets down to its barest, basest essentials.

Mardi Gras is always the day before Ash
Wednesday: in 2002 it falls on Feb 12, in
2003 on March 4, and in 2004 it's on Feb 24.

You need stamina to survive carnival, which gets increasingly frenzied as it progresses. To have the most fun, you'll want to go with the flow: catch a couple of the big parades, rifle the thrift stores and costume outlets (see p.256) for fabulous **disguises** and **masks** (you'll feel left out if you don't), keep your eyes open for flyers and listen to the local radio (WWOZ; see p.11) for news of the best gigs and parties. Official events, parade schedules and routes are advertised in the press and in the glossy handbook **Arthur Hardy's Mardi Gras Guide**; for a more portable, and slightly hipper, alternative, pick up the folding **Mardi Card**. Both are widely available at newsstands and stores throughout the city.

For a history of Mardi Gras, see p.306.

The parades

More than sixty krewes organize major **parades** in the weeks leading up to the big day: huge, overblown events, featuring colorful, motorized floats and masked riders hurling "throws" (see p.274) to the shrieking hordes. Though they occur throughout the city, the biggest parades head downtown and attract hundreds of thousands of people. The crowds, and the size of the floats, make it impossible for the parades to pass through the French Quarter; they head instead along broader, safer roads such as Canal and St Charles. The busiest parade days are the two weekends before Mardi Gras itself.

Parades follow routes of up to six or seven miles and can take at least two hours to pass any one point, their multi-tiered floats joined by the city's famed high-school marching bands – whose ear-splitting blast of drums and brass can be heard for miles – along with weirdly masked horsemen, stilt walkers and the **Second Liners** who dance behind. Night parades may also be accompanied by black **flambeaux carriers**, whose nerve-wracking swirling and leaping is rewarded by a scattering of quarters thrown by the crowds.

Visitors who don't fancy scrabbling on the sidewalk for plastic trinkets pay for places on **stands**, often linked to a hotel or restaurant, where $10 or so gets you a good view and an elevated vantage point for catching throws. In the less congested areas outside downtown, families colonize whole swathes of sidewalk with picnic boxes, folding chairs and stepladders. Others hop around, dipping in and out of side streets to catch up and overtake the rumbling floats. Good **viewing areas** include Canal Street, which sees the densest crowds, and St Charles Avenue, especially between Melpomene and Jackson, where there's more of a local scene. Bear in mind when staking your place that parade schedules tend to be approximate – Zulu, in particular, who parades first thing on Mardi Gras day, is notorious for setting off two or three hours late.

There's a great Mardi Gras exhibition
at the Presbytère; see p.29.

MARDI GRAS

BEADS AND THROWS

One of the best things about New Orleans' Mardi Gras parades is that you get to participate. While marveling at a particularly inventive, elaborate or just plain funny float (and bitching about the lame ones) is part of the fun, most people are here to do more than just watch. Everyone, from the wiry, hyper kids with jabbing elbows to the fierce old ladies hovering above the crowds on customized stepladders, are out to catch "throws". Be they strings of beads, fluffy toys, beakers, bikini briefs or doubloons (tin coins marked with krewe insignia) – once the masked float-riders start throwing them, the leaping and screaming and begging begins. Competition among spectators is fierce, and the krewe members milk the hysteria for all it's worth, teasing and taunting the hoi polloi below them. Souvenirs vary in worth: the bright, cheap strings of beads that adorn balconies everywhere are the most common, while Zulu spears and bizarrely garbed Zulu coconuts – handed out rather than thrown – have become the most prized. While old-guard krewes – including Rex – tend to be more restrained with their throws, the super krewes (see p.312) are the most excessive. Endymion float-riders are known for their generosity, showering the streets with bagfuls of fat beads, perilous towers of plastic beakers and a rainstorm of doubloons, while Orpheus can always be counted on to come up with something new – their "virbloon" mini-discs, launched in 2000, put a millennial spin on tradition. Individual float-riders provide their own throws; it is not unusual for a super krewe member to spend at least $1000 on beads.

Lundi Gras

Lundi Gras, the day before Mardi Gras, is one of the liveliest of the season. Things get going at around 10am, when some of the city's best musicians, most of whom

Though street maskers had been tossing candy up to women on French Quarter balconies since the 1830s, the first parade throws appeared in 1871, lobbed at spectators by a member of the Twelfth Night Revelers dressed as Father Christmas. By the early twentieth century riders were slinging ribbons, confetti and glass beads as a matter of course – much to the umbrage of commentators who complained that it made "hoodlums of the boys and mendicants of the girls, both failing to enjoy the real beauty and grandeur of the floats in their wild desire to get something for nothing".

Nowadays this "wild desire" has reached feverpitch. Throw frenzy rages long after the parades have rumbled past, triggering a drunken flirtation ritual whereby complete strangers, already heavily laden with beads, approach each other begging to swap some particular string in exchange for another. Over the years the stakes have become higher – today those women on French Quarter balconies, out-of-town co-eds, most of them, respond to the challenge to "show your tits!", chanted by goggling street mobs, by pulling up their shirts in exchange for strings of beads and roars of boozy approval. In recent years the guys – gay and straight – have started to join in, eagerly pulling down their pants at the slightest provocation. Though stripping off uptown, where carnival is more of a family affair, would certainly be frowned upon, in the French Quarter pretty much anything goes. New Orleanians leave these antics to the tourists: anyone desperate to see (or join) the show should head for Bourbon Street – a tacky strip at the best of times, and sheer drunken mayhem during Mardi Gras.

MARDI GRAS ●

will have been gigging till daybreak for the past fortnight, play at **Zulu**'s free party at Woldenberg Park by the river. It's an outstanding event, featuring Second Line parades, food stalls and two music stages. After a few hours lying on the grass, snacking on fried chicken and cold beer, listening to R&B, jazz and blues, it's time to leap up again and rush off to see the king and queen arrive by boat. When they've disembarked, you can head just around the corner to the **Plaza d'España**, where at 6pm, in a formal ceremony unchanged since Rex first flounced onto the scene more than a century ago, the mayor hands the city to Rex, King of Carnival. Everyone cheers, and the businessman in the golden robes, page-boy wig and false beard shakes his scepter graciously. Then follows a ceremonial meeting between Zulu and Rex, which recognizes the popularity and political importance of the black krewe while bowing to the historical supremacy of Rex. The party continues with big-name bands and fireworks, after which people head off for the **Proteus** and **Orpheus** parades or to embark on yet another frenzied evening of live music. Most clubs are still hopping well into Mardi Gras morning.

For more about the Mardi Gras krewes, see p.307.

Mardi Gras

The fun starts early on Mardi Gras day, when walking clubs, made up of local musicians, writers and sundry lowlife, stride through uptown on their ritualized bar crawls. Meanwhile, on the other side of town, the fabulously costumed **Mardi Gras Indians** gather to parade, preparing for their afternoon standoffs in Tremé. **Zulu**, scheduled to set off at 8.30am – but usually starting much later – heads from uptown to Canal Street, its float-riders daubed in war paint and dressed in grass skirts. Their wild burlesque is trailed by the motley **Krewe du Jieux** walking parade, organized by members of the Klezmer Allstars (see p.228). The refined **Rex** parade, dominated by the

ALTERNATIVE KREWES

The spirit of old Mardi Gras, when maskers took to the streets to create their own parades and parties, is kept alive today in the city's many alternative, or unofficial krewes. Chief among them is the anarchic Krewe du Vieux (from Vieux Carré, another name for the French Quarter). Their irreverent ball, "the Krewe du Vieux Do" – basically a wild party, open to all – is the first of the season, starting with a weird and wonderful march that weaves its way from the Faubourg through the French Quarter. Makeshift costumes and bizarre mule-hauled mini-floats satirize current local affairs and scandals, while the funkiest brass bands blast the roofs off. As usual with New Orleans' walking parades, anyone is welcome to join in, and within minutes the krewe members are trailing a raggle-taggle Second Line behind them. Uptown, the Krewe of OAK's parade (read: bar crawl) climaxes at the *Maple Leaf* (see p.233) for live music and food well into the early hours. Costumes reveal as much flesh as possible, as the krewe's name ("Outrageous And Kinky") suggests.

And then there's the Mystic Krewe of Barkus, made up of dogs, a thousand or so of whom trot proudly through the French Quarter – all spiffed up on some spurious theme (Saturday Bite Fever, say, or perhaps Joan of Bark), and presided over by their own king and queen. The dogs, along with owners and onlookers, then stop by the *Good Friends* gay bar (see p.267) to be toasted by city officials before scampering off to a happy party in Louis Armstrong Park.

colossal Boeuf Gras, hits Canal Street in the afternoon, followed by a flotilla of trucks filled with families and children flinging leftover and discarded beads.

Ironically, by the time Rex turns up, most people have had their fill of the official parades. The wildest party is

MARDI GRAS

going on in the **French Quarter**, which is teeming with masked, costumed merrymakers, bead-strung tourists, strutting drag divas, tit-flashing teens and banner-carrying Baptists preaching hellfire and brimstone. Most of the action is on the streets – indeed, many bars and restaurants close for the day – but some **restaurants** offer special packages whereby you pay $50 or so for a day pass that includes food, drink and, crucially, use of the restrooms.

To read about New Orleans' Mardi Gras Indians, turn to p.310.

Though it's best to do as most people do and drift spontaneously through the maelstrom, there are a couple of high points to know about. The surreal **St Ann walking parade**, a circus-like procession of the most extraordinary costumes, gathers in the Bywater and hits the Quarter at around 11am, usually stopping for drinks at the *R-Bar* (see p.213) before marching down Royal Street to Canal. Anyone is welcome to prance through the streets with them; you'll fit in best if your costume is wild, beautiful or creative. Meanwhile, on the corner of St Ann and Burgundy, the outrageous gay costume competition known as the **Bourbon Street awards** (see p.267) gets going at noon. This is one to watch rather than join – unless, of course, you're a drag queen who has just happened to wander by in a twenty-foot-high sequinned seahorse ensemble.

Late afternoon, hipsters head to the Faubourg, where **Frenchmen Street** is ablaze with bizarrely costumed carousers and drummers in a scene as skewed as any medieval misrule. The fun continues throughout the Quarter and the Faubourg until **midnight**, when a siren wail heralds the forceful arrival of mounted police who sweep through Bourbon Street and declare through megaphones that carnival is officially over. Some bars do stay open later, but most people, masks askew, are drifting home by 1am. Like all good Catholic cities, New Orleans takes carnival very seriously. Midnight marks the onset of Lent, and repentance can begin.

JAZZ FEST

The internationally acclaimed **New Orleans Jazz and Heritage Festival** (**Jazz Fest**) is held during the last weekend (Fri–Sun) in April and the first weekend (Thurs–Sun) in May, at the Fair Grounds racetrack near City Park. Started in 1969 as a small-scale celebration of local roots music, it has mushroomed to become an enormous affair, rivaling Mardi Gras in size and importance. Detractors complain that it has suffered as a consequence, and that corporate sponsorship has done little to improve the quality of the festival, but gripes about overcrowding and occasional poor acoustics apart, it's still a fantastic show, attracting a mellower audience than Mardi Gras; the "jazz" of the title is taken as a loose concept, with a dozen stages hosting R&B, gospel, funk, blues, African, Caribbean, Latin, Cajun, folk, bluegrass, reggae, country, Mardi Gras Indian and brass band music. Here, even more than at any other of New Orleans' festivals, the **food** is as big a deal as the music, with dozens of stalls dishing up truly spectacular local cuisine.

The **Fair Grounds site** stays open from 11am to 7pm. While some people book up for all seven days, others prefer to pace themselves; there's plenty going on in town throughout the festival, including free in-store performances by Jazz Fest acts at local **record stores**. The second Thursday at the Fair Grounds, traditionally one of the quietest days of the festival, before the weekenders have hit town, is a favorite with locals; the second Saturday, on the other hand, has been known to draw more than 100,000 spectators. In the **evenings**, in addition to the official big-name concerts staged all over town, smaller **clubs** feature superb line-ups and unofficial jam sessions into the early hours.

With some ninety bands playing each day, most Jazz Festers have to make tough decisions, foregoing a few of their favorites rather than dashing from stage to stage in a doomed attempt to catch them all. Don't overlook the interviews and workshops staged in the **Grandstand** – the tranquil, air-conditioned building is a great place to cool off and calm down, and it also benefits from proper, flushing toilets. **Schedules** are listed a couple of months in advance on the **Web site** (ⓦ *www.nojazzfest.com*), and during the festival itself in the *Times-Picayune* and *Gambit*. The best program, however, comes free with the music paper *Offbeat*, whose Web site (ⓦ *www.offbeat.com*) also features a Jazz Fest preview page and messageboard.

Tickets, available from Ticketmaster (ⓣ 522-5555 or ⓦ *www.ticketmaster.com*), cost $15 per day; you can also buy them for $20 on the day at the Ticketmaster stand in Tower Records (see p.262) but you may have to wait in a long line, and they charge a handling fee. The official evening concerts, which book up fast, cost between $25 and $35. To **get to the Fair Grounds**, hop on a shuttle bus from downtown ($10 roundtrip), or try your luck finding a taxi; they hike their rates during the festival and drop off at designated ranks near the Fair Grounds.

For more details, call ⓣ 522-4786 or check the festival's Web site (see above). And if you're interested in volunteering to be a steward, call ⓣ 558-6144.

A FESTIVAL CALENDAR

The following list covers a wide spread of festivals, but is by no means exhaustive; for a **full rundown**, including details of sporting events such as New Year's **Sugarbowl** game (see p.88), contact the **New Orleans CVB** (☎1-800/672-6124 or 566-5011, ⓦ*www.neworleanscvb.com*). **Neighborhood events** are announced on WWOZ radio station (see p.11).

JANUARY 6 TO THE DAY BEFORE ASH WEDNESDAY

Mardi Gras (see p.269).

MARCH

St Patrick's Day

New Orleanians celebrate the Irish saint's day (**March 17**) in fine style, starting on the Friday before with a French Quarter walking parade that sets off from *Molly's at the Market* bar (see p.210). The next day, another parade heads through the Irish Channel – the blue-collar neighborhood between the Garden District and the river – with float-riders throwing vegetables to a green-bead-clad bunch of roisterers swigging green beer and jello shots. On March 17 itself, there's a street party in the Irish Channel, organized by

Parasol's, 2533 Constance (see p.216; ⓦ*www.parasols.com*).

St Joseph's Day/Super Sunday

The Sicilian saint's day, which falls on **March 19**, roughly halfway through Lent, is a big deal in this most Catholic of North American cities. Churches build massive altars of food, groaning with bread, fig-cakes, cookies and stuffed artichokes, while devout worshippers continue the tradition of taking out newspaper ads inviting the public to come and admire their family shrine and to share food. The French Quarter parade is more sedate than many; contact the American-Italian Renaissance Foundation for more details (ⓦ*www.airf.com*). The Sunday closest to St Joseph's (**Super Sunday**) is also the only time outside Mardi Gras that the **Mardi Gras Indians** (see p.310) take to the streets.

A FESTIVAL CALENDAR: JAN–MARCH

Tennessee Williams Literary Festival

This superb five-day festival, in **late March**, attracts internationally known actors and writers – recent attendees have included Richard Ford, Margaret Atwood and John Berendt. Though ground zero is the French Quarter's Petit Théâtre du Vieux Carré (see p.238), many of the readings and discussions – on subjects as varied as presidential speeches, Elvis, and the gothic elements of jazz – are held in local bars. Related events include masterclasses, a book fair, concerts, walking tours and performances of Williams' plays. The finale, the *Streetcar Named Desire* shouting contest, in which overwrought Stanleys compete in Jackson Square to holler "Stellaaaa!" as loudly as they can, has become a cult. Recently, Stellas have begun to shout for Stanley, too, so it all gets wonderfully noisy. Prices aren't low – $35–45 for panels and masterclasses – but the organizers are always looking for volunteer ushers, stewards and ticket-takers. For schedules and full details, check ⓦ*www.tennesseewilliams.net* or call ⓣ581-1144.

MARCH/APRIL (WEEK AFTER EASTER)

Spring Fiesta

Perfect for nosy parkers and decorative-arts fans alike – five days, spread across two weekends, during which the public is invited to ogle the interiors of many of the loveliest private homes in the French Quarter and Garden District. It's all rather genteel, with guides dressed up in hooped skirts and a classical concert series. For details, call ⓣ581-1367.

EARLY APRIL

French Quarter Festival

Lively, free music festival that has come to rival Jazz Fest (see p.279) for the quality and variety of music – classical, world, brass, R&B, trad jazz

– on offer. For three days the Quarter is even more vibrant than usual, with stages and food stalls along Royal and Bourbon streets, in Jackson Square and Woldenberg Park, plus free gigs, parades, workshops, tours and fireworks. Contact ☎ 522-5730 or Ⓦ *www.frenchquarterfestivals.org*

END OF APRIL TO BEGINNING OF MAY

Jazz Fest See p.279.

JULY

Essence Music Festival
What started in 1995 as a one-off event organized by the eponymous African-American magazine, has become a big deal, bringing in visitors from around the country for the best in black music, writing and theater. Contact ☎ 523-5652.

SEPTEMBER

Southern Decadence
New Orleans' biggest gay extravaganza, held over five days on and around **Labor Day** (first weekend of the month), brings nearly 100,000 people to the gay bars and clubs of the French Quarter. It culminates in an unruly costume parade of thousands on the Sunday afternoon, organized by the *Golden Lantern* bar (see p.266). For a peek at what to expect, check Ⓦ *www.southerndecadence.com*

New Orleans Gay and Lesbian Pride
Surprisingly, with its significant gay population, New Orleans' Pride event, held at the **end of the month**, is a relatively small affair, based in Louis Armstrong Park. Contact ☎ 943-1999 or Ⓦ *www.gayneworleans.com*

Words and Music
Refined week-long event, held at the **end of**

September, focusing on the work of Faulkner and other Southern writers, with panels, workshops and readings, as well as music events and cocktail parties. It's organized by Faulkner House Books (see p.250; ℡ 524-2940, ⓦ *www.wordsandmusic.org*).

OCTOBER

Swampfest

Terrific music festival held in Audubon Zoo on the **first two weekends** of the month. Celebrating the music and food of southern Louisiana, it features big-name Cajun and zydeco bands, crafts demonstrations and some truly fantastic food stalls. Contact ℡ 581-4629 or 1-800/774-7394.

Art for Art's Sake

The city's major art event occurs on the **first Saturday** of October. Highlights include gallery receptions in the Arts District and on Magazine Street, a block party along Julia Street and a closing gala at the CAC (see p.87; ℡ 523-1216, ⓦ *www.cacno.org*).

New Orleans Film and Video Festival

Though it's no Sundance, this well-regarded festival, a week-long event held in **early or mid-October**, showcases big-name independent features and short experimental works. The major premieres are screened at the Landmark and Prytania cinemas (see p.240), while independent shorts show at the Southern Rep Theater (see p.238). Call ℡ 523-3818 for details or look at ⓦ *www.neworleansfilmfest.com*

Halloween

Thanks to its long-held fascination with all things morbid, and the local passion for partying and costuming, New Orleans is the perfect place to celebrate Halloween (**October 31**). Pale-faced Goths start descending a week or so before the big day, attending their vampire conferences and covens;

gruesome Haunted Houses pop up all around town, moonlit walking tours skulk through the cemeteries, and clubs, bars and restaurants host costume competitions. The best public events include the wild, arty "Decadence" bash, a free party usually thrown somewhere in the Bywater (flyers start appearing in the hipper Faubourg and Quarter bars a week or so before); the walking parade organized by *Molly's* bar in the Quarter (see p.210); and the thousands-strong masked fundraiser for Lazarus House, a local AIDS hospice. On the night itself, get dressed up and head to the Faubourg, where you'll find the scariest street party in town.

OCTOBER/ NOVEMBER

- - - - - - - - - - - - - - - - - -

Tremé Arts and Cultural Festival

A weekend event held at the end of October or beginning of November, featuring the best in jazz, R&B, blues, swing, gospel, brass and Mardi Gras Indian music. Stages and stalls are rigged up on the grounds of St Augustine's Church, just a couple of blocks from the Quarter; sit back on the grass, tuck into a big plate of fried chicken cooked by the women of the church and wash it all down with a cold beer. Also receptions, parades and short walking tours of Tremé. Contact ☎ 944-7278.

DECEMBER

- - - - - - - - - - - - - - - - - -

Creole Christmas

Though the entire city looks gorgeous during the festive season, garlanded with lights and beribboned wreaths, the French Quarter really pulls out all the stops. Events include tours of patios and private homes; candlelight caroling; jazz masses at the cathedral; cooking demonstrations, and prix-fixe feasts, known as reveillons, put on by the finest Creole restaurants. City Park has its own festival of lights and an ice rink open for the season, while many of the River

Road plantations host festive tours complete with carolers and mulled wine. For information, check ⓦ *www.frenchquarterfestivals.org*

New Year's Eve
New Orleans, which always throws a good party, is a fantastic New Year's destination. Festivities are concentrated around Jackson Square, with fireworks over the river and a whole lot of reveling throughout the French Quarter.

City directory

AIRLINES Aeroméxico ☏ 1-800/237-6639; American ☏1-800/433-7300; British Airways ☏ 1-800/247-9297; Continental ☏ 1-800/525-0280; Delta ☏ 1-800/221-1212; Northwest ☏ 1-800/225-2525; Southwest ☏ 1-800/435-9792; TWA ☏ 1-800/892-2746; United ☏ 1-800/241-6522; USAir ☏ 1-800/428-4322.

AMERICAN EXPRESS 201 St Charles Ave (Mon–Fri 8.30am–5pm; ☏ 586-8201).

AREA CODE ☏ 504.

ATMs Most of New Orleans' banks, and many of its bars, have ATMs; most accept bank cards linked to the Cirrus or Plus systems, for a fee of between $2 and $4 per transaction.

BANKS AND EXCHANGE New Orleans has few bureaux de change, though there is one at the airport (daily 6am–7pm). To change currency you're better off heading for a bank (Mon–Fri 9am–5/6pm, Sat 9am–noon); bring photo ID.

CAR RENTAL National firms represented in New Orleans include Alamo ☏ 1-800/327-9633; Avis ☏ 1-800/331-1212; Budget ☏ 1-800/527-0700; Enterprise ☏ 1-800/736-8222; Hertz ☏ 1-800/654-3131; and National ☏ 1-800/227-7368. Most have offices at the airport and downtown; rates vary, so call around.

CREDIT CARDS To report lost or stolen credit cards: Amex ☏ 1-800/528-4800; Mastercard ☏ 1-800/826-2181; Visa ☏ 1-800/336-8472.

EMERGENCIES ☏ 911 for police, fire and ambulance.

GYMS AND SPAS Day membership ($12) to the Downtown Fitness Center, in Canal Place (see p.242), gives you access to classes, weights, sauna and steam room (Mon–Fri 6am–9pm, Sat & Sun 9am–6pm; ☏ 525-2956), plus use of the rooftop pool at the *Meridien Hotel* on Canal St (☏ 527-6750). They also offer 3-, 5- and 7-visit passes ($30/$45/$55). As for spas, Belladonna, 2900 Magazine St (Mon–Fri 9am–8pm, Sat 9am–6pm; ☏ 891-4393), offers alternative treatments, including massage and aromatherapy, from $40; in the Quarter, try Earthsavers, at 434 Chartres (Mon–Wed, Fri & Sat 10am–6pm, Thurs 10am–8pm, Sun noon–5pm; ☏ 581-4999).

HOSPITALS New Orleans Charity Hospital, 1532 Tulane Ave (☏ 568-2311).

INTERNET ACCESS Access is free at the cybercafé at the CAC (see p.202). In the Quarter, *Bastille Internet Café*, 605 Toulouse St (daily 10am–11pm; ☏ 581-1150), is the cheapest ($2.50 per 15min, $7.50 per hr). Kinko's, 762 St Charles Ave (☏ 581-2541; 24hr) in the CBD charges 25¢ per minute.

LAUNDROMATS Washing Well Laundryteria, 841 Bourbon St (Mon–Fri 7.30am–6pm, Sat till 2pm; ☏ 523-9995), offers same-day laundry and dry cleaning, though it's not cheap. Checkpoint Charlie's, the 24-hour bar in the Faubourg (see p.212), has coin-op machines at the back.

LIBRARIES The New Orleans Public Library is at 219 Loyola Ave (Mon–Thurs 10am–6pm, Fri & Sat 10am–5pm; ☏ 529-7323, ⓦ www.nutrias.org). In the Quarter, the Williams Research Center, 410 Chartres (Tues–Sat 10am–4.30pm; ☏ 598-7171, ⓦ www.hnoc.org) is a good resource for local history and jazz.

OPTICIAN Orleans Optical, 819 Canal St (Mon–Fri 9.30am–5.30pm; ☏ 523-3385), sells frames and lenses and does repairs.

PHARMACIES The Rite Aids at 3401 St Charles (☏ 895-0344) and 4330 S Claiborne (☏ 895-6655) are open 24hr; there's also a 24-hour drive-through Walgreen's at Claiborne and Napoleon (☏ 891-0976). Also Walgreen's at 900 Canal St (Mon–Fri 7am–9pm, Sat 9am–6pm, Sun 10am–6pm; ☏ 568-1271) and in the Quarter at 134 Royal St (daily 7am–midnight; ☏ 522-2736) and 619 Decatur St (daily 8am–midnight; ☏ 525-7260). The Royal Pharmacy, 1101 Royal St (Mon–Sat 9am–6pm; ☏ 523-5401) is a lovely old place with a soda fountain (not in use).

PHONECARDS Semans House, just off Canal at 115 Royal St (☏ 529-6000), sells cheap national and international phonecards.

PHOTO PROCESSING Avoid the cowboy outfits along Canal Street and the first blocks of the French Quarter; try Walgreen's (see above, under "Pharmacies"), or French Quarter Camera, 809 Decatur St (daily 9.30am–6pm; ☏ 529-2974).

POLICE There's a police station at 334 Royal St in the French Quarter. In emergencies call ☏ 911.

POST OFFICE The main post office is at 701 Loyola Ave (Mon–Fri 7am–11pm, Sat 7am–8pm, Sun noon–5pm; zip code 70140 for General Delivery). An equivalent service, along with fax, photocopying, FedEx and the like, is offered by French Quarter Postal Emporium, 1000 Bourbon St (Mon–Fri 9.30am–6pm, Sat 10am–3pm; ☏ 525-6652) and Royal Mail, 828 Royal St (Mon–Fri 8.30am–6.30pm, Sat 9.30am–5.30pm; ☏ 522-8523).

TAX New Orleans' sales tax is 9 percent, or 12 percent on hotel bills. For foreigners, the Louisiana Tax-Free shopping (LTFS) scheme reimburses the tax on all goods that you can

OPTICIAN–TAX

take out of the country. Most participating businesses display a sticker; it's worth asking if you don't see one. Show your passport and they'll give you a voucher, redeemable – with the sales receipt – at the LTFS booth at the airport (daily 7am–6pm). Refunds of less than $500 are given out in cash on the spot; higher sums will be mailed. There's a small handling fee.

TICKETS Ticketmaster (☎ 522-5555) has a booth (daily 10am–7.30pm) in Tower Records, 408 N Peters St.

TIME New Orleans is on Central Standard Time, six hours behind Greenwich Mean Time. Daylight-Saving Time when clocks go forward an hour, runs from the first Sunday in April to the last Sunday in October.

TIPPING New Orleans' economy is based on tourism and the service industry, yet wages tend to be low. Wait staff in restaurants expect tips of around 17.5 percent, higher if you've had particularly good service. Bar staff should get 15 percent, or a dollar per round, whichever is higher; taxi drivers 15 percent; hotel porters about $1 per piece of baggage; and housekeeping staff $1 per night.

WEDDINGS Though it may not yet rival Las Vegas as the hip place to get hitched, New Orleans is a great destination for weddings. If you get overtaken by the romance of it all, French Quarter Wedding Chapel (☎ 598-6808) offers same-day ceremonies and vow renewals, throwing in cake, bubbly and photos for as little as $99. You can pledge your troth in a courtyard, by the river, in a cemetery or even outside St Louis Cathedral (only the great and the good can afford to get married inside). They'll even help you obtain the Louisiana license. If the conventional path is not for you, the Voodoo Museum (see p.56) can provide a genuine voodoo priest or priestess to conduct alternative lifestyle and commitment ceremonies.

CONTEXTS

A brief history of New Orleans

T he history of New Orleans is inextricably tied up with that of the **Mississippi River**, which has been its *raison d'être*, the source of its fortunes and its potential destroyer. In 1543, **Hernando de Soto**, exploring the Gulf of Mexico as part of the relentless Spanish quest for gold in the Americas, encountered the river somewhere close to Natchez, in today's state of Mississippi; he died of a fever before he could establish any claim to the land, however, and more than a century passed before another expedition was dispatched to the Gulf. This time it was **France**, the most powerful nation in Europe, who hoped to establish a foothold on the shoreline, and thus form a link between French territories in Canada and the West Indies.

The French colony

In 1682, while France and England were grappling over the lucrative fur trade in the Mississippi valley, Robert Cavalier, **Sieur de la Salle**, journeyed down the Mississippi from

Quebec. Reaching the mouth of the river, he planted a cross claiming the entire Mississippi valley for France and named it **Louisiana** in honor of his monarch, Louis XIV. La Salle returned to France a hero and was sent back two years later, hoping to build a city; he lost his way, however, landed on the Texas coast, and was eventually assassinated by his men as they headed overland toward Canada in a vain search for the river.

Under Québecois brothers Pierre le Moyne, **Sieur d'Iberville** and Jean-Baptiste le Moyne, **Sieur de Bienville**, in 1698 the French sent a second expedition to establish a colony from where they could trade with the Spanish in Mexico and block the westward expansion of the British. They settled along the coast, setting up inland trading posts at Natchez and Natchitoches; the capital was Biloxi, in present-day Mississippi.

In 1717, preoccupied with the war in Europe, Philippe, Duc d'Orléans – regent for the 5-year-old Louis XV – handed over responsibility for the development of Louisiana to Scottish financier **John Law**. Through a clever boosting campaign, Law's Company of the West engineered a major investment scam, in which shareholders were sold stakes in a promised gold- and silver-filled paradise peopled with friendly natives who would work for free. This so-called **Mississippi Bubble** burst in 1720, bankrupting many of its investors; by then many of them had already left Europe for Louisiana, only to be stranded without the wherewithal to return.

Meanwhile, Bienville, now governor of the colony, was ordered to establish a city near the mouth of the Mississippi. As it was almost impossible to navigate the treacherous lower reaches of the river, impeded by swamps, snags and sandbars, he chose a site some hundred miles upriver, on a portage that led to Lake Pontchartrain. Seeing the twin potential for defense and trade afforded by this convenient route between the river and the Gulf, Bienville had high hopes for his city, and named it **La Nouvelle Orléans** for the French regent.

Progress was slow for the early settlers, who, in the face of hurricanes and epidemics, painstakingly cleared the cane-break and set about building levees in an attempt to protect the banks from annual flooding. In 1721, engineer **Adrien de Pauger** laid out a military-style grid-plan on the morass – a layout that remains intact in the French Quarter. A year later, Bienville persuaded the French to shift the colonial capital from Biloxi to New Orleans; within five years or so the population doubled, more streets were built and drainage vastly improved.

The first **colonists** were a mixed bunch: convicts and aristocrats from France, French-Canadian adventurers and, between 1719 and 1730, a massive influx of **slaves** from Africa and the West Indies. These were joined by the **free people of color**, educated and wealthy Francophones, most of whom were slave-owners from the West Indian colonies and who, unlike the enslaved blacks, held property rights and a limited amount of political power. Given the large slave population, in 1724 Bienville adopted the **Code Noir** as used by the French to govern Saint-Domingue (Haiti). The code laid out laws establishing the rights and responsibilities of both enslaved Africans and their owners, and while placing restrictions on slaves – including a ban on mixed marriages and property ownership – it also afforded them rights unknown in Anglo colonies. Crucially, as well as being allowed to sell their skills independently, New Orleans slaves were given Sundays off. Thus grew the Sunday gatherings in **Congo Square**, a patch of land behind the city where the slaves danced, drummed and traded in their thousands. The only place in the nation where slaves were permitted to gather freely, Congo Square was a breeding ground for jazz and for the spread of

THE FRENCH COLONY

voodoo throughout the city; although the Code Noir pronounced **Catholicism** to be the official religion, slaves used the gatherings to maintain and strengthen their own rituals and beliefs.

Due to internal wrangling, Bienville was recalled to France in 1725. Almost immediately, relations with the local Native Americans – with whom Bienville had been on reasonably good terms – deteriorated, climaxing in 1729 with an alliance between the Natchez and a group of slaves that led to a massacre at **Fort Rosalie**, some 150 miles upriver from New Orleans; 250 colonists were murdered and 450 women, children and slaves kidnapped before the French executed the rebels and virtually decimated the Natchez tribe.

Although he returned to govern in 1731, Bienville resigned for good in 1743 under pressure from his rivals, who held him personally responsible for the floods, droughts, epidemics and Native American uprisings that blighted the colony. His replacement, the Québecois **Marquis de Vaudreuil**, brought to this shabby outpost the fashions, customs and corruption of the French court; New Orleans' first theatrical production was staged soon after, and balls and musical performances filled the calendar. Meanwhile, as Bienville had predicted, the city steadily grew to become a major **market** for the lumber, bricks, tar, tobacco, indigo, hide and sugar being taken from the interior to the West Indies, the eastern seaboard and Europe, and the cargos of silk, wines, cocoa, spices and silver coming in from overseas.

The Spanish era

In 1754, the **French-Indian War** (which merged with what became known in Europe as the Seven Years' War) broke out between the French and English, grappling over their American colonies. After England seized Canada in 1760, Louis XV signed the secret **Treaty of Fontainebleau**, handing New Orleans and all Louisiana west of the Mississippi over to his cousin, Carlos III of Spain, for safekeeping. Carlos, for his part, was keen to establish a buffer between the encroaching British and his colony in Mexico. In 1763, the **Treaty of Paris**, which ended the Seven Years' War and effectively marked the end of France's involvement in North America, handed England all French territory east of the Mississippi except New Orleans – which only then did Louis XV reveal he had already passed over to the Spanish.

The people of New Orleans were not happy with their new Spanish status. Some attempted to form a republic, calling for the overthrow of the first Spanish governor, **Antonio de Ulloa**. In October 1768, Ulloa fled to Cuba to be replaced by **Alexandro O'Reilly**, an Irish soldier of fortune who had worked his way up the Spanish ranks. Arriving with some three thousand troops, O'Reilly promptly executed the rebels in the Place d'Armes.

Despite early resistance, however, New Orleans benefited from its period as a Spanish colony; sensibly, the governors maintained French as the official language and allowed French culture to remain intact. The Code Noir, however, was replaced by the Spanish system: slaves could now buy their freedom, and eventually thousands of slaves, mostly women and children, were **freed**. The Spanish also adopted an open **immigration** policy, which tripled the city's population. Newcomers included Anglo-Americans escaping the American revolution in the east, French Acadians banished by the British from Canada, and aristocrats fleeing revolution in France. New Orleans also became a haven in the 1790s for refugees – whites and free blacks, along with their slaves – escaping slave revolts against the French in **Saint-Domingue**.

THE SPANISH ERA

As in the West Indies, the Spanish, French and free people of color in New Orleans formed alliances to create a distinctive **Creole** culture, partly in an attempt to distinguish themselves from the newcomers. The Creoles, widely known for their love of the good life, were also busy amassing great fortunes and political power; after 1795, when local planter Etienne de Boré perfected the sugar granulation process, the **sugar plantations** boomed and their owners, the wealthiest men in the colony, came to dominate the political scene. Meanwhile, inspired by the events in Saint-Domingue, slaves instigated a revolt at Pointe Coupé, one hundred miles upriver from the city; though its perpetrators were executed immediately, the Spanish were not able to rid the colony entirely of revolutionary ideas, and the threat of further **slave insurrection** was never far away.

In Europe, **Napoleon**, as part of his strategy to reassert French presence in the New World, offered the Spanish a kingdom in Tuscany in exchange for Louisiana. The Spanish, fearful of rendering vulnerable their territory in Mexico, agreed on the understanding that he would not turn it over to another power, and in 1800 the countries signed the secret **Treaty of San Ildefonso**. In 1803, however, Napoleon, fighting the British in Europe, realized that any attempt to hang on to his New World possessions required him to spread his armies too thinly. Imminent bankruptcy left him with no choice but to sell.

The Louisiana Purchase and "Americanization"

US President Thomas Jefferson, for his part, had been keeping his eye on New Orleans for some time, keen to control the length of the Mississippi River, which was fast developing as the nation's major commercial waterway. In 1803, under the terms of the **Louisiana Purchase**, he bought from Napoleon all French Louisiana, which stretched from the mouth of the river up to Canada and west to the Rocky Mountains, for $15 million – doubling the size of the United States and nearly bankrupting the nation in the process.

The Americans had bought a city of eight thousand people – a mixture of French, Spanish, Caribbean, Latin American, African and German settlers. More than four thousand were black slaves or free people of color; half of the property in the French Quarter was owned by free blacks, many of them single women. After the purchase, demographics shifted again as traffic using the port doubled. Redneck boatmen – derided as "Kaintocks" by the Creoles – poured into the city on cumbersome flatboats, bringing goods from the interior to be traded or exported on great sea-going vessels, while fortune-seeking Anglo-Americans settled upriver from the French Quarter in what became known as the **American sector**. In 1804, fearing the spread of revolution from the West Indies – where the success of the Saint-Domingue slave revolts had led to the formation of the independent black state of Haiti – the Americans **banned the external slave trade**. Instead, slaves were bought from other states, literally "sold down the river" to New Orleans.

An exception was made in 1809 and 1810, however, when ten thousand French-speaking refugees from **Saint-Domingue** were invited, with their slaves, to settle in the city. Governor Claiborne's response to the subsequent doubling of New Orleans' **free black population** was to place numerous legal restrictions upon them, and many sold up and left for France or Mexico. Those who stayed continued to flourish, despite the efforts of the American administration, well into the antebellum era.

The arrival of the slaves, meanwhile, also gave **voodoo** a firmer foothold in New Orleans and led to another **revolt**.

THE LOUISIANA PURCHASE AND "AMERICANIZATION"

In January 1811, hundreds of slaves, led by Haitian Charles Deslondes, marched toward the city from forty miles upriver, razing plantations as they went. They were met eighteen miles out by US troops; most of the slaves were killed, while the others were beheaded and their heads displayed on spikes along the River Road.

In 1812, the same year that Louisiana achieved **statehood**, the United States declared war on the British; on January 8, 1815, the **Battle of New Orleans** was fought about two miles downriver of the city by General Andrew Jackson and a motley volunteer crew of Creoles, Anglo-Americans, free men of color, Native Americans and pirates. The battle made Jackson a hero; soon afterward, however, news reached the city that the Americans had already won the war and that a peace treaty had been signed two weeks before the battle took place.

The year 1812 also saw the first **steamboat** puff its way down the Mississippi. This revolution in river traffic – steamers, able to travel both upriver and downriver, took days to travel distances that had taken flatboats months – marked the beginning of the city's greatest days as a port.

The antebellum years

The **antebellum years**, between 1820 and the onset of the Civil War, are known as New Orleans' golden era. In this period the city grew to become the major **slave-trading** center in the South and its **port** boomed, exporting tobacco, grain, indigo, cotton and sugar and importing luxuries from Europe and the Caribbean. By the 1850s, commerce had made New Orleans the second largest city in the nation, bursting with a mix of Creoles, Anglo-Americans and ever more arrivals from Europe. Major **construction programs** on massive Greek Revival edifices like the Mint and the Custom House reflected the city's self-importance and its resources.

It was also a time of great cultural and **recreational activity**. New Orleans was renowned for its theaters and ballrooms, many of which featured European-trained musicians and hosted the notorious **quadroon balls**, where, under a system known as *plaçage*, white men would take young quadroon girls (one-quarter black) as their mistresses, sometimes setting them up in homes of their own. And in the 1850s **Mardi Gras** took on a new, organized form with the appearance of a night-time parade of Anglo-Americans calling themselves the "Mistick Krewe of Comus".

Not all was golden in the golden era, however. Though it's easy to exaggerate the **antipathy** between the Creoles and the Anglo-Americans, it is true that cultural and language barriers had led to bad feeling, and in the early 1800s the Creole-controlled city government had made conspicuously little effort to aid the progress of the new American districts. Thus, in 1836, the Americans called for a division of the city into three **municipalities** – the Vieux Carré, the American sector, and the outlying areas – each governed by its own council. The arrangement lasted until 1852, when the Anglo-Americans, who now dominated the legislature, called for reunification.

With so much invested in a smooth-running **slave economy**, government began to heap heavy restrictions upon slaves – who, by 1838, made up more than fifty percent of the population – and in 1852 manumission was finally deemed illegal. **Free blacks**, meanwhile, whose existence was seen as a threat to the economic system, continued to be stripped of rights they had enjoyed for generations: banks stopped selling stocks to these flourishing "fmcs", who were also banned from holding public meetings. In the 1700s, divisions in New Orleans had been largely based upon questions of class, money or education; now, under

THE ANTEBELLUM YEARS

the Americans – who looked upon free blacks with the same disdain and fear as they did the slaves – color became the crucial issue.

Meanwhile, the emergence in the 1850s of the fiercely anti-Catholic and anti-immigration "**Know Nothing**" party – so-called because of their covert and suspect methods – led to frequent **political violence** and even, in 1855, armed insurrection when the party attempted to topple the Democratic municipal government. The city also faced frequent hurricanes and drastic **floods**, which periodically wiped out entire plantations, along with countless fatal **epidemics** of yellow fever, typhoid and cholera – in the summer of 1853 alone some eight thousand people were felled by disease. Between June and November, those who could afford it left for the plantations or visited family in Europe, leaving the poor and the weak to die.

The Civil War

By 1861, New Orleans was the largest **cotton** market in the world, and wholly dependent upon the slave economy. Louisiana joined the **Confederate states** on January 26; just three months later, New Orleans' General Pierre Gustave Beauregard ordered the first shots of the Civil War at **Fort Sumter** in Charleston Harbor.

By May 1861, the Union fleet had blockaded the mouth of the Mississippi and a year later the city was under **military rule**. White New Orleanians didn't react well to the occupation, and were particularly displeased with Major Benjamin **"Beast" Butler** (see p.84), notorious for his severe measures against those who remained loyal to the Confederacy. The slaves, however, joined forces with free men of color to demand electoral and civil rights; in 1862 they started a Francophone newspaper, *L'Union*, which proposed full emancipation.

Reconstruction and its aftermath

In April 1865, Lee's **surrender** at Appomattox ended the Civil War and the Thirteenth Amendment pronounced the emancipation of all slaves. While the Northern states embarked upon a period of industrialization and expansion, the defeated South was left to deal with a disintegrating social structure and a destroyed economy.

In 1867, the federal government passed the **Reconstruction** laws, placing the South under military rule until political stability was achieved. There followed in New Orleans an unprecedented period of violence when, as in the rest of the South, anyone working to transform the city came under attack as a "carpetbagger" (a Northern opportunist out for political and financial gain) or a "scalawag" (a Southern collaborator). Returned Confederates, having lost their property, were further humiliated by not being able to hold political office; their former slaves, meanwhile, had new voting rights, were involved in government and played a central role in the new Metropolitan police force. Supremacist whites promptly formed militia such as the **White League**, who undertook brutal campaigns against the government and the newly integrated schools, and who, enraged by the seizure of a boatload of their weapons, fought with the police at the **Battle of Liberty Place** (see p.72) in 1874 – just one in a string of race riots, street battles and large-scale massacres that devastated the city. In the face of systematic abuse, New Orleans' **black population**, backed by a few relatively liberal whites, eventually won more civil rights than anywhere else in the South. But they never achieved real power and when Reconstruction ended, in 1878, the previously free blacks of New Orleans were worse off than they had ever been.

The city faced serious economic decline in the late nineteenth century, due in part to the arrival of the **railroads**, which diminished river traffic, and to heavy debts incurred during the Civil War and Reconstruction. The death knell for the ideals of the post-Civil War government came in 1896, when the Supreme Court ruling in **Plessy vs Ferguson** upheld the conviction of Homer Plessy, a black New Orleanian, for attempting – as part of a wider civil disobedience campaign – to sit in a whites-only train carriage. Allowing for "separate but equal" facilities for blacks and whites, the ruling effectively took away the few civil rights that had been won during Reconstruction and legalized segregation throughout the South, a state of affairs that was to exist for more than sixty years.

The twentieth century and today

In the early years of the twentieth century New Orleans achieved a certain notoriety nationwide for its red-light district, **Storyville**, the spectacular parades and balls of **Mardi Gras** and its indigenous music, **jazz**. And although the **Depression** hit here as hard as it did in the rest of the country, it also heralded the resurgence of the French Quarter, which had disintegrated into a slum since the Civil War. Partly due to the energies of the many artists and writers who had moved in during the 1920s, the **Vieux Carré Commission** – the first organization of its type in the nation – was established to preserve the architecture of the old quarter, and under President Roosevelt's New Deal, the **Works Progress Administration** (WPA) restored a number of its most important buildings. Meanwhile, the local political arena was dominated by Roosevelt's avowed enemy, the quasi-fascist Governor **Huey Long**, whose radical "Share the Wealth" programs were funded by strong-arm tactics, political patronage and financial corruption. Wildly popular with the state's sharecroppers and despised by the old-guard elite, Long was assassinated outside the Baton Rouge capitol in September 1935.

By the 1950s a rash of **petrochemical** plants along the river had almost wiped out the old sugar plantations. Financial security, however, was hindered by the racial violence and fear that infected the American South during the **Civil Rights** era: whites and middle-class blacks responded to desegregation by fleeing to the suburbs, leaving black communities downtown to be slashed and razed to make way for interstates and freeways. After **Hurricane Betsy** ripped through the city in 1965, New Orleans seemed to have little left to fight for. Salvation came, it seemed, with the 1970s **oil boom**, which saw a rash of corporate towers shoot up in the Central Business District. When the oil boom inevitably ended, however, in the mid-1980s, New Orleans faced one of the toughest periods in its history, with a lifeless economy, a crack cocaine plague and a sky-high crime rate, and, to cap it all, a notoriously corrupt police force.

Things shifted, however, with the election of Mayor **Marc Morial**, son of the city's first black mayor, "Dutch" Morial, in 1994. In the early years of the twenty-first century, New Orleans was enjoying a strong, popular, black-dominated city government, whose highly publicized police force clean-up program, in the context of a relatively stable economy based upon tourism, injected the city with renewed confidence.

THE TWENTIETH CENTURY AND TODAY

Mardi Gras

M ardi Gras was brought to New Orleans in the 1740s by **French** colonists who continued the European custom, established since medieval times, of marking the imminence of Lent with partying, masking and feasting. Their slaves, meanwhile, were celebrating **African** and **Caribbean** festival traditions, based on musical rituals, masking and the donning of elaborate costumes.

For the practicalities of visiting New Orleans
during Mardi Gras, see p.269.

It was in the mid-nineteenth century that official Mardi Gras took its current form. In 1857, a mysterious torchlit procession, calling itself the "Mistick Krewe of **Comus**, Merrie Monarch of Mirth", took to the streets, initiated by a group of wealthy, white Anglo-Americans who had recently moved to the city from Alabama. Comus was an all-male, secret society, and its parade was strictly members-only. Based on the theme of Milton's *Paradise Lost*, it featured elaborate floats and masked riders dressed as the demon actors of the epic poem – very different from earlier processions, which tended to descend into rowdy affairs, with masked revelers flinging flour, mud and bricks.

Almost immediately, the concept of the **krewe**, a secret carnival club whose mythological name afforded it a spurious gravitas, was taken up enthusiastically by the Anglo elite. More and more krewes were formed, each electing their own king and queen – usually an older business man and a debutante – who, costumed and masked, and attended by a fairytale court, would reign over a themed parade and a ceremonial ball, centred around that great nineteenth-century obsession, the *tableau vivant*. As the secret krewes grew, street masking and public balls – "unofficial" carnival – became the domain of the poor, the black, and the fallen women.

Though official carnival trailed off during the Civil War, it gathered strength during the city's violent **Reconstruction** era. In 1872, newspapers published an arcane announcement heralding the imminent arrival of a so-called "**King of Carnival**", ordaining that "under penalty of Royal displeasure" the city be closed down for the day and handed over to him. On Mardi Gras morning, the masked **Rex** arrived by riverboat, to preside over a brilliantly executed parade, which though it boasted none of the dazzling floats created by Comus, featured hundreds of maskers and mounted horsemen.

Composed of leading civic figures, Rex was formed partly to greet the Russian Grand Duke Alexis Romanoff, who was visiting the city for Mardi Gras that year. Despite his claim to be "king" of carnival, Rex himself, usually a philanthropist or public leader – and always born in New Orleans – bowed to the venerable Comus; while Rex's motto is *pro bono publico* ("for the good of the public"), Comus' is *sic volo, sic iubeo* ("as I wish, I command"). Comus and Rex, along with newly formed krewes **Proteus** and the satirical, right-wing **Knights of Momus**, came to dominate organized carnival, their self-appointed monarchs sweeping through crowds of subjects on parades that wallowed in romantic, exotic and exalted themes. Dominated by the white supremacists whose resistance to the Reconstruction government often exploded into violence, the krewes also used their parades to attack the Republicans and the newly liberated blacks.

Meanwhile, **unofficial carnival** reeled on: a number of smaller, informal groups satirized the pomposity of the big krewes and more than once the Comus parade was blocked by jeering hordes. By the end of the century women were masking in gangs, dressed as men and carrying sticks to beat off attacks; newspapers complained that "few [of the street revellers] are of a class among whom one would care to mingle socially". The underworld held their own masques, or "French balls": raucous, drunken affairs that were curtailed in 1917 when the Storyville red-light district closed down (see p.64).

Throughout much of the nineteenth century, the role of **black** New Orleanians in official carnival was limited to that of torch-carrier, float-hauler or band-member. Blacks had always celebrated carnival within their own communities, however; in 1823 one visitor reported "some 100 negroes . . . following the king of the wake", who wore a crown made from "oblong, gilt paper boxes . . . tapering upwards like a pyramid . . . from the end hang two huge tassels". In the 1880s, groups of black men began to organize themselves into **Mardi Gras Indian** tribes (see p.310), leading their own, often violent, processions through local neighborhoods. Though formal black carnival clubs were known from as early as the 1890s, Zulu, the best-known **black krewe**, was established in 1909, when a band of laborers formed a benevolent society, called themselves The Tramps and paraded with a king dressed in rags. At the same time, gangs of black prostitutes went out on the town as **Baby Dolls**, prancing through the streets in bloomers and bonnets and sucking pacifiers; this tradition soon spread, and even today you will see white men roaming the Quarter on Mardi Gras day dressed as big babies.

In 1916 The Tramps changed their name to the **Zulu Social Aid and Pleasure Club**, and paraded in black-face on palmetto-shaded floats. Two years later the king parodied Rex's portentous arrival on the Mississippi by arriving in a tugboat along the New Basin Canal, waving a hambone as a scepter, and as each year passed Zulu's lampoon of white carnival – and the reclamation of black stereotypes – intensified.

By the 1940s Zulu had become one of the most important black organizations in the States, and in 1949, local boy **Louis Armstrong**, who had left the city as a young man, rode as king. Satchmo's appearance pushed Mardi Gras, and the city, into the public eye – less publicized, however, was his post-carnival avowal that he would never again return to his hometown, sickened as he was by its segregation and racism. Today Zulu is one of New Orleans' biggest krewes, and its Mardi Gras day parade, a raucous cavalcade of black-face savages in wild Afro wigs, is among the most popular of the season.

After a hiatus during World War I, when masking was once again banned as potentially subversive and the organized krewes stopped parading, carnival was revived during the **Jazz Age**. By 1925 Rex, Comus, Momus and Proteus were parading once more, while crowds of citizens took to dancing in the streets, accompanied by small jazz bands on motorized trucks. Many of the official parades also featured brass bands, followed by dancing **Second Liners**. Proteus, Comus and Rex continued to parade throughout the Depression; meanwhile, newer krewes, like Hermes, were being formed to attract tourists to carnival, while writers like Lyle Saxon worked hard to resurrect interest in the dwindling art of street masking.

In 1941 the **Krewe of Venus** was the first female krewe to parade, dodging the heckles and food thrown at them by the crowds. The early 1960s saw the first **gay carnival ball**, thrown by the Krewe of Yuga, which was raided by

THE MARDI GRAS INDIANS

New Orleans' Mardi Gras Indians are not, in fact, Native Americans, but low-income black men who organize themselves into tribes, or "gangs". Today there are some thirty tribes, each with between ten and fifty members, who, on Mardi Gras morning ("that day" in Indian parlance) parade through local neighborhoods in fabulous, extravagant costumes and headdresses. Though there are reports of groups of New Orleans blacks "masking Indian" as early as 1872, the standard story starts in the 1880s, when Becate Battiste, of Native American and African blood, turned up in a bar in Tremé with a bunch of friends and announced themselves as the Creole Wild West. Why they did so, and why the tradition spread, is unclear. Some say it developed out of a widespread craze for all things Native American after the Buffalo Bill Wild West show, complete with genuine Plains Indians, stopped in the city during its nationwide tour of 1884. Others argue that it harks back to the early days of the settlement, when indigenous tribes harbored and intermarried with African slaves, and that the tradition of masking Indian stretches back to the eighteenth century, albeit on a far smaller scale. Many see the tradition in the broader context of the African diaspora throughout the New World: in Trinidad, Haiti and Brazil, blacks celebrate carnival by donning huge feather headdresses, playing percussion and chanting.

The first New Orleans Indians dressed simply – copying the apparel of local tribes and Caribbean Amerindians – and fought gang wars on designated "battlefronts". Since the 1950s, however, largely due to the efforts of Tootie Montana – a descendant of Battiste and chief of the Yellow Pocahontas for fifty years – they have competed instead with dances and chants and for the "prettiest" costume. These "suits" – which are worn in layers, so sections can be revealed one by one –

can weigh as much as 100lb, their tunics, leggings and moccasins heavy with beads and rhinestones (favored by the uptown gangs) and sequins (downtown-style). Each ensemble is topped with a towering feather headdress known as a crown; those worn by the Big Chiefs, quivering with more than 350 feathers, are colossal. Traditionally, suits, painstakingly designed and hand-sewn by the Indians at a cost of thousands of dollars, aren't recycled from one Mardi Gras to the next, though they will be worn again at gigs and special events.

Gangs set out early on Mardi Gras morning, led by the spy boy, who looks out for other tribes, and the flag boy, who alerts Big Chief when his rivals come into view. When tribes meet – usually swamped by Second Line crowds – they gather in circles and communicate with dances, hand gestures, percussion-rattling and improvised calls-and-responses, which go on until Big Chief gives the signal for it all to stop. Influenced by Native American, Haitian and African chants, and peppered with mysterious pidgin and patois, the songs lament lost tribe members, recall past battles and brag about fine suits. Mardi Gras Indian music has been a key influence on the New Orleans sound, and many famous carnival records, including the much-covered favorites Iko Iko and Hey Pocky Way, were originally Indian compositions.

At Mardi Gras the tribes parade through local neighborhoods where tourists, although tolerated, aren't particularly welcome. General spectators are likeliest to see them on the Sunday closest to the Italian St Joseph's day (March 19; see p.281), known as Super Sunday – which happens to coincide with a voodoo festival – when downtown and uptown tribes take to the streets in a more structured procession. Also, many of the more famous groups – the Wild Magnolias, in particular, led by the formidable Big Chief Bo Dollis – play gigs around town in the run-up to Mardi Gras and during Jazz Fest.

the police. In 1969, when the city was facing one of its most difficult economic periods, **Bacchus** emerged on the scene – a very different kind of krewe, less concerned with exclusivity than with cheerful excess.

Bacchus' debut parade boasted the biggest floats, a widely trumpeted celebrity king (Danny Kaye) and, in place of the hush-hush ball, a public extravaganza open to anyone who could afford a ticket. Thus began the era of the **super krewes**, with members drawn from the ranks of New Orleans' new wealth – Bacchus founders included float-designer Blaine Kern and Irish restaurateur Owen Brennan – who were barred from making inroads into the gentle-men's-club network of the old-guard krewes. Super krewe parades are characterized by expensive, flashy floats, alight with state-of-the-art fiber optics, and members are known for their generous throws (see p.274). Other super krewes include **Orpheus**, established by Harry Connick Jr in 1993, which always boasts the longest string of marching bands and a well-known musician as king. In 1998, Orpheus' 125ft-long Leviathan float, with its constellation of 54,000 flashing lights, outshone even Bacchus' King Kong family, and has been a feature of their parade ever since.

In 1992, after months of widely publicized and bitter wrangling, the city government instigated a **nondiscrimination policy** for the parading krewes, requiring that, in order to be granted a parade license, they sign affidavits confirming their organizations to be open to all people, regardless of race or religion. While the super krewes, who in any case were held to be more democratic, agreed to the new conditions – as did Rex – Comus, along with Momus and Proteus, refused to comply, insisting that their membership be kept secret. From 1992 until 1999 none of them paraded, though they continued to stage their elaborate balls, as exclusive and all-white as ever; in 2000 Proteus finally stood down, and since then has taken a prime Lundi Gras parade slot.

Books

Few cities in the United States have inspired as many stories as New Orleans. Since its earliest days, many of its greatest writers – Kate Chopin, George Washington Cable, Sherwood Anderson, Tennessee Williams et al. – have been **outsiders**. Inspired by the stirring, sensual city, so unlike the rest of America, echoing with centuries of memories and ghosts, they composed some of their best work while living here. Others, locals like John Kennedy Toole and Anne Rice, capture the essence and spirit of their home town in a range of styles as diverse as the city itself.

Though a definitive modern **history** of New Orleans has yet to be written, many authors have dealt with its key themes, including the free people of color, Reconstruction and Mardi Gras. Some of the liveliest histories available today were written in the 1930s, by figures such as Lyle Saxon and Robert Tallant, leading lights in the regeneration of the French Quarter.

For details of New Orleans' literary festivals, see p.280. For bookstore listings, see p.249.

Most of the following titles, all of which are in print, should be available in North America and the UK. Unless otherwise stated, all publishers listed are based in the United States.

BOOKS

Fiction, poetry and drama

Brooke Bergan, *Storyville: A Hidden Mirror* (Asphodel Press). Punctuated by E.J. Bellocq's haunting photographic plates of the prostitutes of Storyville, New Orleans' nineteenth-century red-light district, Bergan's lyrical quest to find truth, meaning and beauty in the past weaves together poetry, oral reminiscences and folklore.

George Washington Cable, *The Grandissimes* (Penguin UK). In the nineteenth century, Cable was regarded as one of the finest writers in America and *The Grandissimes* was his masterpiece. A labyrinthine saga of Creole family feuds, it's a superb evocation of the complex relations between the city's free men of color and Creoles, its voodooists and slaves; written during Reconstruction, but set in the years following the Louisiana Purchase in 1803, even at the time of publication it read like a nostalgic evocation of a lost era. One of Cable's chief aims, to represent without sentimentality the dying Creole culture, also informs the short stories of *Old Creole Days* (Pelican), in which the patois can take some getting used to.

Kate Chopin, *The Awakening* (The Women's Press, UK). Subversive story of a married Creole woman whose fight for independence ends in tragedy. Swampy New Orleans, around 1900, is portrayed as both a sensual hotbed for her sexual awakening and as her eventual nemesis.

William Faulkner, *Mosquitoes* (Dell). Faulkner fans delight in the poetry, pace and vision of this satiric account of the wealthy bohemian set in the 1930s French Quarter; detractors dismiss it as a work of overblown hubris.

Ellen Gilchrist, *In the Land of Dreamy Dreams* (Little, Brown & Co). Brittle, diamond-sharp stories spanning four decades of betrayal, lust and loss among New Orleans' uptown elite, penned by one of the modern city's finest chroniclers.

John Miller and Genevieve Anderson (eds), *New Orleans Stories* (Chronicle). Superb collection of extracts from some of the best writers on the city, including John James Audubon, Mark Twain, Lyle Saxon, Tennessee Williams, Ellen Gilchrist and Anne Rice.

Michael Ondaatje, *Coming Through Slaughter* (Picador). Extraordinary, dream-like fictionalization of the life of doomed cornet player Buddy Bolden, written in a lyrical style that evokes the rhythms and pace of jazz improvisation.

Walker Percy, *The Moviegoer* (Vintage). Much-lauded novel in which movie buff Binx Bolling cracks under the strain of a privileged uptown upbringing. Profound tale of the search for meaning and redemption in an essentially empty world? Or an existentialist drone in which too little happens? Take your pick.

Anne Rice, *Interview with the Vampire*; *The Witching Hour*; *Lasher*; *Memnoch the Devil* (all Ballantine) and many more. Rice's gothic tales of vampires, witches and evil spirits make

good use of the city as a location; the vampire chronicles, featuring the brooding hero Lestat, are the most psychologically complex. Perhaps her finest novel, however, is the lesser-known *Feast of All Saints* (Ballantine), a fascinating historical saga set among the Creoles and free people of color of antebellum New Orleans, dealing sensitively and intelligently with issues of race, sexuality and gender.

Josh Russell, *Yellow Jack* (Norton). Gothic portrayal of the decline and fall of Claude Marchand, an ambitious daguerrotypist who perishes under the spell of voodoo and illicit desire in the decadent and death-plagued New Orleans of the 1840s.

Julie Smith, *New Orleans Mourning*; *The Axeman's Jazz* and many more (all Ivy Books). Pacey detective novels featuring misfit New Orleans cop Skip Langdon sleuthing her way through the city's myriad social strata. The first in the series, Edgar Award-winning *New Orleans Mourning*, is by far the best, a tale of uptown murder set

FICTION, POETRY AND DRAMA

against a backdrop of carnival, corruption and cross-dressing.

John Kennedy Toole, *A Confederacy of Dunces* (Penguin UK). The quintessential New Orleans novel, an anarchic black tragicomedy in which the pompous and repulsive antihero Ignatius J. Reilly wreaks havoc through an insalubrious and surreal New Orleans.

Tennessee Williams, *A Streetcar Named Desire*; *Vieux Carré* (New Directions). *Streetcar*, an overwrought tale of perverse desires and brutality in the sultry city, has become one of the seminal works in American drama. The film version (see p.335), though iconic in itself, doesn't do the play justice. Written thirty years later, *Vieux Carré*, a semiautobiographical account of Williams' early years in a dilapidated New Orleans boarding house, is as bleak in its vision as *Streetcar*, if somewhat lower-key.

Christine Wiltz, *Glass House* (Louisiana State University). Pageturner centering on the complex relationships between a rich white woman, her black maid, her maid's son and a host of multiracial characters. Treading carefully through a slew of potential minefields, Wiltz deftly portrays the mistrust, violence and racism that beleaguer New Orleans, while offering a hopeful vision of a future based on humanism and empathy.

History and biography

Christopher Benfey, *Degas in New Orleans* (Knopf). A slightly misleading title for an engaging history that draws upon the novels of George Washington Cable and Kate Chopin, as well as the paintings of Edgar Degas – who stayed with family in the city in 1872 – to draw a memorable picture of the Creole experience during Reconstruction.

John W. Blassingame, *Black New Orleans 1860–80* (University of Chicago). Scholarly survey of the political and social life of blacks in the city during Reconstruction, covering both the experience of the educated, urban free men of color and the newly freed plantation slaves.

Garry Boulard, *Huey Long Invades New Orleans* (Pelican). Gripping account of one of the most dramatic moments in New Orleans' twentieth-century history, when, in 1934, the "Kingfish", Louisiana's populist and notoriously corrupt governor, sent in troops to wrest control of the city from its old-money, old-guard elite.

John Churchill Chase, *Frenchmen, Desire, Good Children and Other Streets of New Orleans* (Touchstone). Chatty, fast-paced and highly readable, if occasionally inaccurate, popular history of the city, using its weird and wonderful street names as a lynchpin.

Frank de Caro (ed), *Louisiana Sojourns* (Louisiana State University). Chunky collection of travelers' tales; the chapters on the Mississippi River and New Orleans include extracts from Mark Twain, Frances Trollope and Simone de Beauvoir, among many others. Perfect background reading.

Mary Gehman, *The Free People of Color of New Orleans* (Margaret Media). Concise history of the city's free black population, from the first days of the colony, via the ravages of the Civil War and Reconstruction, up to the advent of "Jim Crow" segregation laws in the 1890s.

William Ivy Hair, *Carnival of Fury* (Louisiana State University). This enthralling attempt to document the life of a black laborer who shot 27 whites in 1900 does a good job of illuminating the racial tensions that wracked post-Reconstruction New Orleans.

Al Rose, *Storyville* (University of Alabama). Sizeable volume on New Orleans' notorious late nineteenth-century red-light district, packed full of photographs, newspaper reports and extracts from the famed "blue book", and scattered with oral accounts. Informative and fun, though the tone, at once prurient and puritanical, can be jarring.

Lyle Saxon, *Fabulous New Orleans* (Pelican). Compelling, evocative historical vignettes by one of the major lights in the renewal of the French Quarter in the 1930s. The account of a late nineteenth-century Mardi Gras,

HISTORY AND BIOGRAPHY

as seen through the eyes of the author as a young boy, is as fresh today as when it was written. Other works by Saxon include *Lafitte the Pirate* (Pelican), a rollicking biography of the buccaneer, and *Gumbo Ya-Ya* (Pelican), a collection of Louisiana folk tales.

Mark Twain, *Life on the Mississippi* (Penguin). America's wittiest and wisest chronicler turns his attention to New Orleans in chapters 41 to 50 of this marvelous travel book. Bringing to life as only he can the bustling waterfront, the steamboat men and the river, Twain also dwells on the city's intriguing death customs and its cemeteries, and on the oddity of Mardi Gras and the Southern accent, taking in some tasty fish dinners along the way.

Christina Vella, *Intimate Enemies: The Two Worlds of the Baroness Pontalba* (Louisiana State University). Detailed, sprightly biography of one of the colonial city's most fascinating figures. The saga of the baroness' eventful life, divided between New Orleans and France, makes gripping reading.

Samuel Wilson Jr, Patricia Brady and Lynn D. Adams (eds), *Queen of the South: New Orleans in the Age of Thomas K. Wharton, 1853–1862* (Historic New Orleans Collection). Wharton, one of the major architects of antebellum New Orleans, kept detailed diaries of his life in the rapidly expanding city. Edited and reproduced here, backed with fine illustrations, they form a fascinating account, with much discussion on architecture, but also covering epidemics, political violence, race relations, social life and the weather.

Christine Wiltz, *The Last Madam: A Life in the New Orleans Underworld* (Faber & Faber). Wiltz's biography of Norma Wallace, the last of the city's "landladies", who presided over a French Quarter prostitution empire for more than forty years, is a vivid evocation of the Quarter in its sleazy, low-living heyday. Smart, glamorous and above all powerful, Wallace makes a great subject, and this is a lively read, drawing upon testimonies from movie stars, gangsters, crooked cops, hardheaded

HISTORY AND BIOGRAPHY

prostitutes and political bigwigs, as well as Wallace's own memoirs, tape-recorded two years before her suicide in 1974.

Mardi Gras

James Gill, *Lords of Misrule* (University of Mississippi). Excellent, informed exploration of the role of Mardi Gras in maintaining racial divisions in New Orleans, beginning with carnival's earliest days and closing with detailed accounts of the furious city council debates over desegregation of the krewes in the early 1990s.

Reid Mitchell, *All on a Mardi Gras Day* (Harvard). Like James Gill's book (see above), this is a first-rate cultural study of New Orleans carnival, tracing its long history as a political battleground. Well written, vivid and accessible, with chapters on race, gender and class.

Henri Schindler, *Mardi Gras New Orleans* (Flammarion). Exquisite coffee-table book from the art director of many of the old krewe parades. Nostalgic for what he calls the lost era of Mardi Gras artistry, Schindler touches on every aspect of carnival from its Creole days up until the 1950s, illustrating with rare photos and vintage designs. His *Mardi Gras Treasures: Invitations of the Golden Age* (Pelican) focuses on the elaborate invitations and dance cards designed between 1870 and 1930.

Michael P. Smith, *Mardi Gras Indians* (Pelican). Coffee-table book detailing the history and cultural significance of New Orleans' unique Mardi Gras Indians. Their lavish costumes, debuted each year on Mardi Gras morning, are captured in the book's fabulous photographs.

Architecture

Randolph Delehanty, *Ultimate Guide to New Orleans* (Chronicle). A dozen architectural tours of the city, written in a lively and personal style by the curator of the Ogden Museum of Southern Art.

Malcolm Heard, *French Quarter Manual* (University of

Mississippi). Outstanding volume, packed with old photos, plans and literary extracts. Not only an illuminating guide to the baffling array of styles that make up the French Quarter's vernacular architecture, but also a lively read.

Richard Sexton and Randolph Delehanty, *New Orleans: Elegance and Decadence* (Chronicle). Luxurious coffeetable book with fabulous photographs and intelligent captions detailing the city's distinctive aesthetic style through private homes and gardens.

S. Frederick Starr, *Southern Comfort* (Princeton). Beautifully illustrated coffee-table book, surveying the development of the Garden District in the nineteenth century and telling the stories of its developers, architects, craftsmen and residents.

Music

Danny Barker and Allyn Shipton, *Buddy Bolden and the Last Days of Storyville* (Cassell). Highly entertaining, anecdotal stories of New Orleans' early jazz scene by one of its leading lights. The much-loved Barker,

who died in 1994, was well known for his chatty style, which perfectly encapsulates the spirit of the music he played.

Joshua Berrett (ed), *The Louis Armstrong Companion: Eight Decades of Commentary* (Schirmer). Broad selection of essays, interviews, letters, reviews and autobiography, revealing one of the world's most influential musicians in all his complexity. It's a fine introduction to the subject, featuring lots of previously unpublished material: standouts include Armstrong's own lament about defeatism and negativity in his fellow black men.

Jason Berry, Jonathan Foose and Tad Jones, *Up from the Cradle of Jazz* (Da Capo). Copious, fascinating account of the genesis and the heyday of New Orleans R&B; written in the 1980s, the tone is a little dated now, but it's a compelling read all the same.

Jeff Hannusch, *I Hear You Knocking: The Sound of New Orleans Rhythm and Blues* (Swallow). Another title that suffers a little from being written in the 1980s, this delightful mixture of anecdote and scholarship still holds its own as one of the best books there is about New Orleans music. Short chapters outline the careers of the city's great stars of the 1950s and 1960s, with sections on piano players, producers, blues singers and female stars. Accessible, brimming with enthusiasm and a rocking good read to boot.

Art, Aaron, Charles and Cyril Neville with David Ritz, *The Brothers Neville* (Little Brown & Co). Readable autobiography from New Orleans' favorite musical brothers. Telling their own stories, each Neville comes across with a distinctive voice, and although most of the book concentrates on the 1950s and 1960s, their testimonies paint a vivid picture of the music industry – particularly its racism – and life on the mean streets of New Orleans over the last fifty years.

Mac Rebennack (Dr John) with Jack Rummel, *Under a Hoodoo Moon* (St Martin's Press). Addled but very readable autobiography from New

Orleans' inimitable "Night Tripper", maestro of the city's distinctive piano funk. His prelude, which calls the book "a testament to funksterators, tricknologists, mu-jicians, who got music burning in their brains and no holes in their souls", sets the tone.

Satchmo, *My Life In New Orleans* (Da Capo). Published originally in 1954, and written in Armstrong's distinctive hep-cat style, this is a great evocation of what life was like for a poor, talented and ambitious young man trying to hit the big time in New Orleans, starting with his birth and ending with his departure to Chicago to play with his idol Kid Oliver.

Charles Suhor, *Jazz in New Orleans* (Scarecrow Press). Concentrating on a neglected period in the city's jazz history – the years from the end of World War II to the 1970s – these articles, written by a local music writer and drummer, are particularly strong in their coverage of individuals who were central in the re-emergence of Dixieland jazz.

MUSIC

New Orleans music

The high-spirited, soulful **music** of New Orleans has had an impact on North America and the world out of all proportion to the city's size. Though no single reason can explain why New Orleans gave birth to jazz a century ago, no other city was so ideally situated to synthesize the traditions of the Old World and the New. Not only did it pass from French, to Spanish and into American hands, but it was home from its earliest years to large populations of both African slaves and free people of color. As an international port, it was also exposed to the manifold rhythms of Latin America and the Caribbean.

Thanks to the Code Noir, adopted in Louisiana in 1724 (see p.295), New Orleans was the only city in the United States in which slaves, including first-generation arrivals from Africa and Haiti, congregated freely together. Right up until the mid-1800s, at weekly gatherings in **Congo Square** (see p.295), slaves would sing in African languages, play African instruments and perform African dances. As well as being joined by free people of color and local Houmas tribes, they became a tourist attraction for whites, watched by crowds of Anglo-American New Orleanians and visitors from further afield. The Yankee architect Benjamin Latrobe, for example, in 1819 commented on the dancing, the drums and a "curious . . . stringed instrument which no doubt was imported from Africa", which sounds like a forerunner of the banjo.

An even more direct influence on the emergence of jazz, however, was **brass band** music. New Orleans' first brass parade took place in 1787, to celebrate a meeting between Governor Miro and the Houmas. By 1820, each ethnic group had its favorite ensembles, who competed in occasional "battles of the bands". In 1838, the *Picayune* observed "a real mania in this city for horn and trumpet playing". That mania only increased, with marching bands featuring prominently in **Mardi Gras parades** and being hired for public occasions of all kinds – including, famously, funerals.

Meanwhile, from the early nineteenth century onward, formal, classically trained **orchestras** would play the latest European dance tunes in the ballrooms, and the city also boasted a thriving opera house. The cultural links between Louisiana and France remained strong, and many musicians completed their schooling in Europe.

After the **Civil War**, brass band music grew ever more popular throughout the United States, spurred by a craze for the rousing tunes of bandmaster John Philip Sousa. The voices of newly freed slaves were now also being heard, albeit largely at first in bowdlerized minstrel and vaudeville shows. In New Orleans, the merging of musical traditions was hastened by an influx of ex-slaves from rural Louisiana, as well as migrants from the North, and immigrants from Germany and Italy. In addition, in the bitter aftermath of **Reconstruction**, the city's extraordinarily complex system of social and racial gradations, based on subtle differences in skin tone and degrees of European, Caribbean or African ancestry, became eroded. As a result of the Supreme Court ruling in the *Plessy vs Ferguson* case (see p.304), which led to the legal categorization of all people of color as "negroes", mixed-race Creoles and black musicians found themselves competing for work and, inevitably, playing together.

Jazz

Toward the end of the nineteenth century, the music that became known as **"jazz"** developed out of the incorporation of African and Caribbean rhythms into both brass band and popular dance music. This was often a very literal process, as young, unschooled musicians from the "spasm" bands who played homemade instruments for tips on the streets would graduate into formally constituted brass bands. Increasingly, in turn, brass band musicians joined the adhoc groups who were now providing the entertainment in the clubs and dance halls. In part because they supplied the sheer volume essential in crowded indoor venues, trumpets, cornets, trombones and clarinets swiftly replaced the violin as lead instruments, playing above a rhythm section of perhaps guitar, bass, drums and piano.

Legend has it that the defining moment in jazz history came in 1897 when the smooth, sophisticated sound of Creole multi-instrumentalist **John Robichaux** was rendered passé by the "hot" new sound of the anarchic, flamboyant cornet player **Buddy Bolden**. In fact there's no evidence that Robichaux, whose band thrived for at least two decades and featured many of the seminal figures of early jazz, was any less talented or popular than Bolden. Bolden did, however, provide the archetype of the tortured jazz genius: he was declared insane following his erratic behavior during a Labor Day parade in 1906 and never played again.

Few jazz groups seem to have played in the brothels of **Storyville**, New Orleans' red-light district, which flourished between 1897 and 1917 (see p.64). Most brothels employed solo pianists, often known as professors. Storyville was not so much the "birthplace" of jazz as the incubator for a particular kind of jazz – piano-based, ragtime-derived and Caribbean-influenced. Its most famous exponent, **Jelly Roll Morton**, was later to claim, "I myself happened to be the creator of jazz in 1902".

In the absence of the fabled Edison cylinder said to have been cut by Buddy Bolden around 1900, no one now knows what the first jazz bands sounded like. New Orleans musicians were responsible for the earliest jazz **recordings**, twenty years later, but by then the music had expanded far beyond the city. Following the closure of Storyville, which coincided with a clampdown on live entertainment throughout the city, there was a mass exodus of musicians to Chicago and then New York, where they helped start the Jazz Age of the 1920s.

Freddie Keppard, whose band took Chicago by storm in 1914, refused to be recorded on the grounds that other musicians would copy his style. Instead, the first jazz band to make a record, in New York in 1917, was a group of white New Orleanians called the **Original Dixieland Jazz Band**. Their million-selling *Dixie Jass Band One-Step* inspired black New Orleans bands such as those of **Edward "Kid" Ory** (in California) and **Joe "King" Oliver** (in Chicago) to try their hands. Oliver's Creole Jazz Band cut the first definitive jazz classics in 1923, then broke up acrimoniously, but his second trumpeter, **Louis Armstrong**, went on to form the Hot Fives – which occasionally grew to become the Hot Sevens – in New York. Jelly Roll Morton was also in Chicago by 1923 and reached his creative peak recording there with the Red Hot Peppers in 1926.

New Orleans itself soon came to be seen as a backwater, far from the cutting edge of jazz, and even those New Orleans musicians who had achieved success elsewhere found it hard to adapt in the Big Band and swing era of the 1930s. Several jazz pioneers dropped into obscurity and despair – Oliver, for example, died as a janitor in Savannah in 1938 – while those who managed to crest the incoming

JAZZ

wave, such as Armstrong and the saxophonist Sidney Bechet, displayed a marked reluctance to return home to the South.

As academic interest in jazz grew, however, New Orleans came to be seen as a repository of "authentic" jazz. Hence the excitement over the "rediscovery" of a former Oliver and Armstrong sideman, trumpeter **Bunk Johnson**, in the early 1940s. Dental problems had precluded Johnson from playing for ten years, so the well-wishers who paid for his teeth to be fixed felt that he could not have been corrupted by modern styles. His re-emergence did him little long-term good, but the jazz revival continues to this day, with the New Orleans, or **Dixieland**, style being regarded as "traditional".

Rhythm and blues

In the late 1940s, New Orleans once again spearheaded the creation of a radical new form of popular music. While the blues had never been a major force in the city, its electrified cousin, **rhythm and blues**, certainly was. In collaboration with the bandleader and producer **Dave Bartholomew**, a shy young bar-room pianist, **Antoine "Fats" Domino**, announced himself as *The Fat Man* in 1949. Together they went on to sell a hundred million records worldwide, with hits including *Ain't It a Shame* and *Blueberry Hill*. Domino's sound changed little over the years, but its crossover appeal with young white audiences meant that he came to be regarded as a rock'n'roll rather than an R&B star.

Thanks to Fats Domino's huge international success, New Orleans became a major **recording center**. Cosimo Matassa's studio at Rampart and Dumaine churned out a stream of hits, not only from Domino himself but by emulators such as Lloyd "Lawdy Miss Clawdy" Price, and even Little Richard from Georgia, all of whose greatest material was recorded in New Orleans. However, the most influential figure within the city itself was Henry Roeland Byrd. A former tapdancer and boxer who reinvented himself in 1949 as pianist **Professor Longhair**, "Fess" was a one-man synthesis of all that made New Orleans funky. One bandmate defined his style as "a Caribbean left hand and a boogie woogie right hand", Jerry Wexler of Atlantic Records hailed him as "the Picasso of keyboard funk", and the professor himself said his music consisted of "offbeat Spanish beats and Calypso downbeats". His genius remained unrecognized and unrewarded for most of his life, but his legacy includes three of New Orleans' greatest party records: *Tipitina*, which gave its name to the uptown club where he gave his final performances before his death in 1980, the carnival anthem *Go to the Mardi Gras* and the extraordinary, intoxicating *Big Chief*.

During the early 1960s, New Orleans churned out an almost inexhaustible stream of R&B and pop hits, thanks largely to composer-producer-pianist **Allen Toussaint**, who was responsible for Jessie Hill's *Ooh Poo Pah Doo*, Ernie K-Doe's *Mother-in-Law*, former boxing champion Lee Dorsey's *Working in a Coalmine* and *Holy Cow*, and the young Irma Thomas' *It's Raining* and *Ruler of My Heart*. Toussaint later achieved fame as a solo artist and continues to work in the city, promoting new talent on his NYNO record label and making rare live appearances.

The 1960s to the present

The city's music scene all but collapsed in the mid-1960s, however, as recording studios went broke and clubs closed down. Some blame a "clean-up" operation by district attorney Jim Garrison; others say it was the advent of rock music that delivered the hammer blow. Among musicians who left town was session man Mac Rebennack, who, while working for Sonny and Cher in California, developed a musical persona based on the nineteenth-century voodoo man **Dr John**. Failing to find anyone willing to play the part, he took on the role of the "Night-Tripper" himself. Though albums from 1967's *Gris-Gris* onward may have gone overboard on depicting New Orleans as a mysterious, voodoo-riddled and otherworldly realm, he was scrupulous about honoring the city's musical heritage, working with Professor Longhair and employing such prime talent as troubled keyboard wizard **James Booker**.

Over the last 25 years, four major factors have restored New Orleans music to its current healthy state. The first was the success of the Neville brothers. The eldest, Art Neville, recorded *Mardi Gras Mambo* with the Hawkettes in 1954 and was also (as he remains) a member of the Meters – nowadays known as the funky Meters – while the pure-voiced Aaron cut an all-time **soul** classic in 1967's *Tell It Like It Is*. They only came together as a group with brothers Charles and Cyril for the *Wild Tchoupitoulas* album in 1972. A critical if not a financial triumph, that superb tribute to the music of the **Mardi Gras Indians** (see p.310) resulted in the formation of the **Neville Brothers**, still the city's best-known band.

In addition, New Orleans continues to produce major-league jazz stars, even if most of them swiftly move on to the international arena. The extended **Marsalis** family – especially trumpeter Wynton, the virtuoso classicist, and the funkier saxophonist Branford – were the great success story of the 1980s, while another young trumpeter, Nicholas Payton, was the discovery of the 1990s.

The third factor was the emergence in the 1990s of new, young **brass bands** whose raw energy must surely be a match for the spasm bands of a century ago. Groups such as the Dirty Dozen, who started out in the 1970s as a kazoo band, paved the way for the revival, but the first of the new generation to achieve a commercial impact, with an exciting, raucous sound that extended from traditional standards to Michael Jackson covers, was the **ReBirth Brass Band** in the 1980s. Charismatic performers such as the ubiquitous **Kermit Ruffins** started their days in the ReBirth and have justifiably become solo stars since, while in their wake came young brass bands like the New Birth and the Lil Rascals, and hip brass-hop bands **Soul Rebels** and **Coolbone**.

Finally, mention has to be made of the city's flourishing **rap** scene, spearheaded in the 1990s by multimillionaire home boy **Master P**, whose No Limit label has achieved mind-boggling success. Pioneer of New Orleans' dance-oriented hip-hop style known as bounce, the Master paved the way for a flurry of local rap talent – including young titan **Mystikal** – and perhaps more than any other performer in recent years has pinned New Orleans securely back on the international music map.

Discography

Various Artists, *Crescent City Soul: The Sound of New Orleans 1947–1974* (EMI). None of the dozens of compilations of New Orleans R&B is perfect – there's just too much material to choose from – but this four-CD set is as close as any, including essentials such as *The Fat Man* (Fats Domino), *Mother-in-Law* (Ernie K-Doe) and *Ooh Poo Pah Doo* (Jessie Hill), plus another 116 cuts besides.

Louis Armstrong, *The Hot Fives (and Sevens) Volumes 1–3* (Columbia). Definitive collection of the 1925–28 recordings whereby New Orleans' greatest son brought jazz onto the world stage.

James Booker, *Resurrection of the Bayou Maharajah* (Rounder). Culled from his legendary solo gigs at the *Maple Leaf* bar between 1977 and 1982, this cornucopia of electrifying keyboard genius features extended medleys, improvisations and rambling, introspective interludes. There is no better example of Booker's flurrying New Orleans triplets and his unfailing R&B instinct.

Coolbone, *Brass-Hop* (Hollywood Records). This funky, hard-hitting 1997 experiment in rap-brass fusion benefits from a slick LA production job; if you prefer a rougher sound, try the Soul Rebels' *Let Your Mind be Free* (Mardi Gras Records).

Doc Cheatham and Nicholas Payton, *Doc Cheatham and Nicholas Payton* (Verve). Two great trumpeters breathe fresh life into jazz standards, in a gloriously elegiac meeting that was recorded in 1996 when Cheatham, who has since died, was 91 and Payton was just 23.

Dr John, *Goin' Back To New Orleans* (Warner Brothers). Accompanied by a fabulous roster of postwar greats, Dr John takes a vibrant, inspirational journey through a century of New Orleans music.

Fats Domino, *My Blue Heaven: The Best of Fats Domino* (EMI).

You'd need a box set to do Fats full justice, but this twenty-track anthology has the major hits.

Bob French's Original Tuxedo Jazz Band and Friends, *Livin' the Legacy* (Royal Tuxedo Records). Recreating the jazz house party atmosphere of *Donna's* Monday nights (see p.221), this quintessentially New Orleans CD features not only the classy work of masters Dave Bartholomew and Bill Huntington but also younger talents, notably slick trumpeter Leon Brown and vocalist Tricia Boutté.

Jelly Roll Morton, *The Chicago Years* (Louisiana Red Hot Records). The Red Hot Peppers' finest moments, recorded between 1926 and 1928, and lovingly restored to near-pristine condition.

Mystikal, *Let's Get Ready* (Jive). From the hard man of New Orleans rap, this is the CD that got everyone talking, beating Madonna's *Music* to the top of the US charts in 2000.

The Neville Brothers, *Treacherous: A History of the Neville Brothers* (Rhino). This exciting, eclectic compilation of

Nevilles' highlights stops in 1985, but it takes in Art's 1954 *Mardi Gras Mambo*, Aaron's sweet soul ballad *Tell It Like It Is* from 1967 and two stand-out tracks from *The Wild Tchoupitoulas* 1972 album of Mardi Gras Indian music (see p.311).

Professor Longhair, *Fess: The Professor Longhair Story* (Rhino). Sumptuous two-CD selection of the best of Fess, worth the price for 1964's *Big Chief – Part 2* alone.

ReBirth Brass Band, *The Main Event: Live at the Maple Leaf* (Louisiana Red Hot Records). The ReBirth's raucous, uplifting brass rearrangements and Second Line stomps make the *Maple Leaf* the place to be on a Tuesday night (see p.233); this CD is the next best thing, blasting the boys' inspired improvisational genius into your own front room.

Kermit Ruffins, *The Barbecue Swingers Live* (Basin Street Records). The hardest-working musician in New Orleans, versatile trumpeter Kermit Ruffins is in peak, convivial form on this 1998 live CD, which ranges from traditional brass to rap.

Irma Thomas, *Time Is On My Side: The Best of Irma Thomas* (EMI). The young Irma Thomas sings her heart out on stunning songs like *Time Is On My Side*, *Ruler of My Heart*, and *It's Raining*, recorded in collaboration with producer Allen Toussaint in the 1960s.

Wild Magnolias, *Life is a Carnival* (Metro Blue). Mardi Gras Indian funk at its most accessible, with guest appearances from Dr John, Cyril Neville, Russell Battiste and Allen Toussaint, and a host of other local luminaries.

Greg Ward

DISCOGRAPHY

New Orleans films

New Orleans has captured the imagination of film-makers since 1918, when the first Tarzan movie, *Tarzan of the Apes*, was filmed in the nearby swamps with members of the New Orleans Athletic Club swinging through the trees in ape costumes. It's a supremely photogenic city, particularly in the French Quarter, which lends itself perfectly to steamy, noirish visions and haunting Gothic nightmares. On top of that, its countless romantic associations – Mardi Gras, the Mississippi River, the lost culture of the Creoles, the pirates, the prostitutes, the voodoo queens – offer rich pickings for storytellers.

All the King's Men (Robert Rossen, 1949). Thinly veiled biopic of 1930s Governor Huey Long – popularly known as the "Kingfish" for his catchphrase "Every man a king" – whose hard-nosed radical politics, bully-boy tactics, and blatant corruption led to his murder in 1936. A gripping insight into Louisiana's notoriously corrupt political system.

Always for Pleasure (Les Blank, 1978). Outstanding, impressionistic documentary whirl through New Orleans' street parades, jazz funerals and Mardi Gras festivities. Performances include turns by Professor Longhair and the Wild Tchoupitoulas Mardi Gras Indians.

The Big Easy (Jim McBride, 1986). Dennis Quaid shot to fame as the maverick New Orleans cop who plays cat-and-mouse in the French Quarter with uptight assistant DA Ellen Barkin. Great fun, not least for Quaid's preposterous Cajun accent.

The Buccaneer (Cecil B. de Mille,1938). Based on Lyle Saxon's book *Lafitte the Pirate*, this riproaring swashbuckler, starring Fredric March, shamelessly romanticizes the role of Lafitte in Andrew Jackson's victory against the British in the 1815 Battle of New Orleans.

Down by Law (Jim Jarmusch, 1986). From its moody opening shots, panning across decrepit streetscapes, to the stylish soundtrack from Tom Waits and John Lurie, Jarmusch's monochrome hymn to New Orleans lowlife is a treat. Waits and Lurie are the jaded jailbirds making a bid for freedom, led by their *faux-naïf* cellmate, Roberto Benigni in an early American role. New Orleans is shown at its dissipated best, populated by pimps, corrupt policemen and tear-stained lushes.

Easy Rider (Dennis Hopper, 1969). Hippy anthem to life on the road, with hirsute bikers Dennis Hopper and Peter Fonda riding their Harleys cross-country in search of freedom. New Orleans, where they pick up a couple of hookers and freak out in St Louis No. 1 Cemetery, represents the death blow to their dreams. For all the acid-trip posturing, the New Orleans scenes do give an oddly true-to-life impression of the city's decadence and decay, and, in particular, the sheer weirdness of carnival.

The Flame of New Orleans (René Clair, 1941). Marlene Dietrich is fabulous as a Russian émigré posing as an heiress in this romantic drama set on the Mississippi steamboats and in the gambling dens and barrelhouses of nineteenth-century New Orleans.

Interview with the Vampire (Neil Jordan, 1994). Movie version of Anne Rice's first vampire novel, with Tom Cruise as the malevolent Lestat, and the puffy-faced Brad Pitt less convincing as his victim/consort Louis. The complexities of the

NEW ORLEANS FILMS

novel don't quite make it onto the screen, though Kirsten Dunst as the tragic child vampire Claudia is undeniably affecting.

Jezebel (William Wyler, 1938). Classic melodrama set in antebellum New Orleans. Bette Davis shines as the rebellious heroine – the sort who wears scarlet dresses to society balls – who must lose the man she loves (Henry Fonda, suitably lily-livered in the role) to yellow fever.

JFK (Oliver Stone, 1991). Three hours of Stone's conspiracy theory paranoia can be a bit much, and Kevin Costner is dull as New Orleans DA Jim Garrison, investigating the Kennedy assassination, but the supporting cast – including Gary Oldman as Oswald – put in some polished performances, and there are some great location shots.

King Creole (Michael Curtiz, 1958). Elvis is at his darkest, pouting best as a hustler in this drama of gangsters, sleazy nightclubs and doomed love. The black-and-white city looks great, and the songs, including the title number and *I'm Evil,* are among the King's finest.

My Forbidden Past (Robert Stevenson, 1951). Passions run high in 1890s New Orleans, when bad-to-the-bone heiress Ava Gardner schemes to seduce a lazily sexy Robert Mitchum away from his wife.

Panic in the Streets (Elia Kazan, 1950). Pacey film noir, in which bubonic plague-carrying murderer Jack Palance is hunted down along New Orleans' seedy waterfront.

Piano Players Rarely Ever Play Together (J. Palfi Stevenson, 1982). Magnificent documentary which brings three generations of piano maestros – Tuts Washington, Professor Longhair and Allen Toussaint – to play together for the first time. Their interaction in the build-up to the performance, and the interplay of their different musical styles, are fascinating in themselves, but Longhair's sudden death during filming, and the footage of his jazz funeral, serve to make it an even more poignant document.

And the music, of course, is fantastic.

Pretty Baby (Louis Malle, 1977). Seductive portrayal of the Storyville bordellos of the early 1900s, seen through the eyes of a virgin prostitute (Brooke Shields) and tortured photographer E.J. Bellocq (Keith Carradine). Filmed on location at the *Columns Hotel* (see p.168).

A Streetcar Named Desire (Elia Kazan, 1951). In a tortuous attempt to comply with the Production Code, which controlled censorship in Hollywood, Tennessee Williams' drama about nymphomania, hysteria and homosexuality loses something in the film version. Still fabulous, though, with fine performances from Method actors

Marlon Brando and Kim Hunter, and from Vivien Leigh, all rolling eyes and wilting feather boas as the troubled Blanche Dubois. New Orleans – the little you see of it outside Stanley and Stella's shabby apartment – is suitably steamy.

Wild at Heart (David Lynch, 1990). At the time of its release, Lynch's surreal, dark style was all the rage; with hindsight, however, the self-conscious bizarreness palls somewhat. Nicolas Cage and Laura Dern ham it up as the passion-crazy lovers fleeing Dern's evil mother; New Orleans, a nightmare of violet shadows and lacy iron balconies, is just one stop on their demented roadtrip through the Deep South.

INDEX

S

Index of background boxes

Stay in touch with us!

ROUGHNEWS is Rough Guides'
free newsletter.
In three issues a year we give you
news, travel issues, music reviews,
readers' letters and the latest
dispatches from authors on the road.

I would like to receive ROUGHNEWS: please put me on your free mailing list.

NAME . . . .

ADDRESS . . . .

Please clip or photocopy and send to: Rough Guides, 62-70 Shorts Gardens,
London WC2H 9AH, England

or Rough Guides, 375 Hudson Street, New York, NY 10014, USA.

ROUGH GUIDES: Travel

ROUGH GUIDES: Mini Guides, Travel Specials and Phrasebooks

Seattle
Sydney
Tokyo
Toronto

German
Greek
Hindi & Urdu
Hungarian
Indonesian
Italian
Japanese
Mandarin
  Chinese
Mexican
  Spanish
Polish
Portuguese
Russian
Spanish
Swahili
Thai
Turkish
Vietnamese

MINI GUIDES

Antigua
Bangkok
Barbados
Big Island of Hawaii
Boston
Brussels
Budapest
Dublin
Edinburgh
Florence
Honolulu
Lisbon
London Restaurants
Madrid
Maui
Melbourne
New Orleans
St Lucia

TRAVEL SPECIALS

First-Time Asia
First-Time Europe
More Women Travel

PHRASEBOOKS

Czech
Dutch
Egyptian Arabic
European
French

AVAILABLE AT ALL GOOD BOOKSHOPS

ROUGH GUIDES:
Reference and Music CDs

AVAILABLE AT ALL GOOD BOOKSHOPS

100
Essential
CDs

Eight titles,
one name

ROUGH GUIDES

Sorted

ROUGH GUIDES

Will you have enough stories to tell your grandchildren?

©2000 Yahoo! Inc.

Yahoo! Travel

DO YOU YAHOO!?

Rough Guides
on the Web

www.travel.roughguides.com

We keep getting bigger and better! The Rough Guide to Travel Online
now covers more than 14,000 searchable locations. You're just a click
away from access to the most in-depth travel content, weekly
destination features, online reservation services, and an outspoken
community of fellow travelers. Whether you're looking for ideas for
your next holiday or you know exactly where you're going, join us online.

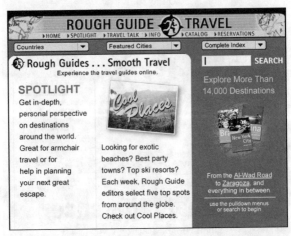